D0456031

AIN'T MISBEHAVIN'

TACTICS FOR TANTRUMS, MELTDOWNS, BEDTIME BLUES AND OTHER PERFECTLY NORMAL KID BEHAVIORS

ALYSON SCHAFER

COUNTY LIBRARY
TILLAMOOK, ORE.

WILEY

John Wiley & Sons Canada, Ltd.

Copyright © 2011 by Alyson Schafer

All rights reserved. No part of this work covered by the copyright herein may be reproduced or used in any form or by any means—graphic, electronic or mechanical—without the prior written permission of the publisher. Any request for photocopying, recording, taping or information storage and retrieval systems of any part of this book shall be directed in writing to The Canadian Copyright Licensing Agency (Access Copyright). For an Access Copyright license, visit www.accesscopyright.ca or call toll free 1-800-893-5777.

Care has been taken to trace ownership of copyright material contained in this book. The publisher will gladly receive any information that will enable them to rectify any reference or credit line in subsequent editions.

Library and Archives Canada Cataloguing in Publication Data

Schafer, Alyson, 1963-
Ain't misbehavin' : tactics for tantrums, meltdowns, bedtime blues and other perfectly normal kid behaviors / Alyson Schafer.

Issued also in electronic format.

ISBN 978-0-470-67909-8

1. Parenting. 2. Child rearing. 3. Child psychology. I. Title.

HQ769.S1957 2011   649'.1   C2010-907552-8

ISBNs: 978-0-470-96355-5 (ePdf); 978-0-470-96357-9 (eMobi); 978-0-470-96356-2 (ePub)

Production Credits
Cover and interior design: Michael Chan
Typesetting: Pat Loi
Cover images: Alex Nirta
Author photo: Henry Mendel
Printer: Solisco Tri-Graphic Printing Ltd.

John Wiley & Sons Canada, Ltd.
6045 Freemont Blvd.
Mississauga, Ontario
L5R 4J3

Printed in Canada
1 2 3 4 5 (SOL TRI) 15 14 13 12 11

ENVIRONMENTAL BENEFITS STATEMENT
Using 9850 lbs. of Rolland Enviro100 Print instead of virgin fibres paper reduces John Wiley & Sons Canada, Ltd. ecological footprint by:

TREES	SOLID WASTE	WATER	AIR EMISSIONS
84	5320	50,215	11,683
FULLY GROWN	POUNDS	GALLONS	POUNDS

It's the equivalent of :
Tree(s) : 1.7 american football field(s)
Water : a shower of 10.6 day(s)
Air emissions : emissions of 1.1 car(s) per year

CONTENTS

Acknowledgments..vii

Preface: How to Make Lemon Bars and Raise a Child........................ix

Chapter 1:   **Parenting Primer**..1
     Belonging...1
     Encouragement..2
     Family Fun...2
     Family Meetings..2
     Firm and Friendly..3
     Four Dances of Misbehavior........................3
     Mutual Respect..5
     Natural and Logical Consequences.............6
     Never Do for a Child What a Child Can Do for Herself..........7
     Punishments and Rewards Are Old School.........7
     Respect...8
     Take Time for Training (TTFT)......................8

Chapter 2:   **The Classics—a Democratic Approach to Overcoming Those Typical Trials**...................................9
     Sulking...9
     Whining...12
     Crying..14
     Cheating..15
     Lying...17
     Tantrums...19

Chapter 3: **Sleeping—the Democratic Approach to Getting Wee Ones to Winky Land**..**27**
Won't Fall Asleep Unless Parent Lies with Them 28
Wakes Every Few Hours during the Night.........................31
Crawls into Your Bed at Night..33
Night Terrors and Nightmares...34
Afraid of the Dark..36
Comes Out of Room after Being Tucked In 38

Chapter 4: **Potty Training—and the Democratic Approach to Toileting** **41**
Holds Bowels...42
Will Only Move Bowels in a Pull-Up..................................46
Refuses Diaper Changes 47
Won't Use Public Toilet 50
Accidents at Playdates 52
Won't Use the School Washroom......................................53
Still Pooping Pants at Age Six, Seven, Eight or,
    Yikes!, Nine 55
Still Wetting the Bed at Age Seven (or Eight or Nine).........57
Refuses to Wipe 59
Refuses to Wash Hands 61

Chapter 5: **Fretting Over Food—the Democratic Approach to Ending Food Fights** **63**
The Pokey Eater 64
The Food Strike..67
Overeating...73
The Picky Eater 76
Will Eat Only If in Front of the TV....................................78
Gags or Spits Food Out...81
Won't Give up the Bottle 82

Chapter 6: **From Trough to Table—the Democratic Approach to Table Manners** **85**
Won't Set the Table When It's Their Job............................86
Won't Come to the Table When Called 90
Gets Up and Down from the Table 92
Who Invited Tom Foolery to the Table? 96
Talks with Mouth Full..99
Refuses to Clear Plate...100
Toys at the Table 103

Chapter 7: **Social Skills—the Democratic Approach to Socializing Your Little Barbarian**..........................**105**
Won't Say Hello...106
Won't Say "Please" and "Thank-You" 108
Won't Kiss Grandparents 111

Tells Your Company to Go Home 112
Potty-Mouth 114
Curses and Swears Like a Sailor 115
Rude, Rude, Rude 118
Spitting 120
Gives Attitude and Tone 122
Doesn't Play with Friends Invited Over...........................124
You Hate Your Child's Friends 125
Has No Friends 127
You Think Your Child Is Being Bullied 129
Your Child Is a Bully..132

**Chapter 8: Health, Hygiene and High Fashion—the Democratic
Approach to Managing One's Body........................... 135**
Won't Brush Teeth..136
Refuses Hair Brushing..140
You Can Never Get the Ponytails Right 141
Hates Water and Getting in the Tub 143
Will Only Wear One Favorite Pair of Pants—
    and They're Dirty 145
Refuses to Wear Socks 147
Won't Take Medicine 148
Sticks Hands in Dirty Diapers 150
Disagreements about Wardrobe 152
Won't Get Dressed...155
Won't Put on Pajamas at Bedtime 157

**Chapter 9: Bad Habits—and the Democratic Approach to
Breaking Them 159**
Hair Twirling...160
Hair Sucking 161
Masturbating Tots 163
Nose Picking...165
Thumb Sucking 167
Love Objects...169
Pacifier Dependence...171
Loves Eating Glue, Playdough, Etc. 174

**Chapter 10: Bedroom Brawls—and the Democratic Approach to
Settling Space Issues 177**
Won't Make Bed in the Morning.....................................177
Won't Put Clothes in the Laundry Hamper 181
Won't Let Sibling into Bedroom 183
Won't Let You in Bedroom..185
Destroys Bedroom during Time-Outs 186
Writes on Walls..189
Siblings Share a Room, but They're the Odd Couple........191

Chapter 11: The Plugged-in Kid—the Democratic Approach to Managing the Wired World **193**
Inappropriate TV viewing 194
Addicted to Gaming...198
Acts Aggressively after Watching Violence 200
Disregards Screen-Time Limits 201
Wants a Cell Phone 205

Chapter 12: School 101—the Democratic Approach to Academic and Social Issues at School **209**
Has Poor Grades...210
Doesn't Pay Attention in Class 213
Homework Hell 215
Doesn't Care about School or the Subject Matter 219
Hates the Teacher...220
Always Late for School...222
Switching Schools...229
They're Autocratic—We're Democratic 230

Chapter 13: Extracurricular Activities—the Democratic Way to Manage the Angst **233**
The Overscheduled Child 234
The Dropout Kid..236
Goes to Lessons but Won't Participate 240

Chapter 14: Kids and Coins—the Democratic Approach to Money Matters **243**
Mommy, Buy This for Me! ("Dammit" Implied).................244
Complaining about the Amount of Allowance 246
Savings or "Slavings"? 251
Loses Money 253

Chapter 15: Sibling Fighting—and the Democratic Approach to Ending It **255**
Sibling Fighting Cheat Sheet 256
Fighting in the Car..257
Mommy, He Stole My Toy! 260
Can't or Won't?...262
The Physical Factor: When Siblings Physically Fight.........265
My Toddler Is Too Rough with the Baby...........................267
Name-Calling and Being Mean.......................................270
Is Jealous..273

Chapter 16: The Best Practices Democratic Family Checklist........**275**
Best Practices Family Checklist 275

ACKNOWLEDGMENTS

It's always a team effort to write a book. The author is the "front person," but I want readers to know I represent a terrific group of people, all of whom were a vital part in the chain of events that took my initial idea and walked it through the gazillion little steps to your hot little hands.

Big thanks to my two editors: Leah Fairbank, who kicked this book into action, and Liza Finlay, who took it over the finish line with me. A gal couldn't ask for better collaboration partners. Thanks to Pam Vokey, Alison Maclean, Judy Phillips, Erin Kelly, Katie Wolsley, and Meghan Brousseau, all with Wiley, for managing the process and making it all go smoothly and look beautiful.

Then there is the cast of characters who have been my encouragers and teachers. Some even admit to being my dear friends: Frank, Kathy and Cindy Walton, Wes Wingett, Louise Gireaux, Tim Hartshorne, Erik Mansager and Jane Pfefferle, Drs. Joyce and Gary McKay, Daniel Eckstein, Steve Maybell, John Petersen, Dan and Marilyn Dalton, Richard Kopp, Tim Evans and Gerri Carter, Jody McVittie, Linda Jessop, Patti Cancellier, Dina Emser, Betty Lou Bettner, Dr. Eva Dreikurs Ferguson, Bryna Gamson, Edna Nash and my closest advisors, the late Larry Nisan and his team—Chris

Nisan, Michael Vesselago, Peter Morse and Kathy Vance, all of the Psychotherapy Institute of Toronto.

To my sisterhood of momma bloggers, writers and business supporters that help make my soapbox a little higher so I can get my parenting message out farther: Kathy Buckworth, Ann Douglas, Erica Ehm, Jennifer Kolari, Emma Waverman, Theresa Albert, Sharon Vinderine, and Kathryn Howell. Too numerous to mention individually but way too important to leave out: my Twitter followers. Yes, it's all you folks, too. I @loveyou for all your RTs and enthusiasm.

To my late parents, Dick and Sylvia Knight, who were hell-bent on family meetings, and stuck with them even when they were going poorly, who offered up our family for counseling demonstrations to the public and who inspired me to share Adlerian ideas with other families as an adult. To my grandmother, Edith Dewey, who brought Dr. Rudolf Dreikurs to Ontario.

I want to give thanks to my daughters, Zoe and Lucy. I never meant for them to be the poster children of my parenting career, and I tried my best to respect their privacy and let them have their share of misbehaviors and mistakes like any other kids going through childhood (without me saying, "Don't act like that—you'll ruin my reputation!"). But it seems they've thrived under this way of parenting and have never felt the need to give me a run for my money. Instead, they cheer me on every day and tell me I am doing important work.

And to my circle of friends who jump in as extended family when I need them. And when you're writing a book, you need them! Dirk Bouwman, Julie Weiss, Colette Annetts and Mark Kitchen and, yes, even their children, Reilly and Liam Kitchen.

Hooray, everyone! We did it. I share this success and celebration with you all.

Alyson

HOW TO MAKE LEMON BARS AND RAISE A CHILD

For the most part, parenting is still lumped into the category of "soft topics," falling somewhere between recipes and fashion in our papers and news broadcasts. "How to make lemon bars" and "Is your teen depressed?" are buried on page 221, just before the real estate ads.

We're raising the next generation of humanity, for Pete's sake, and there is no doubt in anyone's mind that, as a society, we're struggling with how to go about it. Yet, there seems to be more Sudoku puzzles than parenting columns being printed.

As a parenting expert and psychotherapist, I speak with parents who have the warmest hearts, the greatest ambitions, and yet they have the biggest frustration about how best to deal with their children.

I have been in their shoes. My children are 15 and 16 now, but when I was a young, newbie mom, I experienced first-hand my toddler's ability to morph into a boneless, limp, rag doll. She would lie defiantly in the foyer while I politely requested, and then pathetically begged and eventually yelled to "get those snow pants on RIGHT THIS MINUTE because now you've made me late for my meeting! Look at how mad you've made mommy. Happy now?"

I felt terrible for yelling. Well, that's a lie. It felt good actually—that's why I did it. It was cathartic to yell. In the moment, it had a nice, "I'll show you who's boss" feel to it. Yelling helped me feel like my 23 month old didn't have me in a choke hold. But the guilt feelings would come as time passed and I calmed down. "Not a proud parenting moment," as we say, but honestly, I was stuck; I didn't know what else to do.

Why didn't I know what to do?

Yes, loving our kids is intuitive, but parenting them is a learned skill, and despite being the child of not one but two parent educators, I still hadn't learned the techniques I needed. How weird is that?

It's true. When I was a child, my parents taught parenting classes in our living room. (I used to make money babysitting the children of the parents in their classes.) They didn't use threats or bribes. No sticker charts on my childhood fridge. I wasn't even grounded. What *did* they do, then? Sadly, I didn't have a clue. I could not recollect a single parenting technique from my own childhood to replicate with my kids.

I decided to pick up the parenting book my parents had taught from. It was still on their living room bookshelf. That book was *Children: The Challenge* by Dr. Rudolf Dreikurs. Today, over a million copies have been sold, and the Library of Congress cited it as one of the most seminal books of the century.

Wow! I was awestruck. As a new mom wanting to do right by her children and having enjoyed an awesome family life myself, I was blown away by what I learned. It wasn't the light and fluffy stuff of lemon bars and Sudoku at all. It was psychology and anthropology and sociology and the humanities all rolled up into a single philosophy. But more importantly, it provided actual techniques for raising mentally healthy, happy, cooperative children.

And I wanted to learn more, More, MORE! So I signed up for Adlerian parenting classes, began teaching at an Adlerian nursery school and, while there is no such thing as getting a postsecondary degree in parenting, I did get my masters degree in counseling at the Adler School of Professional Psychology in Chicago.

The entire time I was learning, I was teaching. I couldn't discover something new that was helpful and *not* tell my mom friends at the drop-in. (I must have been annoying, huh?) The point is, how can you know something so important and then keep it to yourself? That felt selfish to me, like hoarding. I felt I just *had* to share. How far could I spread the good news? How many parents and children could I help?

So I gave classes, and I launched a call-in parenting program for cable TV, and I wrote two parenting books.

In the first book, *Breaking the Good Mom Myth* (*BTGMM*), I tackle, on the most meta level, the parental baggage and "myth-conceptions" about parenting—the ones that end up doing more harm than good. Then, in my second book, *Honey, I Wrecked the Kids* (*HIWTK*), I dug deeper into the biggest parenting challenges and misbehaviors. (After all, if they didn't misbehave, we'd love this parenting thing! Who doesn't love reading stories at bedtime all snuggled up together? It's when you try to leave and turn out the lights that we wonder why we didn't control ourselves on that fateful all-inclusive trip to Mexico, now immortalized by your daughter Margarita.)

Well, that book was full of the theory and techniques for handling misbehavior and your emails came flooding in: you wanted more. Specifically, you wanted more real-life problems with quick-and-dirty solutions. You wanted a veritable bible of misbehaviors, an encyclopedia of parental troubles and tactical remedies—categorized and labeled for easy, daily use.

Well, I heard you, so, voilà! Book three. Throughout this book you'll find feature boxes and lists that will bring you up to speed on the concepts introduced in the other books. Read over the "parenting primer" to review the concepts you'll need to know and then jump in! You'll find that, no matter how much reading you've already done, this book will be effective in giving you parenting strategies that are both respectful and effective.

Are you ready? Let's go solve the common problems of the parenting world.

CHAPTER 1

PARENTING PRIMER

Belonging · Encouragement · Family Fun · Family Meetings ·
Firm and Friendly · Four Dances of Misbehavior · Mutual Respect
· Natural and Logical Consequences · Never Do for a Child
What a Child Can Do for Herself · Punishments and Rewards
Are Old School · Respect · Take Time for Training (TTFT)

The concepts in *Ain't Misbehavin'* are based on psychologist Alfred Adler's Individual Psychology and Dr. Rudolf Dreikurs' child-guidance principles. You can read more about these in my earlier books, *Breaking the Good Mom Myth* and *Honey, I Wrecked the Kids.*

But here you'll find a quick primer of the main points of democratic parenting arranged alphabetically. The primer will give some context to the advice you'll read in the coming pages and act as a handy reference tool.

BELONGING

We are social creatures who strive to find our place of significance in our social groups. We only feel belonging when we know our place and feel unconditional acceptance from the group. The family is the child's first and most important social group. Help the child gain a sense of belonging by utilizing the "Ps & Cs"—participation and contribution. This makes children feel a part of the family team. Find their strengths and talents and help the children put them to use in the family. Show unconditional love always, by separating the deed from the doer: "I love you; it's your hitting I don't like."

ENCOURAGEMENT

All children are born in an "inferior" (immature) state to the adult version of the species: they can't walk, talk or tie a shoe, but they push on to overcome these inferiorities. They are intrinsically motivated to mature, grow, develop and become a more complete version of themselves. That said, children can become discouraged, or lose their courage. They may fear that if they try new things they may reveal their inadequacies and inferiorities. Children can confuse failure in a task as being a failure in their personal worth. Without courage to face life's challenges, the discouraged child will avoid, evade or find shortcuts. Parents should avoid all forms of punishment, avoid being discouraging, disparaging or showing pity. Don't knock children for their mistakes. Learn to be an encourager! Encouraged people know their worth is unwavering. They know they are worthy now as they are, not conditionally "when they . . ." or "if they . . ." (achieve something). Encouraged children don't see their mistakes and shortcomings as failures to their worth as a person.

FAMILY FUN

Fun is the glue of the family. When families have fun together, they bond, they become cohesive, they become a group. It's team building. When the group is tight, the members care more about the whole group than their personal interests, and that's critical in soliciting social interest and cooperation from our children. So, if all you do is amp up your fun time, you'll see immediate changes in your children. How great is that?

FAMILY MEETINGS

The cornerstone of democracy is allowing people to have a voice in the creation of the rules that govern them. In our families we can do this by having weekly family meetings. Children like having input, and they are more likely to go along with rules that they helped create. Decisions should be made by consensus (not majority rules), and they can be revisited and tweaked each week until they work for everyone. Family meetings help us to reframe "discipline issues" as "problems that need solutions." See chapter 5 for more on family meetings.

FIRM AND FRIENDLY

Democratic parenting is respectful leadership that requires parents to be both firm and friendly at the same time.

> **Firm:** we set clear and reasonable limits, boundaries and expectations for our children's behavior.

> **Friendly:** we teach and enforce these limits with a warm, caring, friendly demeanor. There is never a reason to raise your voice to a child. All these tactics will be more effective without parental tone or attitude.

FOUR DANCES OF MISBEHAVIOR

All behavior has a purpose. Remember I said that every child is trying to find her place and significance in the group? Well, sometimes a child misses the turnoff for "cooperation" and takes an alternate path to the ultimate destination: significance. These are known as "misbehaviors," or as I prefer to call them, "mistaken approaches."

The parents typically think their children's behavior is a problem, but from the children's perspective, their behavior is actually a solution to a problem. The children's (mis)behavior solves the problem of finding significance through one of four means: undue attention seeking, power over others, revenge or avoidance.

The way we respond to our children's misbehavior is key. We have to recognize our involvement in these repeated interactional patterns. It's our responses to their behavior that determine if children are successful at reaching their mistaken goal. If they are *not* successful in eliciting their goal from us, the behavior will be abandoned. If we give them the reaction they seek, they'll deem their strategy successful and repeat it.

Because it takes two to create these cycles of behavior, I like to think of them as four dances we do with our children. Let's look at the four patterns a little closer:

1. UNDUE ATTENTION DANCE

The child seeking undue attention has the mistaken belief that she is important and significant only when she is in the limelight. If the child was neglected early in life, she may lack solid attachment and struggle to feel a connection with her parent; so she seeks it through undue attention. More commonly, however, the child has simply had too much attention in her early years, so she'll come to expect it constantly.

You may ignore her when your child behaves properly, but if she acts up, you're right there to correct her, nag her and remind her. The child responds easily to these verbal corrections and tends to listen and settle down, only to start up again, or move on to some other annoyance to get your attention. Even a lecture or getting yelled at is better than being ignored, in her mind. To recognize the attention dance, you should be aware of when you're feeling irritated and annoyed or worried about your child's behavior. The general rule of thumb is to ignore the undue attention-seeking behavior and instead show your child positive avenues for feeling connected with you so that she doesn't have to take the creative path on the negative side of life.

2. POWER DANCE

The power dance is all about winning. The parent and child are akin to two people at either end of a tug-of-war rope, each trying to beat the other. The outcome of the fight will determine who is the puppet and who is the puppet master.

The power dance makes a parent feel angry, provoked, challenged or defeated. You'll think, "You aren't getting away with that!" or "I'll show you." Unlike in the undue attention dance, when parents respond in the power dance, the child doesn't stop temporarily. Instead, things escalate in a one-upmanship manner. The child is seeking self-determination to avoid being put under your thumb. She is saying, "I'll do what I want" or "You can't make me." We have to stop fighting with these children. We have to cease and desist using domination to control their behavior. Instead, we need to win their cooperation and help them find positive empowerment in their lives.

3. REVENGE DANCE

You will know if the child's goal is revenge because you will be hurt by her. That is what the child hopes to accomplish. She wants to hurt you as she feels you have hurt her. Usually, we've done this by beating the child in a power struggle. If you feel you don't like your child anymore, you are in a revenge dance. This child needs to know you love and care about her, so crank up the loving and listening so that you can heal the relationship.

4. AVOIDANCE DANCE

This dance is the end of the line for discouraged kids. They are so sure they can't find their place in the family that they give up. Instead of trying and failing in life, they turtle their heads and avoid. You'll recognize this dance because you'll feel exasperated and hopeless. You feel like giving up too. If the doom cloud is floating over your relationship with your child, it's time to get professional help. This child needs encouragement, and the parents do too. It's hard for a discouraged parent to encourage a child.

MUTUAL RESPECT

Social equality is the inalienable right of all humans. Everyone, children included, deserves to be treated with respect and dignity regardless of their age, race, religion or gender. Parents should treat their children with respect so that they learn to respect themselves and others. Parents should also act in ways that win the respect of their children.

NATURAL AND LOGICAL CONSEQUENCES

Children learn best experientially. Consequences allow children to be free to make choices but also to experience the consequences of their behaviors for themselves.

Natural consequences refer to the natural laws that govern the natural world: gravity, heat, pressure and so on. Children learn natural laws very quickly:

> You don't lift your foot high enough → you trip on the edge of the carpet.
>
> You don't get your fingers out of the way → the cupboard door will pinch them.
>
> You don't dress properly → you get cold.
>
> You don't eat enough → you get hungry.

Parents want to protect their children from the discomforts of experiencing natural consequences, but by doing so they interfere with learning. Of course, this is not a good way to teach if the natural consequence is too severe. Use your judgment, but a bump, bruise, shiver or hunger pang is fine.

Logical consequences are about the social laws that govern our families, classrooms and culture. We have to create logical consequences, so these take more thinking. A good logical consequence meets the 3R requirement and helps tie freedoms and responsibilities together to maintain respect for the social order. These 3Rs are:

> **R**easonable
> **R**elated
> **R**evealed in advance

Here are two examples of the 3Rs in action:

> *Example 1:* Bikes need to be in the garage after they are used. If it is left on the driveway, the bike will be put away for a day.

> *Example 2:* Cars need to be peaceful in order for driving to be safe. If the car gets too boisterous, it's no longer safe to drive and the car will be pulled over and stopped.

Again, it's not the threat of the consequence that makes these effective teaching tools for child guidance; it's the child experiencing the consequence that results in the learning.

NEVER DO FOR A CHILD WHAT A CHILD CAN DO FOR HERSELF

Often referred to as NDFACWACCDFH. Okay, kidding, but I thought this section was getting a bit dull and I chant this line *a lot* to parents. If you're doing the child's jobs, you're acting in servitude and the child is evading responsibility. In fact, your child may become confused by your help. Be consistent. It helps children learn. They feel more secure when life is predictable and clear.

PUNISHMENTS AND REWARDS ARE OLD SCHOOL

Punishments and rewards are tools designed to make a child acquiesce to your authority. Their aim is to create obedience, conformity and servitude. The obedient child is unable to think for himself, is susceptible to peer pressure and is at risk for being mistreated by untrustworthy adults. Ruling by means of oppressing eventually leads to a revolt. Children learn domination as a fruitful method of getting one's way, and fail to learn cooperation with others. Punishments and rewards hurt the child's self-esteem and harm the parent-child relationship. Instead of creating obedient children, my child guidance system has a higher ideal: to raise cooperative and caring children who learn from their experiences rather than through fear of rejection or corporal punishment.

RESPECT

Respect encompasses respect for self and others, but also respect for the social order. One cannot simply do whatever one pleases—that would lead to anarchy and social instability. Freedoms and responsibilities must go together.

TAKE TIME FOR TRAINING (TTFT)

A child gains feelings of security by facing challenges and overcoming them. It's about feeling capable of handling life situations. So, as soon as you see signs of readiness or interest, let the child practice some Take Time for Training (TTFT) skills such as putting on his own clothes, pouring his own juice, picking up his toy, doing his own laundry and managing his own homework. Pick a task that is just difficult enough that the child is not so sure he can do it on his own, but one that you are fairly sure he'll succeed at if he tries. Never stop looking for what your child is ready to learn and master next on the path to autonomy and mastery.

CHAPTER 2

THE CLASSICS—A DEMOCRATIC APPROACH TO OVERCOMING THOSE TYPICAL TRIALS

Sulking · Whining · Crying · Cheating · Lying · Tantrums

Every parent has to deal with them—the usual smattering of undesirable behaviors that mark a typical childhood. You know, the sulking, whining, crying, lying and cheating. Oh, and let's not forget tantrums. In this chapter, we'll examine these classics and learn what to do about them.

In every case, we need to remember that behavior is goal-directed and serves a purpose. Only discouraged children take on these creative (although mistaken) approaches and, ultimately, our parenting job is to alleviate discouragement by becoming more encouraging; we need to help our children solve these problems through constructive, cooperative methods. Too often, children are at a loss about how to get their way or have their needs met through positive avenues—we've got to build those roads for them, so they don't take the shortcut across the field of misbehavior. Let's start rerouting.

SULKING

You've told your daughter she can't go to her friend's house for a sleepover because there is no parent home. She crosses her arms, makes a sour face and pushes past you out of the kitchen. You join her on the couch and she *hrrrmps* at your arrival. Every question is answered with a minimal, monosyllabic answer, and you feel like a black cloud has invaded your house, blocking out all the happiness for the rest of the weekend. The sulk is on!

UNDERSTANDING THE PROBLEM

Sulking is a wonderful form of passive or silent power. You have enforced a limit or a boundary, said no, and your child is protesting. She is angry with you and your limits. But instead of exploding in a tantrum, she implodes with a quiet sulk. It's basically a silent tantrum.

Sulking is directed at you, the parent, with the intention of punishing you back by creating a negative emotional state in you: usually guilt or upset. The child is hoping you'll change your mind about the "no," or that you'll compensate her in some other way— make it up to her with some other privilege as a way to cheer her up or make her feel better.

SOLUTIONS

Understand that the child really is upset and angry. We want kids to talk about their disappointment. Perhaps your daughter feels you are being ridiculously strict for requiring parental supervision. Perhaps she is concerned about being socially ostracized because no one else's parents have this limit. Maybe she's worried she'll be left out, and that not going to the sleepover means people may talk behind her back. Perhaps she feels that you don't trust her—and that hurts her.

How will you know, if the child shuts down and sulks? How can we help kids navigate life if we don't know what issues are plaguing them? Communication is key, and we have to get behind the sulking to find out what's bothering the child. Here's how.

Practice active listening. For example: "I see you're really disappointed. Can we talk about this more? I want to understand." Remember that active listening is about understanding them, not defending your point of view. Listening actively requires that you paraphrase back to your child what she is communicating—including both the facts of the situation and the emotions she's feeling. (See chapter 10, p. 188 for more details on how to be an active listener.)

If the child is not willing to talk at the moment, see if she'd like some time to deal with the disappointment and maybe talk again about it later. Don't let it go too long, though. The child is seriously angry, and you have to address the issues or they'll fester. Once you feel you understand the child's point of view, you can respond with I-messages rather than you-messages.

Examples:

Instead of:
"You're too young."

Try:
"I feel nervous when you are at someone else's house with no adult supervision because, while you use good judgment yourself, a group can get out of hand. I'd rather you wait till you are older or an older person is near by for 'crowd control.'"

Instead of:
"You're not responsible enough."

Try:
"I am not ready for you to do that yet."

Don't cave. The sulker is hoping you'll feel sorry for her and change your mind about the "no" that has her disappointed. If you succumb, the child will learn that sulking is an effective way to get you to back down. Don't make this mistake.

Don't compensate. If you feel guilty, you may try to cheer up your child by offering something to make her happy, like preparing hot cocoa or offering to take her out for ice cream. We contribute to our children's happiness, but we are not responsible for it. If unhappy moods produce parental presents, your child is more likely to get into foul moods for the benefits they produce. Kids have the right to be disappointed; you have the right not to be bothered by it. Sometimes life is just disappointing. Don't teach them to expect a consolation prize every time they experience life's shortcomings.

Don't mind. It's okay for your child to sulk, but usually sulking requires an audience. If the child is unwilling to talk and continues to sulk about in stony silence, ask her to leave, or remove yourself from the situation. Without an audience to observe the quiet storm, it's not worth the effort. But please—don't forget active listening!

Be a model. Be aware of your own behavior. Do you give the silent treatment when you are upset with your child or partner? Show kids a better way to face difficulties by modeling open communication, and don't withhold your love when you're angry with someone.

WHINING

For most parents, it's like nails on a chalkboard. It's the high-pitched whiiiiiine. Do any of these sound familiar? "Youuuuuu do it, Mommy." "Uppy, I want uppy." Funny how a tone of voice can be our undoing.

UNDERSTANDING THE PROBLEM

Whining is a demand for both your attention and service. It's like a universal kids' solvent that has the strength to take down the walls of Jericho. It's just so annoying that parents find the easiest way to get their child to stop is to come a crumblin' down. We'll do *anything* to stop the whining.

SOLUTIONS

Ask for the behavior you would like. Instead of saying, "Stop whining!" try, "I'd be happy to get you a juice if you'd use your regular voice." Have you said that a million times already, and it's not working? Then drop the strategy. The child knows what you're doing and it's not going to work. Remember: attention-seeking behaviors are all about enticing you to nag and remind, so if you find yourself falling into that pattern, stop. Move to the next strategy.

Ignore. I know it's hard. But pretend that your ears have lost the ability to hear in the whine zone, and that your receptors pick up only regular tones. Simply don't respond. (And I bet the child will stop whining.) But don't get angry either. If the child sees that you're upset, he'll know he is being heard even though you're not replying.

Catch the child being good. Reinforce how much you appreciate being asked nicely. For example: "It's a pleasure getting you a juice when you ask so pleasantly. I feel so appreciated when you make your requests so respectfully."

Take Time for Training (TTFT). Help your child learn to get his own juice or put on his own socks. Show her how to push a stool up to the counter so she can reach the tap for her own water. Lower the cups in the cupboard so she can help herself. Be excited about your child's growing independence and ability to manage himself or herself: "Look at you! You know how to do that all by yourself. You are so capable!" Children seem to get a lot of mileage for being incapable and needing our help. Let's switch that up so inability gets less of our energy and being capable brings a shower of positive attention.

Connect with a hug. Don't comment on the whining, but simply say, "Would you like a hug?" You'd be amazed how far that gesture can go in reducing whining.

Be proactive. Whining can peak when we are busy attending to other matters. If you know you have to cook dinner or spend time doing work on the computer, plan some cuddle connection time *before* you embark on your tasks: "I have to start supper soon. Do you want to have a cuddle before I go off and do that?" Or, if possible, involve the child by asking him to help you with your task.

CRYING

Everyone cries. I just cried watching "We Day" on TV: twenty thousand kids chanting about how they can change the world. Totally moving. I also cried yesterday when I pinched my finger in the car door. It hurt! And I cried a lot when my parents were sick and dying. Sometimes I still cry because I miss them.

UNDERSTANDING THE PROBLEM

There is nothing wrong with any emotion. Our feelings are our facts, and we have to honor our children's feelings. Not just the positive emotions but also the so-called negative ones.

It would be doing children a disservice to teach them not to feel negative emotions. They'd feel there was something wrong with them for feeling angry, hurt, sad, disappointed or discouraged. We want to help our children normalize the experience of having a whole rainbow of emotions, from the very low to the very high, and from the very dark to the very bright.

However, children are still learning coping styles, communication skills and problem solving and, since their repertoire is limited, they can easily cry as a default. It's the response their tears garner from you that will determine if they have a secondary realization—that tears may be a useful social strategy in reaching one of their goals. That's when tears become a tool, a shortcut to achieving their purpose rather than facing life's challenges.

SOLUTIONS

Avoid dismissive statements. Never say, "Don't cry," or "Boys don't cry," or "Be a man" or "Suck it up." These are dismissive statements that hurt.

Practice active listening. Try to reflect back the feeling behind the tears. For example: "You seem sad," or "That was an ouchy!" or "You're feeling disappointed."

Give them permission to feel. For example: "It's okay to be sad sometimes," or "It's okay to feel disappointed" or "Yes, sometimes life makes us angry."

Coach them. Ask kids to speak up. When children are communicating with their tears, help them use language instead—"I see you're upset; do you need to speak up?"

Don't bend. If children learn that crying will get you to change a limit or boundary, they will turn on the waterworks as a means of getting their way: if asking for a cookie gets a "no," try crying and see if that will work! Parents seem to be convinced that being upset is harmful for children—that psychologically there is some need to always be happy. Hello? Reality check. It's okay to be disappointed that a fun day has come to an end and now it's time for bed. But crying should not get children a free pass. Stick with the rules and routines and allow them to cry about it. When tears fail to get parental attention, the crying ceases. We can help by addressing the child—not the tears.

Be open-minded and problem solve. If your child is unhappy and crying about something, you need to hear his point of view and help him express his feelings and work collaboratively to find solutions as a family. That doesn't mean that the child will necessarily get his way, but he has a right to be heard. Use your family meetings (see p. 71) to solve issues and come up with solutions that work for everybody. Maybe it is time to talk about changing bedtime because it's been the same time since your child was eight and now he's twelve. Make rules and agreements together to preserve family harmony.

CHEATING

"Hey, you didn't roll a six! That was a four." "I saw that—that was out of bounds!"

Do you have a child who cheats? At sports, on tests, in games? That pushes our buttons in a serious way, doesn't it? We immediately envision our child behind bars, wearing a striped jumpsuit. Relax. Your child isn't on the road to becoming a criminal.

UNDERSTANDING THE PROBLEM

Cheating is the ultimate shortcut to success. The cheating child's behavior is no different from the corporate cheating we saw with Enron and in Ponzi schemes. Cheating is the ultimate lack of courage. When people are consumed with a need to win, to be on top, they'll do anything to get it—even if it involves corruption.

In competitive families, more and more we parents are setting up the conditions that produce cheaters. We say, "Winning isn't everything," but we give 20 bucks for every A on a report card. We say, "Winning isn't everything," but we have parents beating up hockey coaches because of a bad call. We say, "Winning isn't everything," but our children know we don't mean it.

SOLUTIONS

Use encouragement. We have to address the child's mistaken belief that "I must be first and best at any cost." Children who use this logic don't see a second-place standing. Rather, they think, "If I am not number one, I am useless, I am worthless." These kids believe that they secure their worth by being the best, and that idea is supported when we use praise instead of encouragement.

Praise is a verbal reward. Some external authority figure judges the performance of the child and determines if it meets the mark, and if it does, the child gets a reward: money, a sticker, or whatever, but—most importantly—approval and love.

We send the message "You're okay when . . ." (when you get an A, when you score a goal, when you win the tournament, when you build a tower 10 blocks high). Perfection becomes the ultimate goal, the key to feeling important and worthy. How you get there is not important.

With encouragement, children hear a totally different message. They hear: "You're worthy already. You're lovable already. Success or failure doesn't change my love for you or your worth as a human being. You can't fail. There is no such thing as human failure. You are already everything you need to be." With this belief, children are freed up from the mental anguish of trying to constantly prove their worth, which might be fleeting, and instead focus on what they want to do: What needs to be done? What skills will I master? With encouragement, children are motivated by the joy of the process, with the improvements they see as parents notice their efforts instead of their accomplishments.

So stop praising and start encouraging. (See the table titled "Praise versus Encouragement" in chapter 15 for more on the differences between praise and encouragement.)

Be a good role model. Be aware of your own ambitious attitude and need for perfection and winning.

Address cheating. For example: "I don't like playing if people cheat. The game is not fun for me when we play that way. I won't play if there is cheating."

Practice active listening. For example: "Your teacher said you were cheating on the exam? What happened?"

🌱

Help your child understand that it is through *effort* that he will achieve his goals in life. Only through hard work and industriousness do people reach their goals. Shortcuts always catch up with us in the end. That means parents have to be more interested in their children's efforts than their final achievements—and that is a hard one for some parents to give up.

LYING

"Did you break the window? Is that your glass left in the living room? What do you mean 'no'—you're lying!"

Understanding the Problem

What kid in his right mind is going to say, "Yes, I broke the lamp," when he knows he's going to get punished? Kids are not masochists, for crying out loud! Lying is a sloppy solution to getting out of a tough spot: we want our kids to learn other ways of dealing with mistakes.

Solutions

Don't set your child up for a lie. Instead of asking: "Did you break the window?" Try: "The window is broken, we need to talk about what happened."

Don't get upset when your child tells you she made a mistake. Stay cool when you hear, "I broke the window" or "I left my bag at Chloe's." Instead, thank your child for her willingness to tell you: "It took a lot of courage to tell me that. I am glad you trust me enough to come to me with your problems."

Don't punish; problem solve. If you don't want kids to lie as a solution, help them learn to solve problems. For example: "What should we do about the broken window?" Help them make reparations and amends if needed. You can say, "This upset me," but you must show the child that you are an ally in life as she faces ever-growing problems. If you want your child to come to you with issues like failing school, drugs, pregnancy, etc., you have to show her *now*, with the little problems in life, that you are a safe person to trust with her issues. Don't blow up. Keep your influence by keeping the relationship a safe place to be imperfect.

Don't call the child a liar. This is a label. Children internalize these labels and then start to move in line with our expectations. You'll end up with more lying, not less.

But What If . . .

My child doesn't lie about breaking things or making mistakes, but he fabricates stories. I picked my son up from school and the teacher congratulated me on the new baby. What new baby? Apparently, my son shared at circle time that he had a new baby brother! What the heck?

This kind of lying is not about avoiding punishment, but rather to impress peers. This need to impress is a creative solution to the problem of gaining social acceptance or status in the group. For story-telling children, we have to help them find positive ways to feel secure about themselves, just as they feel social recognition through their own strengths and putting their strengths to use in a constructive way.

Sample Script

"You don't need to make up things to impress your friends. They already find you likable and lovable just the way you are." (Again, load on the encouragement instead of the praise.)

"If you like sharing at circle time, maybe we could ask you to make up a fun, fictional story and share it with the group as a story time. You could call it, 'Why I wish I had a baby brother,' or something else, like 'The day the elephant ate the banana.' You could make up a great story to share with the group." Now the child is getting positive attention through his quality and strength of being a storyteller, and it's being used to benefit the group by entertaining them instead of false ego striving.

TANTRUMS

Oh, the explosive outbursts that shatter the peace of our homes! For many parents, it's the dreaded tantrum that keeps them walking on eggshells all day long. Or keeps them from having company or arranging playdates for their child. Sometimes your kid just goes off for no apparent reason. You made macaroni and he wanted a hot dog. You gave her the blue cup and she wanted the red one. You'd think you just cut her leg off! The child falls to the floor, wailing—or worse, lashes out violently, like a tornado of destruction. What do you do now?

Nothing? Well, not quite.

UNDERSTANDING THE PROBLEM

Statistics show that toddlers are the most violent humans on earth, with an act of aggression happening as frequently as every three minutes. Okay, that's depressing news. The point is, there is a developmental piece at play here. Tantrums peak at around age three, partially because kids are still learning to emotionally regulate, still learning to communicate and still building coping strategies and problem-solving skills. At the same time, they are living large and pushing the boundaries on growing their autonomy and mastery, which, not surprisingly, are still fairly limited. All in all, it's a time of high frustration.

When something doesn't go the child's way, she expresses her anger over the reality of the situation by exploding. "I don't like it, I don't want it! This is not how I wanted things to go! I want *my* way." Tantrums are an active, outward display of power in the form of protest.

Once a tantrum has started, the best strategy is to remain calm and let it run its course. Indeed, you're best to concentrate on eliminating tantrum triggers, some of which you may not even be aware of—hence, the feeling that the tantrums happen out of the blue. Not so. Let's look at some factors and be proactive.

SOLUTIONS

I've broken the solutions down into four time frames:

1. About to blow
2. Mid-blow
3. After blow
4. Preventative measures (between blowups)

1. About to Blow

Don't cave! If you change the rules because of someone's mood, he'll use tantrums as a form of manipulation. Hold firm, but stay pleasant.

Practice active listening. Quickly, right when it looks like your child may wig out on you, drop to eye level, maybe touch him lovingly (if he doesn't recoil) and verbalize what the child is feeling and experiencing:

> "You're disappointed. You really wanted that tower of blocks to be much higher and it fell down on you. How frustrating!"

> "Ah, we are having such a good time at the park and it's hard to stop having fun—that is so maddening!"

> "Your ice cream fell off the cone! You were enjoying that cone so much, and looking forward to the next lick, and now it's a mess on the ground. How disappointing!"

Active listening helps develop emotional intelligence by giving names to feelings. It also helps your child feel that you actually "get" what he is experiencing so he feels affirmed and emotionally supported. This paves the way for being better able to calm himself down.

2. Mid-Blow

Move you, not them. There is no reasoning with a child in meltdown. Don't be upset with him, and don't try to hold and soothe him. Research proves that only increases the time it takes until he settles down.

Instead, move away from the storm. It's always better to remove yourself from the situation than trying to move the child, which will only intensify the situation.

Bring the child a stuffed animal or make some other gesture to show you are not angry and that you want him to be able to find a way to self-soothe and self-calm. Maybe a quick rub on the back, with: "It's okay to be upset, come see me when you're calm." Then get out of there.

But What If . . .

If I move, he follows me!

If the child follows you, try the bathroom technique, which goes like this: You move yourself to the bathroom (or your bedroom) and just before ducking in, say, "Can you calm yourself? Or do I need to go?" If the tantrum continues, simply enter the bathroom and close the door while saying, "When you're calm, I'll know it's time to come out."

The child will bang the door and call under the crack, but keep yourself safe in there, and don't talk through the door. Wait until he tires and calms. Then open the door and say, "I see you're ready!" If he starts up again upon your appearance, close the door and repeat. You may have to do this a few times, and for a few days, but not much beyond that. If this behavior continues beyond a few days, something isn't working and you should stop the strategy.

3. After-Blow

If the child tears a room apart in the height of a tantrum, wait until he is calm again and some time has passed, then be sure he cleans up the mess he's made. Be nice about this. A simple line like, "Looks like you have a job to do . . ." is enough of a prompt to remind him that this is his responsibility. Keep accountability by using a when/then statement: "When your job is done, then I'll know you're ready for supper."

Kids are less likely to pull every book off the bookshelf if they know they'll have to put them back. If the destruction is overwhelming, you might offer to get them started or keep them company, but don't be doing their work.

4. Preventative Measures

Continue skill building. Continue to work on independence, self-sufficiency, communication and problem-solving skills in an ongoing way.

Keep in mind that kids who feel good, do good. Watch for tiredness and hunger as triggers. It's best not to plan a shopping trip if it's going to run into nap or snack time.

Give a heads-up. Kids can have a hard time transitioning from one activity to the other. You wouldn't like your partner to grab you at a cocktail party and say, "Let's go home" when you're mid-story, mid-merlot and having a good time. Your kids don't like to be yanked from the park on your whim either. Instead, give them a heads-up: "We're leaving the park in five minutes" or "After we finish this puzzle, it's time for PJs." This gives kids time to get their heads around it all. Be sure to stick to the planned transition time so they come to understand that you mean what you say and you say what you mean. If the tantrum succeeds in buying them more time, they're more likely to repeat the tactic. Instead, remove your child from the park, for example, by carrying him gently and lovingly to the car (okay, you'll be gentle but he's flailing, so do your best!). Let the child know that if he can't leave the park without getting upset, he'll have to skip the next park visit. Discuss how to improve leaving the park at your next family meeting so you involve the child in finding a solution.

Establish rules and enforce them consistently. If the rule is no jumping on the couch, you need to enforce that rule. If you only sometimes feel up to enforcing the no-couch-jumping rule, it's really not a rule at all. Since your kid won't really think it's a rule, the little kangaroo will likely melt down when you do occasionally remove her: to the child it's an arbitrary and unfair act. She will experience this removal as a personal affront. You're exerting your personal power over her in a "do what I say" way. However, if you remove her consistently from the couch and do so in a friendly manner, it's no longer personal but about the rules of the house, and the upset will diminish with time as she comes to understand that this is a real rule.

You Think . . .	Child Thinks . . .	Try Instead . . .
YOUR UNDERSTANDING OF A CLEAR AND REASONABLE RULE.	THE WAY YOUR CHILD PERCEIVES YOUR RULES BASED ON WHAT REALLY HAPPENS.	CLEAR, CONCISE ENFORCEABLE RULES THAT THE CHILD CAN UNDERSTAND.
Sure, you can have a treat. Just not too many and not too close to supper.	I don't know what "too many" or "too close" means. Basically, Mommy decides when I can't eat treats. I have to appeal to her to get what I what. She is the gatekeeper to my sweets. If I tantrum, I can often get the gatekeeper to open the gate.	One treat a day. We have them at our snack time, which is 3 p.m. each and every day.
Bedtime is at 7 p.m.	Bedtime is really just when my mom gets tired and fed up and says, "That's it—time for bed." I always feel upset. I like life to be predictable, and I take being told to go to bed personally. If I blow up, sometimes I can make tuck-ins start later.	Bedtime is 7 p.m., even when people are happy and still getting along. Bedtime is 7 p.m. even if Daddy just got home. Bedtime is always 7 p.m., and we all know this because the kitchen timer dings.
Sometimes, if it's a nice day and I don't have any work to get to, we play at the playground after school for a bit before coming home for lunch.	I never know when we'll get a chance to stay and play, so I ask every day. If I have a meltdown, sometimes I get to stay and play before lunch.	Together, let's pick one day this week to stay and play before lunch. I'll mark it on our family calendar in the kitchen. I'll pack a little snack and you can wear my watch with a timer to let us know when it's 12 noon and we have to head home.

Add choice. There is always a way to add choice, to give your child some empowerment. You can still maintain control, but believe me, adding a little bit of choice makes a huge difference to a tantrum-prone tot, especially right before you're about to execute an action or consequence. Too often, we think, "That's it! I'm taking action now"—and the child is not told what is about to happen. The consequence is not revealed in advance, so the child feels "duped" or overpowered, and a tantrum ensues.

Examples:

"Can you get off the couch on your own or do you need some help? I see you need some help." (Set the child on the floor.)

The timer dings: "TV time is over. Can you turn off the TV or shall I?"

"Can you get in the car seat on your own or do you need my help? I see you need my help." (Put the child gently in the car seat.)

"It's not okay to write on the table. Can you give me the marker? Can you let go of the marker, or does Mommy have to use force?" (It's okay to pry the child's hand open, but only after you have given the choice of the child handing it over herself.)

Ask instead of tell. Often, you can avert a tantrum by asking instead of telling.

Examples:

"The timer went off. What does that mean? You're right! It's cleanup time!"

"Where do our boots go? You're right! On the mat, high five buddy!"

"What do we do after we eat? Yes! Clear our plates. You really know the routine!"

Say "no" less often. Our little firecrackers hear "no" a lot. Their entire day is peppered with it: no, don't touch, no, don't run, no, don't hit. This negative message tires them. Try to change up your language to be more positive, while still guiding the child.

Examples: of "yes" instead of "no":

"Yes, you may have a cookie—at snack time."

"Yes, we can stay and play at the school—on the day we decided on the calendar."

Ask for the behavior you want to see:

Instead of: "Don't run," *try:* "Walking feet."

Instead of: "Don't hit," *try:* "Gentle hands."

Instead of: "Don't yell," *try:* "Inside voice."

Instead of: "NOOOO!" *try:* "Danger!"

CHAPTER 3

SLEEPING—THE DEMOCRATIC APPROACH TO GETTING WEE ONES TO WINKY LAND

Won't Fall Asleep Unless Parent Lies with Them •
Wakes Every Few Hours during the Night • Crawls into Your
Bed at Night • Night Terrors and Nightmares • Afraid of
the Dark • Comes Out of Room after Being Tucked In

The brain needs sleep. Ever had to fight to keep your eyes open when you're dog tired? It's brutal. So brutal that sleep interruption is actually a form of military torture. Maybe you're feeling a little tortured yourself right now. Parents suffering sleep deprivation are at risk for depression. And then you are *really* no good to your child. The basic idea is that we have to separate out sleep needs from sleep wants and work toward developing good sleep habits for everyone in the family.

Think of it as being similar to the way we transition our children with feeding. Newborns need to be fed every couple of hours, but eventually they grow and develop into children who eat three square meals at the family table. They move along a developmental continuum as their tummies grow and as we socialize them to our family's eating patterns and food choices. We always address their food needs, but we don't cave to their every food want.

Same goes for sleep. Newborns need to sleep pretty near all day, but by the time they are school-aged, they've consolidated their sleep so they no longer nap and they can now manage falling asleep, staying asleep and getting a solid ten hours straight. At least theoretically. In this chapter, you'll learn how to help kids get there.

WON'T FALL ASLEEP UNLESS PARENT LIES WITH THEM

It's 11 p.m. You wake up only to find yourself surrounded by stuffed animals and a tot in Dr. Denton's drooling on your arm. Damn. You've fallen asleep tucking in your tot again. Another evening lost.

UNDERSTANDING THE PROBLEM

No doubt you were tired and decided that lying down with your child while he drifted off to sleep was the quick-and-dirty solution to getting him to sleep. But now this "quick fix" has become a tradition that is robbing you of your evening leisure time, and it's robbed your child of the skills he needs to fall asleep independently. Oops. You've become a sleep prop.

Usually the parents who fall into this pattern have some hidden worry about the child being frightened and alone, or feeling abandoned.

I see it differently. I see children as being very capable, and that only good things result when parents are able to set reasonable boundaries and enforce them. I don't believe children feel abandoned when you train them properly. Children can learn that mommy and daddy love them—that you are secure, loving, predictable adults who are fully present and engaged during the social hours of the day— but you are not willing to socialize or offer unnecessary nighttime services. Children learn the family routine and are being properly socialized to participate in the group norms.

So how do you make the change?

Solutions

I have two methods: gradual transition, and cold turkey. Let's look at both.

Method 1: Gradual Strategy

If your child has never fallen asleep alone then this is the plan for you.

1. *Create a strategy.* Sometime other than bedtime, explain to your child that he is growing up and it's time to start making a plan for how he will learn to fall asleep on his own. Work with him to create a strategy. Staying positive, eliciting his help, and working together cooperatively will improve your chances of success. You'll see how below.

2. *Take Time for Training (TTFT).* If the child doesn't know how to fall asleep on his own, you have to do some training. Ask him to notice if he has a favorite position that he feels the most comfortable in, or what position he finds himself in when waking up. Is it on his tummy? His side? One leg jackknifed up? Ask your child what else feels soothing that can replace you. A teddy bear? A special blanket? Would he like to use a pillowcase that smells like you? Or snuggle with one of your T-shirts? Ask him what he'd like to think about as he winds down and drifts off. Some people count sheep, others think of special thoughts, maybe replaying a special day. Give him some ideas and guidance, and explain that all people have to discover their own private special way of soothing themselves.

3. *Move away over time.* With your child, map out exactly how you plan to gradually move out of his room. For example:

   - Lying down with him until he's asleep
   - Sitting on his bed until he falls asleep
   - Sitting in a chair by his bed but leaving before he is asleep (however, you remain down the hall in, say, your office or bedroom)

- Sitting in a chair by his door, then leaving and remaining nearby
- Sitting in a chair in the hall out of sight
- Not sitting, but staying upstairs

Be sure each night the child knows the plan.

4. *Plan sleepovers instead.* Let your child know that while you'll miss the nightly snuggles, you'll be more than happy to plan monthly sleepovers. Make a fun time out of it: movies, popcorn, stories, giggling and sleeping together. But it's a special date night you plan in advance and put on the calendar for every few months. It's *not* a nightly event.

Method 2: Cold Turkey

If your child falls asleep when a babysitter or grandparent is watching him, then you can clearly differentiate the child's needs from his wants. He wants you to lay with him, but he doesn't *need* you to. He has the skills to sleep independently.

1. *Give a heads-up.* Give the child some warning—maybe a day or a week, so that he can get his head around the upcoming change and you can enjoy your last snuggly nights together.
2. *Be firm and friendly.* Now your job is to follow through. Don't lie down. Don't get irritated or mad, don't start negotiations. Instead, sing your songs, say your good nights, kiss kiss and off you go. Yes, the child will probably cry, get out of bed and follow you (look for tips on dealing with this later in the chapter), or perhaps tantrum. Expect that. This will probably be the first of a few tough nights. What will you do to calm yourself while the child figures out this is a nonnegotiable new boundary? Listen to calming music? Do laundry in the basement? Call a good friend who can help you be strong? Make a plan to help you cope too. Hang in there. It's just a few nights.

WAKES EVERY FEW HOURS DURING THE NIGHT

Some kids are fine at falling asleep, but they are still up every few hours in the night. If they're up, no doubt you're up. Can you even remember the last time you had eight uninterrupted hours of sleep? Oh, don't cry now. I shouldn't have brought it up.

UNDERSTANDING THE PROBLEM

Sleep is a fascinating thing. The brain goes through various cycles, just like your dishwasher, over the course of the night. There is a very thin veil between the awake cycle and the asleep cycle that occurs about every 90 minutes to two hours. At this time, our children will stir and fuss. If we bound out of bed and go settle them, they come to associate this transition with a little night visit.

SOLUTIONS

Wait. Believe it or not, some children are not actually awake, though they may appear to be. They're just stirring. They may have their eyes open, be moving and making sounds, but they are not awake. Your arrival is what actually wakes them. So hold back and see if they resume the quieter phase of sleep.

Wait longer. Maybe the child is now standing up, holding on to the crib rails and wailing. You know she is awake now! At this point you can decide on your course of action.

Consider needs versus wants. If you suspect the child might be sick or hurt, or it's time for a feeding, you must attend to the child's needs. Do so in the quietest, quickest way. Keep the room dark, and keep your interactions to a minimum. You don't want her thinking it's daytime and playtime.

If you're satisfied the child is fine but simply awake, allow her to experience that waking in the night is boring since everyone else is sleeping and no one is around to socialize with her. (Aka: stop your nighttime visits to her room.) Stay in bed and let her fall back to sleep on her own, tears or no tears. Even very young children can put together the pattern that daytime is for visiting, nighttime is not.

But What If . . .

What if I don't agree with letting a child cry? Won't that hurt her and make her less secure?

I hear this concern all the time. Some parents want a no-cry solution to every discipline issue. We are so impressed and concerned when tears appear. I recently read about a two-year-old boy in Thailand who smokes 40 cigarettes a day. His parents say they have to give him cigarettes or else he cries. Crazy, right?

Here are just a few sleep facts to consider:

- Sleep is the time when the brain processes the information and memories from the day. The cognitive advances lost because of lack of sleep are never made up for.
- Sleep is when our neurotransmitter sites are flushed so they function properly during waking hours.
- Sleep is when growth hormone is produced, vital for growing children.
- Sleep is when the nervous system grows and repairs.
- Sleep is necessary for proper brain health.

All of these facts should help you feel more determined and committed to helping your child learn to not wake at night and instead continue naturally through all the brain cycles uninterrupted. We can help support the tendency to stay asleep, rather than awake, by not socializing with our children at night.

I leave it to you to decide when you feel you can let your child cry (again, only if you know she is safe). You know best when you feel your child is ready (and, in fact, when you are ready). However, it may help you to know that between six and a half months and about eight months of age is a great window for sleep training. Physically the brains and bellies have developed enough that they have the capacity to sleep through the night, but they have not yet hit Piaget's milestone of "object permanence." What is that you ask? Well, Piaget was a developmental psychologist who identified stages of cognitive development. Before eight months of age, if an object moves out of the child's sight, they believe it no longer exists. Out of sight, out of mind—literally! After eight months of age, however, the child is able to understand that while mommy may not be in sight she is still around, just in another room. Now the child has a reason to fuss and behave in ways that might elicit mommy to come hither. Sleep training becomes noticeably more difficult now.

How Many Hours of Sleep Do We Need?
Newborn: 16–20 hours a day
3 weeks: 16–18 hours
6 weeks: 15–16 hours
4 months: 9–12 hours, plus two naps (2–3 hours each)
6 months: 11 hours, plus two naps (1.5–2.5 hours each)
9 months: 11–12 hours, plus two naps (1–2 hours each)
12 months: 10–11 hours, plus two naps (1–2 hours each)
18 months: 13 hours, plus one or two naps (1–2 hours each)
2 years: 11–12 hours, plus one nap (2 hours)
3 years: 10–11 hours, plus one nap (2 hours)
4–5 years: 10–12 hours (usually no nap)
6–9 years: 10 hours
10–12 years: > 9 hours
Teens: 8–9.5 hours
Adults: 7–9 hours

CRAWLS INTO YOUR BED AT NIGHT

Some little gaffers are stealthy at making their way into their parent's bed without waking them. It's hard to send them back to their rooms to sleep if you are not even aware they are tucked in with you.

UNDERSTANDING THE PROBLEM

Your brilliant child has discovered the loophole in the system. He can reach his goal of sleeping with you if he deploys after you're asleep. It's a successful strategy. That's why he's keeping it up.

SOLUTIONS

We have to prevent the child from reaching his goal. Since you can't seem to wake, we have to take alternate steps: secure the fort.

When you go to bed, secure the door to your bedroom. Please read this properly. I am advising you to lock yourself in your own room, not the child in his. You can put a lock on the inside of the door, a child-safety handle on the outside, or whatever works to make your room un-enterable.

Tell your child that you'll be securing your door at night, so if he comes to your room, he won't be able to get in. Of course, he'll check that out for himself. When he discovers the door really is locked, he may just go back to bed and that's that! Or he may launch an attack to get back into your bed again. Put your head under the pillow while he bangs and screams, but remain silent. If you start talking to him through the door, that alone can be social payoff enough that the child continues his efforts to get in.

Some parents can't stand saying nothing. If you must, say "It's our sleep time, go to bed, see you in the morning." Expect the protest to get worse after you say this because you just confirmed that you do indeed know the child is there and you can indeed hear him. Of course, he'll work it harder. A chance still exists that you'll cave and let him in. Don't.

Expect to lose some sleep for a few nights, but that is all it will take for your youngster to know that you mean what you say, you say what you mean and you follow through (firm but friendly). You have established and enforced a reasonable boundary, and he'll get that after a few nights of testing.

NIGHT TERRORS AND NIGHTMARES

Does your child wake screaming in the night? What the heck is that about? (I think it's more upsetting to us than them sometimes.) What can we do to help them?

UNDERSTANDING THE PROBLEM

You're dealing with a child experiencing either night terrors or nightmares. Both cause children to scream and be visibly upset, but they are very different phenomena. Let's look at each.

Night terrors usually happen early in the evening, roughly two to three hours after the child goes to bed, during non-REM sleep. Basically, the central nervous system is overworking, just like it does in sleepwalking except instead of walking a fear response is triggered for no reason. All of a sudden, *boom!* The child will sit bolt upright in bed and let out a bloodcurdling scream that would make Linda Blair proud. The child's heart is pounding, he's trembling and inconsolable, and looks possessed. Because night terrors occur in deep sleep, your child won't even rouse or wake. He won't have a clue what you're talking about when you mention it to him in the morning. There is absolutely no thought content associated with night terrors. Believe me, it's a hellish experience for parents to see their child in a state of terror, but it's a complete non-event for the child having the night terror.

SOLUTIONS

What to do?

DON'T try to wake the child. He'll just be confused and disoriented.

The night terror will last only a few minutes—well, 3 to 30. Three sounds okay; 30 would be hard to bear. Stay with the child to be sure he is safe and doesn't injure himself if he starts flailing about.

Preventively, you can help reduce the likelihood of a night terror by making sure the child doesn't get overtired or overstressed. Some experts recommend briefly waking your child in the early evening, prior to when he usually has an episode, so that you are jarring the sleep cycle.

Nightmares happen later in the night, during REM sleep, which is when we are actively dreaming. Your kiddo will wake up screaming and crying, but he'll be responsive and able to be soothed. He'll tell you he had a bad dream.

Solutions

What to do?

DO give the child gentle reassurance and have him settle back to sleep. Use the suggestions listed in the next section, "Afraid of the Dark," to help him learn to calm his own fearful thoughts.

DON'T use this nighttime disruption as a time to change your bed policies. If you feel badly for your child and either tuck in beside him or allow him the comfort of joining you in your bed, you'll be starting down a slippery slope.

• •

The Importance of Dreams

Dreams are important. Psychologist Alfred Adler believed that dreams were representations of the problems we face in our waking life, and that while dreaming we practice or rehearse ways to solve our problems.

• •

AFRAID OF THE DARK

"Mommy, there's a monster in my closet!" Before you run and get the anti-monster spray out, read my suggestions.

Understanding the Problem

Fear of the dark and the scary creatures that might be lurking there are common in young children. It's a sign of a developing mind and a budding imagination. They are of an age when they begin to learn that life is not always rainbows and unicorns.

Being afraid of the dark may also serve the child in getting extra service or attention from her parents:

- She may get a second tuck-in
- You may stay with her until she falls asleep
- You may let her sleep in your bed

If the child sees a benefit in being scared, that can increase the child's likelihood of continuing to get really worked up about her fears. It's a pre-conscious decision, of course. We want our children to learn the exact opposite—to calm their fears independently. Here's how to go about it.

Solutions

Explain. Teach your child that she is thinking up creative thoughts with her imagination, but that there are no such things as monsters and the like. If you start looking for monsters or spraying her room with ghost repellant, you are in essence showing her they *do* exist. What if the spray wears off? Or the spray has expired? The monsters might come out again! Be clear that they don't really exist.

Reassure. Tell the child with calm confidence that it is *your* job as a parent to make sure she is safe, and that you know that she is. You are doing your job just fine, thank-you very much. Your attitude will be infectious.

Teach coping skills. Help your child understand that she feels frightened because she is choosing to think scary thoughts. Explain that if she thinks happy thoughts, she will feel happy feelings. The important point to make is that *she* herself is in control of the thoughts she chooses to think. She is not a passive victim of her runaway brain. She has to work to push out the scary thoughts by working to instead pick happy or calming thoughts. She decides what to think about. If the monster thought comes into her brain, tell her to smack it away, just as if she were popping bubbles. Help her find some good substitute thoughts to have at hand so she knows in advance what she'll think of when the scary thoughts pop into her mind.

🌿

Important note: If a child is being bullied, sexually assaulted or some other traumatic experience is happening, a child will have sleep disturbances, nightmares and other signs of stress, such as not wanting to go to school or appetite changes. Be sure you don't dismiss these signs. There could be a bigger problem that needs addressing. Speak to your child and pediatrician if you think this might be the case.

COMES OUT OF ROOM AFTER BEING TUCKED IN

Sure, you can do a beautiful tuck-in, but *then* the night antics begin. Does the child follow you out of the room? Do you see her sitting at the top of the stairs peering down quietly at you? Maybe she just barges right in and asks you for water, or claims she forgot her teddy or some other creative excuse for being out of bed. How do you make tuck-ins that actually stick?

UNDERSTANDING THE PROBLEM

A child might not dawdle getting into bed, but she can draw out the evening by repeatedly requiring your attention and services after bedtime. If she sees she can engage your company longer by these creative tactics, she will.

SOLUTIONS

Stop engaging. Stop allowing the child's strategies to be effective and prolong the night. Here are a few tactics you can employ.

Ignore the child. If she is sitting on the stairs, don't notice her, look at her or talk to her. Hopefully, she'll tire and bore and go back to bed on her own.

Use actions, not words. Walk the child back to her room, but don't chat and don't offer a second tuck-in.

Offer choice. Instead of threatening "If you come out, I am closing your door!" try offering a respectful choice that allows the child to decide for herself but also respects the limit you've set. For example: "Can you stay in your room on your own or do you need some help?"

If she comes out of her room, walk her back and say, "I see you need some help" and then secure the room with a baby gate or install a childproof handle on the inside. Don't stand there holding the door handle, though. The child will know you're there, and that is still a form of engagement. She will probably be upset with this initially and cry, bang on the door, call out to you. Don't respond. She'll learn that you mean what you say, and that this is an enforced boundary. You are saying to the child: "It's bedtime, this is where you need to be." If she can stay there on her own, great. If not, the gate solves that. You may find her asleep on the floor the first night. However, on the second and third night as you repeatedly enforce this limit respectfully, your child will learn that it's nicer to stay in bed after tuck-ins and that getting out of bed is no longer an effective way of getting more mommy or daddy time.

But What If . . .

What if my child cries so loudly it wakes the baby or the neighbors?

Yes, you have a few noisy nights to endure, but only a few. I suggest you tell your neighbors in advance that you are about to do some sleep training and it might be loud for a short spell. Buy them a bottle of wine or movie passes and thank them for their understanding.

Yes, the baby may wake, but that is no reason to change your strategy. If you constantly remind your crying child to be quiet and not to wake the baby, she'll quickly put it together that being loud and boisterous is one way to have the upper hand with you—and you'll get *more* noise, not less. Instead, since you know you are only going to do this training for a few nights, take the proactive approach of putting the baby to bed somewhere farther from the noise, or simply resettle the baby as you would with any other waking.

CHAPTER 4

POTTY TRAINING—AND THE DEMOCRATIC APPROACH TO TOILETING

Holds Bowels · Will Only Move Bowels in a Pull-Up · Refuses
Diaper Changes · Won't Use Public Toilet · Accidents at Playdates
· Won't Use the School Washroom · Still Pooping Pants at Age Six,
Seven, Eight or, Yikes!, Nine · Still Wetting the Bed at Age Seven
(or Eight or Nine) · Refuses to Wipe · Refuses to Wash Hands

Oh, the crap we go through to potty train.

I suggest parents approach potty training in much the same
way they do baby's first steps and walking. After all, we don't really
teach our children to walk, do we? It's human nature to want to get
off our knees and start using our feet like everyone else. All we do
is cheer them on along the way. Basically, the same goes for gaining
control of our bodily functions.

So why then do we have so many troubles with potty training?
There are whole sections in bookstores dedicated to the topic, and
yet you never see books titled *The No-Cry Walking Solution* or *Teach
Your Child to Walk in One Week*.

Parents somehow see pottying success as a reflection of their
parenting skills. They get very busy with the mechanics and process

and procedures and timelines of it all. And, of course, when things go awry, it all becomes so personal.

I am suggesting that, moving forward, you adapt that "can do," relaxed attitude that I know you had when you watched with awe as your child decided to work from being a crawler to a walker. As we move from diapers to undies, let's be okay with the slowdowns and slip-ups and inconsistencies and just go with the erratic course without getting bent out of shape.

If you are looking for a good book on the "basics," I recommend *Toilet Training: The Brazelton Way* by Dr. Brazelton and Dr. Sparrow. As for the specific problems, let's look at how to get out of those sticky (or should I say stinky?) situations.

HOLDS BOWELS

If I had a dollar for every stool that I helped pass, I'd be a rich woman. This is, bar none, the biggest pottying issue.

UNDERSTANDING THE PROBLEM

It's difficult for us adults to recall a time when we didn't have bowel control. What I find interesting is that, as adults, our bowel habits do tend to be consistent with our overall personality. Controlling people who are rule-bound and who like order tend to have orderly bowel habits. They may have difficulty moving their bowels in public places and prefer to have their, shall we say, "habitual ablutions" at home, in the same washroom, at the same time of day. It's all very orderly.

Little people who put a high importance on rules and orderliness also don't like feeling out of control. And if that sounds like your child, I'll hazard a guess that this characteristic is describing your eldest or only child. No, I am not a mind reader. It really is just a guess, but you can read *Honey, I Wrecked The Kids* to get the full skinny on birth order and personality development. Eldest and only children experience early life in the family in such a way that makes being correct, having rules to make sure you are correct and avoiding mistakes all very important to them. Feeling in control also helps them "get it right."

Children who value control may perceive moving their bowels much the way we adults might perceive vomiting. When was the last time you tossed your cookies? Doesn't it seem almost instinctive to cover your mouth and try to hold it in, even though your entire body is trying to propel your stomach contents out? Somehow we don't like this lack of gastrointestinal control and want to force it to stay down. Similarly, some children fight that feeling of smooth muscle action that sends waves of contractions down the muscles of the colon; so they hold their sphincter tight. Hold it in! Hold it in!

Imagine you have a tot who is already predisposed to being in control and rather type A-ish. Then your attempts to potty train make them feel performance pressure. More stress + more desire for control = less likely to relax and let the nervous system begin smooth muscle contractions.

If you get insistent, the child will not only have performance pressure but also turn pooping into a power struggle: "Mom is commanding me to sit and poop for her! I will defy her and show her that she can't control me. I am the boss of me!" With this mindset, the child perceives pooping in the potty as losing the fight with you.

Don't go down this path. Here is why. If a child starts to hold his bowels, the stool remains in the system longer. It becomes more compact, larger and drier. It's harder to pass this type of stool, and it can lead to a rupture or tear of the skin around the rectum. Now you've got a problem: it hurts when you have a fissure! So who wants to poop if you think it's gonna hurt? Associating moving our bowels with pain and loss of control is a problem on top of a problem. Then, just to make matters worse, the stretch receptors can become "tired" and ignore the constant signaling to move the bowels. The colon stretches beyond its normal size, allowing even bigger stools to form, which are even more painful to pass. This is a phenomenon called megacolon.

Caution: Many parents think their child has diarrhea rather than constipation when they see the liquidy accidents in the child's underwear. However, with megacolon, it's liquid that is seeping out and around the stool.

Solutions

So, all of that background is leading up to why you flipped to this section in the first place—whatcha gonna do now? The answer is to back off. End the power struggle and relax the child. Here's how.

Admit defeat. This doesn't mean she wins, you lose. It means admit that she, and only she, can decide when she wants to potty train, and when she wants to move her bowels. You are respecting that this is your child's business and that somehow you have been micromanaging. Give your child back the power and authority to master her own body in her own way on her own timeline.

- -

Sample Script

"I am sorry. I've been disrespectful. [That will get their attention!] I was trying to manage how you take care of your body when you are so capable of doing that yourself. I apologize. From now on, I'll stay out of your business about using the potty. If you need to go, go. I'll leave that up to you now. Let me know if you need anything from me, okay?"

The end. How easy was that?

Of course, this will work only if you really do believe that your child will manage. If you act like you don't care but secretly do (it's still driving you nuts), chances are your child will pick up on your true intentions—fooling her into thinking you aren't controlling her when you are in fact just applying an "Alyson technique" to win. Ain't gonna work.

- -

But What If . . .

What if I've already done that? I don't force them. Never have!

It's important to know that power struggles are about the distribution of power in the relationship and about trying to be in mutually respectful relationships, with neither party feeling like a slave or a tyrant. You may not dominate your child when it comes to toileting, but she may feel you are still too controlling in other areas of her life. Even though you have not been insistent in this area, symptoms can manifest in toileting because of a global problem in proper power sharing between parent and child. Think of ways to empower your child in all areas of her life while working through this issue.

If she continues to hold, try these tactics:

1. Increase her water and fiber consumption to help keep stools soft.
2. Increase her physical exercise if needed, as that moves things along too.
3. Take her to the doctor if you suspect a stool softener is needed and to rule out any underlying medical issues.
4. After your admit-defeat apology, drop all discussions of potty training. That means:

    • No talking to your friends on the phone about it.
    • No saying, "We're going out; do you want to try to go to the potty before we leave the house?"
    • No saying, "You look like you need to go pooh. Why don't you just try?"

With *no* pressure, we increase our chances of this becoming a *non*-issue. Once the pressure and attention are off, the child will begin to figure out that moving her bowels is her job to master, and the pursuit will become more interesting again—eventually. (It may take a few months at this point, so have patience.)

It's okay to disclose to your child what works for you: "Sometimes I like to read while I wait to go. I find it helps me relax and pass the time while I am waiting. Maybe that is something you'd like to try?" Watch your tone and language, though. It's important you don't demand it, as in: "Here, sit and read a book. That will help." Said in that manner, you'll come across as too controlling.

But What If . . .

What if it takes months? Am I supposed to clean up poopy underwear for weeks?

If your child shows no interest in the potty at this point and she is soiling her pants, simply let her know that she will require a diaper. Underwear is a nice choice, but freedoms and responsibilities go together: "If you want to wear undies, you must show me you are trying to get to the toilet to go."

Otherwise, it's back to diapers and she can try undies again in a few weeks or months. She may be more interested at that time.

Tactical Tip

Children who have a goal of power like choice. Put pull-ups and undies side by side in the drawer and say, "You choose for you." That reinforces the message that it's their business, their choice and they are in control. I would limit the choice only if the accidents are daily and consistent, with no sign of interest or regret for the accident.

WILL ONLY MOVE BOWELS IN A PULL-UP

A common parenting complaint is that the potty training is going fine—no accidents. But then I hear: "Rebecca has been dry for months now. However, there is one little problem. She refuses to poop in the toilet. She doesn't have accidents, but she asks to have her pull-up on for bowel movements. These things are costing me. If she knows she has to go and can ask for a pull-up, surely she can just go use the toilet!"

Understanding the Problem

For some, peeing in a toilet is fine, but pooping is not. It could be that they don't like the potential for a splash, or the feeling of "letting go" in such an open environment. Maybe they want to see what they have done without it "disappearing around the bend." It's hard to get into their mindset, but we have to respect that if they are not interested in pooping in the toilet yet, that's okay. They will some day—and that day will come sooner if we don't push them.

Some children prefer standing up as their pooping position. This is how they've been doing it to this point in their life. Turns out that standing allows the pelvic floor muscles to be engaged, and that makes standing a better position than sitting with feet dangling off a toilet. (If your child is using the big toilet, have a stool for her to rest her feet on while perched on the toilet seat, so she can activate those muscles that require planted feet.)

SOLUTIONS

Simply allow it. Go with it. Remember, we are just the support team. Tell them that if they need to poop, they can do that on the toilet or in a pull-up, but not in undies that need washing. ("You decide for you!") Many children will choose to switch quickly from undies to a pull-up or diaper, poop, then back to the undies. I know, it sounds fruitless. Such a waste of a pull-up to catch a poop and be thrown out mere moments later. Yet, I think you'll find that a few weeks of that routine will move them through this transition stage more quickly than any other tactic.

Pick an end date. Perhaps you could say, "What date would you like to choose as your No More Diapers Day?" Or, if you feel it might work for your situation, you could let them know, "This is the last package of pull-ups in the house. I won't be buying any more after this." Sometimes the child accepts the situation and decides she had better find a different way.

REFUSES DIAPER CHANGES

The smell of a rank diaper drifts your way. You do the classic one-finger maneuver, pulling at their pants to get a visual confirmation of your olfactory guess. Yup, it's a messy one that needs changing. ("Honey, I'm gonna need your help with this one.")

If you've been relying on wresting holds to change your toddler, I've got a new democratic approach that can help. In fact, I use this exact example (a toddler who refuses to get his diaper changed) when I teach about power struggles.

UNDERSTANDING THE PROBLEM

When babies are small they don't fight you over a diaper change, do they? As they age, we continue to assume that we can just stop them in their tracks, tug at their pants and smell their butts—all without a concern for them. But once children have a sense of ownership over their bodies, that is, well, rather disrespectful. They're communicating in their protest that they are ready for more power in this area of their lives.

• •

Children will not engage in power struggles until they are ready and able to be entrusted with more power and autonomy in that particular area of their lives.

• •

SOLUTIONS

Reframe the problem. Instead of getting angry with your child, interpret his resistance as a signal that he's ready for you to let out a bit more leash or to hand over a bit more control. Parents might jump to the conclusion that I mean the child should have *total* responsibility and so scoff at this advice. But what I'm recommending is a gradual transfer of power and responsibility to the child. Let me explain what that looks like at 30 months when you have a child refusing to let you change him:

1. Don't fight. Don't win. Don't lose. That is the golden rule for all power struggles.
2. Ask instead of tell. For example: "Can I check your bum?" Sounds like a little thing, but it tells the child you understand he is the manager of his body. That's empowering and respectful.

3. Offer choice.

    Examples:

    "You have a dirty diaper, would you like me to change it?"

    "Would you like to change your diaper here or upstairs?"

    "Would you like Mommy or Daddy to change your diaper?"
    (Please pick Daddy, please pick Daddy!)

If you've been fighting over diaper changes, your child will initially say no to every choice. That's okay. "No" is a choice he can make. However, we have to go back to basic democratic principles. People are free to decide for themselves. However, they are not allowed to rob others of their right to peaceful enjoyment of their environment.

Translation? Rather than forcing the child against his will to have his diaper changed, let him know he is free to wear a dirty diaper, but that he is not free to wear a dirty diaper on your lap, for example. If the diaper begins to leak, you may have to enforce the limit of "no wet or dirty diapers on the carpet or upholstery. If you'd like to stay in that diaper, you'll need to stay on the hardwood or linoleum."

Without controlling the toddler but still enforcing reasonable limits and boundaries that show respect for yourself and for order, the toddler is allowed to experience the outcomes of his choices. He begins to see the inherent value in a fresh bum—you can go more places and people enjoy engaging with you. Now there is intrinsic motivation to choose a clean bum! Not because you are being forced or coerced. Cooperation will follow.

But What If . . .

He gets terrible rashes if he isn't changed immediately.

Dissolving this power struggle won't take very long—maybe a few days or a week. During that time, a rash may develop. That is a natural consequence of wearing a dirty diaper and will also contribute to the child's intrinsic motivation of wanting the diaper changed instead of resisting a change.

Don't lecture. Instead of: "See! If you had let me change you this wouldn't have happened," try: "I am worried your bottom is going to get sore again from being in that diaper so long. I know that can become painful for you."

There, you've said it. The child has all the information he needs to make a decision. You are not responsible for swaying or convincing him.

Have the child stand up. Being on your back is one of the most submissive positions in body language. You may find less resistance if you change your child in the standing position. It does take some skill on your part, and it's definitely easier with a wet diaper than a dirty one. I've heard some mothers do the job while their child stands in the bathtub.

Distract the child. In case it didn't already cross your mind, there's always good old-fashioned distraction. I am not big on entertaining children every moment of their lives, but I am not so stubborn that I won't give a good idea a chance. Download free cartoons or simple games on your iPhone and hand it over during diaper changes. My parents were old school: I had a basket of toys that could be played with while on my back that came out only at diaper-changing time.

Use humor. Remember to use humor, which is probably my favorite antidote to power struggles. Humor keeps the mood light. Being silly and joking says "I am not fighting, I am not angry." The invitation to fight is not being extended.

WON'T USE PUBLIC TOILET

Believe me, if you look at the majority of public washrooms, you realize your child is actually pretty wise and using good judgment! The problem is, public washrooms are a part of reality, a challenge we all have to face.

Understanding the Problem

Some savvy kids who hate public washrooms wisely bring along a sucker of an adult who will pull a diaper out of her purse, or even a little portable urinal. These solutions are not helpful. They send a vote of nonconfidence to the child. Sure it sucks to use a public washroom, but it's part of life—just like getting needles and stubbing our toes. Show your child you have faith in her ability to deal with life's challenges, just as everyone else does. Special consideration and pity reinforces her belief in her inabilities. Instead, we want to build up her courage!

If you've been carrying a Plan B so your child has *not* had to use public facilities, you'll have to work with your child to develop a new strategy that doesn't include avoidance and special service.

Solutions

If your child's feelings toward public toilets are of a phobic nature, the standard approach is desensitization training: repeated and increasingly difficult exposure to the fear.

For example, if someone is afraid of spiders, therapy might start with something very safe, like having the client look at a picture of a spider. The next challenge might be watching a spider in a glass jar from across the room, then from up close. Take that same approach with public toilets. Start with a public washroom that you're familiar with, one that feels safe and friendly to your child. It's your child's perception that's important, as it's hard to know what part of a public washroom is bothering her.

Is it:

1. *Germs?* Just small exposure through touching the door and us-ing the taps might be a good start in this case. Show your child how to use a toilet-seat cover and hand sanitizer. Explain that exposure to germs helps us build our immune systems. Keep your own sanitation worries on the down low. They could be picking up on your fears.

2. *Strangers?* Use a public washroom that has only one stall, then moving to one that has two stalls, then a row. Move from a quiet bathroom to a really loud, bustling one. Use a similar progression with your proximity: First stay in the stall with her, then stand outside holding the door for her, so she can see your feet and hands. Eventually increase your distance. It's all about baby steps and each success building on the one before.

3. *Loud noises?* Public washrooms often have loud toilets and hand dryers. Sometimes I think it would be quieter and less windy standing next to a 747 preparing for takeoff. Teach them to cover their ears, sing a song, or prepare for the loud noise by counting down: "One, two, threeeeee!" when it's time to flush or activate the hand dryer.

Celebrate your child's growing bravery: "High five! You did it!"

Concurrently work on other experiences that will give your child other forms of mastery in her life so that she feels more confident in her overall ability to face challenges and be in command of herself. Generally, celebrate competency and downplay weaknesses, fears and inabilities.

● ●

Capable versus Incapable: Which Gets Mileage in Your House?

When we become impressed with our children's fears and inadequacies, they tend to express those qualities more. Our children need to be given more admiration and encouragement for their strengths and courage, and less mileage for their neediness.

Remember: needy children may make others feel important and needed, but at what cost to them?

● ●

ACCIDENTS AT PLAYDATES

Oh, great—your child is perfectly trained at home, but at the last three playdates she's been sent home with a little bag of wet clothes. Oops. Do you send her on that fateful fourth playdate?

UNDERSTANDING THE PROBLEM

Using the potty at home is one thing, but when your child is having a playdate at a friend's house, chances are she's having fun and is more distracted. She may think she can just hold it until she gets home to a more familiar surrounding, but she misjudges. Accidents are more likely to happen. And part of potty training is learning to handle accidents.

SOLUTIONS

Show your child how to get out of her wet clothes and to put them in a plastic bag to bring home. If she is early in her training, you can send a bag with a change of clothes in it to the playdate. However, as she gets older and accidents are less frequent, sending a change of clothes in case of an accident is actually a vote of nonconfidence. Instead, let your child discover what happens when she's out and pees her pants. How will she solve that dilemma? She might borrow a change of clothes from her playmate, or perhaps she has to go home to get changed and so misses the end of the playdate. Either way, the child learns that when mistakes happen, she can manage. It wasn't a tragedy; it was a problem she solved successfully. That's a great way to learn that she can, in fact, handle life's curveballs. But that lesson will be taught only if you too maintain this accepting attitude about mistakes—with both potty accidents and other mistakes.

• •
Mistakes are not bad—they are opportunities to learn.
• •

WON'T USE THE SCHOOL WASHROOM

You've worked so hard to potty train your child so he'd be ready for school. Now he is perfectly trained, *except* when he is at school. Grrrr! You're so frustrated. Every day there is at least a dribble in his pants, sometimes more.

UNDERSTANDING THE PROBLEM

So, why *does* a child who uses the toilet at home pee in his pants at school? Well . . .

- The classroom may have a washroom-break time that may not coincide with when your child has to go.
- Toileting is intimate, and the child may not feel comfortable doing his business with others within earshot.
- The bathroom itself may pose problems. Your child may not like that it's just off the classroom and not private enough. Or, alternately, the washroom may be down the hall, and he doesn't feel safe leaving the classroom, even with a washroom buddy.

SOLUTIONS

Don't pressure, punish or shame the child. Here's what to do.

Be patient, and prepare your child. If he needs time to figure out how to manage the school schedule and toileting requirements, expect a few accidents to occur initially. Schoolteachers understand that every child has to adjust. The best help you can give is to teach your child how to manage when an accident happens at school. Teach him how to wipe himself (try a wet wipe instead of toilet paper if that helps) and how to change into a spare set of clothing, independently. Practice at home.

Problem solve. Probe into what is troublesome about the toilet situation at school. Problem solve to find a workable solution. You may have to work cooperatively with the school. For example, with the child who doesn't like his classmates hearing him "go," he could try using the washroom down the hall instead of the one in the classroom. This could be arranged. Some students have made individual arrangements to use the bathroom at recess when others are outside.

Long-Term Strategies

The above ideas are only short-term solutions while you build up the child's confidence and help integrate him successfully into the group so that he feels a sense of belonging at school. Remember, our job is to prepare—not protect—our children. Steady, ongoing encouragement will improve matters with time.

• •

> *Alert*
> If accidents continue at school but not at home, your child may be expressing some form of protest against a teacher. It's be-havioral communication that I'll translate for you: "You harassed me about something and now I'll show you how upset I am by peeing my pants and irking you. Ha! Take that!" If that seems to be the case, try to discuss with the teacher how improving the relationship with your child might help. Share ideas for dealing with your child's behavior that work at home that might also help in the classroom. See if there are activities the teacher might do outside of class time (e.g., playing checkers at lunch, or helping look after the classroom aquarium together) that might build rapport.
>
> Often the teacher whose classroom-management style is strict and autocratic is unwittingly inviting retaliation. As a very last resort, you might request the child be moved to another classroom. Children who seek the goal of revenge manage bet-ter in classrooms with teachers who are more democratic and gentle in their approaches to discipline.

• •

STILL POOPING PANTS AT AGE SIX, SEVEN, EIGHT OR, YIKES!, NINE

Bowel control is usually attained somewhere around the age of four. That is not to say that a youngster might not have momentary mis-judgment that leads to an accident. However, there is a difference between an occasional accident and a child with encopresis—the fancy schmancy medical term for, well, pant pooping.

● ●

Definition
Encopresis is repeatedly having bowel movements in places other than the toilet after the age when bowel control can normally be expected.

● ●

There's a difference between a little kid having an occasional accident and a fully trained older child pooping in inappropriate places! If that is your case, something is smelly in the state of Denmark. Or is that rotten? Either way, I recommend you check with your doctor first to make sure there are no medical explanations. If the doc rules out anything physiological, we are left with a behavioral issue. Hmm. What would have to be true for this behavior to make sense?

UNDERSTANDING THE PROBLEM

Voluntary, willful moving of the bowels in inappropriate places is an outward sign of an underlying psycho-stressor. Basically, I explain it to parents as: "Your child is shitting at you." I think that is clear. It's the mother lode of insults, really, but is in keeping with a more passive style of aggression. The child is demonstrating a form of protest. It may be difficult to pinpoint what exactly she is protesting in her family life, but she sure is sticking it to her parents with this purposeful act of defecation.

SOLUTIONS

In most cultures, anything associated with bowel processing is considered the utmost insult or degradation. Given the severity of the problem, I suggest it's a reason to seek counseling. A counselor will probably want to probe into these areas:

- Is there a matter that you know has upset your child (moving cities, a divorce, a parent who has started dating, a change in childcare arrangements)?
- Are you a family that has an overbearing or controlling style?
- Are you a family that has a chaotic style?

- Is there another sibling in the family that could be perceived as the golden child?
- Does the child with encopresis get in trouble a lot? Or is she thought of as a "going concern"?

These types of issues can all contribute to feelings of deep discouragement, worthlessness, hurt and inferiority.

My advice:

Try to get your child talking. Practice active listening to try to understand what life in her shoes is like. Don't defend, don't fix, just listen. (See p. 188 for more details on how to be an active listener.)

Encourage your child to draw or write in a journal. See if she'll share a picture or a poem or a song to help you understand her feelings.

Express your love through actions. Love is a verb! Find more ways to show love and caring to your hurting child.

Be respectful. This means in all dealings, but especially when disciplining.

If things don't improve in short order, get counseling. While you are waiting for the appointment:

- Never shame your child for pooping her pants.
- Show your child how to manage cleaning up after a poop. Don't be angry when you do this. Simply show her how to get the fecal matter in the toilet, and how to rinse and soak the undies.

STILL WETTING THE BED AT AGE SEVEN (OR EIGHT OR NINE)

Getting a tad tired of washing sheets? When will they ever be dry at night?

There is a genetic component to bed-wetting that people often aren't aware of. A specific hormone is produced that slows the kidneys' functioning and reduces urine production at night. Some people don't produce this hormone until they are much older. If you or your partner were bed wetters or were late training for night dryness, this is probably the case also with your child. (Again, check with a doctor to make sure there isn't some other underlying problem that requires medical attention.) Or, there may be something else at play.

UNDERSTANDING THE PROBLEM

Some children discover through experience that peeing the bed has unexpected benefits: a little visiting in the night, having mom all to themselves while the sibs are sleeping (maybe mom doesn't want to deal with sheets, so the child is allowed to spend the rest of the night in mom's bed). Or to take it in another direction, maybe it ticks a parent off and it's a good way to defeat him or her. Either way, kids may find some usefulness to peeing instead of holding when they get those nighttime urgency signals from their bladder. Now remember, these are pre-conscious thoughts. We can't ask, "Why do you do that?" They don't know: it's inaccessible information to them.

SOLUTIONS

Normalize. We have to help our children understand that it's okay if they have accidents. Never shame them or be upset with them for this.

Take Time for Training (TTFT). Teach your child how to deal with the situation on his own, so it doesn't interfere with your nightly sleep. Show your child how to strip the sheets and make the bed. He doesn't need to do all that work in the middle of the night. It may be sufficient for him to pull the wet sheets off the mattress and leave them until the morning, and then use a backup sleeping bag that's kept in the bedroom—it's easy for a child to get out of his wet jammies and jump into a sleeping bag on the floor at 3 a.m. without disturbing the family. The next day you can teach him how to use

the washing machine. If your children are like mine, they will probably enjoy that responsibility—for a seven year old, it's tantamount
to learning to drive a car! By teaching our children the skills they
need to handle the situation independently, we've parented in a way
that develops both self-sufficiency and social integration. We have
removed any possible social benefit or payoff for getting up during
the night. No one else is disturbed by the bed-wetting.

Teach coping skills. Wetting one's own bed is one thing, but it's social
suicide at a sleepover. You can help your child learn how to discreetly
slip a pull-up on when getting into his PJs. Explain about cutting
back on liquids and emptying the bladder before bed. Teach him the
science of night-peeing so he understands the process and doesn't
blame himself for being faulty or bad or incapable.

REFUSES TO WIPE

It was Molly's turn to host the monthly book club meeting. Her
living room was a cultural mecca of brainy feminists, sipping pinot
noir and nibbling on blue cheese and roasted almonds. Atop the
intellectual chattering, a screaming child's voice bellowed down the
hallway, "MOMMY! WIPE MY BUM!"

Understanding the Problem

Some children don't like to do the wiping job and, frankly, they'd
prefer to outsource it. Maybe they tried themselves, had a bad experience (you can use your imagination here) and decided, enough
of that! Perhaps they don't want to risk trying and failing again, or
maybe they just enjoy engaging you in these services. Let's face it,
many children learn that competency leads to independence and in
many homes "independent" means being left alone or passed over for
less competent siblings. It's easy to deduce that if you want to grab
mom's attention, it's better to feign helplessness than competency.
We are a society that reveres babies and babyness, after all.

Many children see younger children getting the service of their mother and conclude that this service is a form of love. "Show you love me by caring for me" can be a problematic formula. Yes, children need to be shown they are loved, but feeling they are loved only when receiving acts of servitude creates a troubling script for relationships down the road.

Solutions

Take Time for Training (TTFT). Does your child know how to wipe? Here is how I moved that responsibility over to my daughters.

At first, the entire job was mine. Then I taught them all the little details, like how many sheets to pull off the roll, what position to get into, which direction to wipe, to look at your results, to throw the paper in the toilet, and repeat until the toilet paper didn't have anything on it after a wipe.

I would have my kids give it a try first, and then I would be the "pooh checker" and wipe after they were done. Similar to learning to brush your teeth, the toddler's skill is not sufficient to do the job correctly, but if you let her have the first turn, she learns while you make sure the job gets done. As her skills improve, your job gets easier, until the pooh checker is eventually out of a job.

- -
Tactical Tip
Have your child use flushable diaper wipes instead of toilet paper while she is learning to be a good wiper.
- -

Pass the responsibility ball. Once your child has proven she can wipe effectively, you are out of a job. Let her know, "You can wipe your bum all by yourself! You don't need me anymore. That is your job now."

Be consistent. Once you have told your child that wiping is her job, be consistent. Don't confuse her about whose job it really is by stepping in to do this service occasionally—you are not helping her, you are confusing her.

Zingy One-Liner: "I know you'd like me to think you can't, but I know you can!" (Said optimistically if they whine and complain they can't do it.)

REFUSES TO WASH HANDS

Why is it that some children seem allergic to hand washing? Especially after they have just used the toilet. Gross! You can't let them get away with that. They'll spread germs all over their toys.

UNDERSTANDING THE PROBLEM

Yes, cleaning hands after using the toilet is important. Without question. However, it's those "without question" issues that invite power struggles. Remember, with power struggles the issue is not really about hand washing, but rather our attempts to control our children. Instead of insisting, we need to find other ways to stimulate a willingness to cooperate in hand washing.

SOLUTIONS

Make it fun. Buy foaming hand soap and teach them to use the pump themselves. Show them how to wash for the entire length of a short song. Some people sing the alphabet song, but you could make up your own hand-washing jingle using your child's name to personalize it.

Ask instead of tell. Instead of "Hey, hey—wash your hands!" which is a command and will trigger resistance, try asking, "What do we do after using the toilet?" They feel more empowered showing you what they know and when they answer "wash our hands" you can say "You know it!" which is further recognition of their abilities.

Avoid fighting. Try a when/then statement. If your child is really refusing to wash his hands, you can't physically restrain him or make him. Don't fight. Let him leave the washroom, but wait for the first opportunity to use a when/then statement.

Examples:

"Sure you can have a snack—when your hands are washed."

"Sure I'll help you get the Barbie dress on—when your hands are washed."

"Yes, you can play in the backyard—when your hands are washed."

Notice I didn't say, "No snack until your hands are washed." That is a threat. Using when/then statements ensure their hands get washed—eventually—without fighting, the idea being that once the power struggle over hand washing dissolves, the child will be free to wash his hands after using the toilet without feeling like he is losing a fight and submitting to your controlling ways. With no benefit in defeating you, your child can get on with washing up right away like everyone else does. I know it's hard to believe, but in actuality, children really are much more like mindless lemmings, strongly motivated to follow the social norms of the group . . . so long as there isn't a power struggle interfering.

CHAPTER 5

FRETTING OVER FOOD—THE DEMOCRATIC APPROACH TO ENDING FOOD FIGHTS

The Pokey Eater · The Food Strike · Overeating
· The Picky Eater · Will Eat Only If in Front of the TV
· Gags or Spits Food Out · Won't Give up the Bottle

The human body can survive a week without food, but the human mother can go only two hours without fretting over it. Given our current paranoia surrounding kids and nutrition, it's hard to believe we used to send misbehaving kids to bed without their supper.

We all need to relaaaaax about our food issues in general. After all, malnutrition is rare, and most eating problems are actually social, or relational, in nature. If we could just chill a little, we'd return to the joy of eating together—the joy that is wired in our brains as a primal form of bonding with our fellow clans people.

As you read this chapter, keep in mind these two golden rules:

- A parent's job is to buy healthy food, model good eating, prepare nutritious meals and snacks, and serve them at fairly predictable times.
- A child's job is to manage his body, including feeding it.

THE POKEY EATER

There is probably some normal human variation in the speed of eating. Me, I talk a lot while I'm enjoying a meal, so I am usually the last one done and my food is cold, but hey.

Buddhists who practice mindful eating savor every bit by focusing on their food and chewing each bite 40 times (or something like that). Maybe you're raising the next Zen Buddha master and you don't even know it!

However, if you've tabbed to the part of my book called *The Pokey Eater*, rather than picking up *10 Ways to Know If Your Progeny Is the Next Dali Lama*, I'm guessing you have a child whose slowness is bugging you. That emotional reaction is very telling—it's your clue that the behavior is less stylistic than purposive.

• •

"Our emotional response to a child's behavior is in line with the child's intentions."

—Dr. Rudolf Dreikurs

• •

UNDERSTANDING THE PROBLEM

To understand the usefulness of eating slowly, we need to look at the typical parental responses it evokes.

Do you:

a. Sit like a hostage at the table waiting for your child to finish?

b. Nag him to speed up, to take one more bite, to get on with it, to focus?

c. Resort to feeding him yourself, just to pick up the tempo?

d. All of the above.

e. None of the above (confirmation he is a budding Dali Lama).

If you picked a, b, c or d, your child has creatively found a way of getting a lot of parental engagement. This is especially true if your slow eater has a sibling to compete with for the limelight. If the rest of the bros have left the table, this may prove to be precious one-on-one time for the slow eater and his supervising parent. This is also a "you can't make me" passive/resistant power behavior. All our urgings can't speed up his eating. He has sole control over his jaw muscles. So it's a fanciful form of dawdling, really.

SOLUTIONS

Mind your business. The child has the right to eat at any speed he wants, but *not* to hold up others. Allow him to stay at the table as long as he wishes, but don't feel you need to stay and keep him company. Continue on with your post-meal routines and simply ask him to pop his plate on the counter when he is finished.

Stop reminding, urging or nagging your child to take a bite. In fact, stop talking about his eating speed altogether.

Don't label. If his nickname is Pokey, don't call him that anymore. Don't joke with your friends on the phone about how Pokey will pick away at his plate until mold starts to form on the pork chop.

Find other things to chat about. Don't talk at the dinner table about the speed of eating. Engage in positive conversations instead of negative corrections.

• •

Making a Positive Connection at the Table

- Sit down and eat at the same time and at the same table as your children.
- No BlackBerrys or iPhones at the table, please (that goes for parents and children alike).
- Clear your head before coming to the table so you can be fully present and attentive. Be in the moment, really "there" in mind and body.
- Ask personal questions that show you care and want to know your child better: "What is your favorite TV show character? . . . Why?" "What part of going to the zoo did you like best?"

"When is your teacher's baby due?" "Why do people give snakes a bum rap?"

- Ask the kids to look online for table conversation starters or parlor games if you don't feel creative enough to come up with any.
- Ultimately, change up your mealtime atmosphere to be one of fun.

These strategies should help you make eating speed a non-issue. Since you can't control your child's eating speed anyway, don't attempt it (your lame urgings will only set you up for defeat). Without people reacting to his speed, dawdling will no longer serve the child's purpose, and he will likely abandon the behavior.

"No habit is maintained once it loses its usefulness."
—Dr. Rudolf Dreikurs

BUT WHAT IF . . .

What if I don't have all the time in the world? In the mornings we have to get out the door to school for 8:30 a.m. They need breakfast in order to concentrate in class. Lunch is hours away!

If the slow eater is causing you to be late in the morning, try one of these tactics:

Let the routines and schedule be the boss. Set a specific time when the kitchen closes and breakfast time has ended—and be consistent. This way, it's the schedule that dictates when breakfast time is over, not you personally. Having a schedule avoids the dreaded "because I say so" argument that triggers our power-seeking kids into resistance.

For best results, include the children in reaching a consensus about what time breakfast should be concluded in order to make it out the door on time; discuss it at a family meeting (see page 71).

Use a timer. Set the timer on the stove to ring at 8:15. You can moan, "Oh no, Mister Timer says we have to finish up now. Bummer, eh?"

You are externalizing the issue, reinforcing the idea that it's the schedule, not you, making this decision. Now it's the timer that is the meany instead of mom or dad. You're less likely to experience a meltdown reaction.

Of course, if you set a timer for your 14 year old, it's probably gonna make you look like a laughable control freak, so use your best judgment on when to retire the timer tactic.

THE FOOD STRIKE

Children sometimes refuse to eat altogether. First, be sure to rule out any health issues. Children who don't feel well will often refuse to eat, even though no other symptoms have yet appeared. Cutting a tooth, an impending ear infection, sore throat and the lot can interfere with a child's desire to eat. That's the body's way, and it should be respected. Show faith in children's ability to listen to their own bodies and fluctuating appetites (whether they are healthy or not). Don't presume you know their appetite better than they themselves do. We typically don't trust children with this responsibility, yet we are willing to trust infants when we nurse on demand.

A food strike, however, is different. "Food strike" is a term used to describe the child who is healthy but taking a classic power stance that screams: "YOU CAN'T MAKE ME!" to the parents.

UNDERSTANDING THE PROBLEM

What a brilliant child for discovering a behavior that totally unravels her mother. It's passive power in all its glory. The guilt, the worry, the feeling of parental failure! What if she starves? Oh my God, I'm killing my child! If you are four years old, most of life is still arranged and decided for you, so it's easy for a youngster to experience powerlessness in her life. However, if she can make her 40-year-old mother spaz out—well, that does make one feel rather mighty.

What is mom to do? Count to 10 and take some deep breaths, for starters. This is a parenting situation, not a medical crisis (yet). Let's gain some perspective: the first sign of starvation is lethargy.

If your child is alert enough to complain or vociferously and loudly abstain, she's doing just fine.

How did the child discover that food was one of her mother's buttons? Children are learning about their social world and thus are very observant. For them, the roadmap right to mom's hot buttons is posted with 3Ms:

1. Watch MORE closely
2. Respond MORE quickly
3. Respond MORE extremely/severely

Here is how the 3Ms might look with food-related hot buttons:

1. Mom paid extra attention, and babbled on a lot about food and needing to eat, eat, eat!
2. Mom responded immediately to any little hint of "supposed" food issues (the mere suggestion of not being hungry has mom talking about the child not eating enough).
3. Mom responds even more extremely in her measures to deal with issues related to eating—she is in a total exasperated flap, fussing with the day-care workers to get the lowdown on what was eaten at snack, asking constantly if children are hungry, pushing snacks.

Can you see how this mom is highly reactive and responsive to eating? Perhaps she is a dietician by profession or a foodie by hobby. Now that the entire nation has gone all Jamie Oliver, it could be any of us! Her 3Ms around food have taught her kids that eating is her hot button—and so they push it.

Eating is something parents *can't* control. Sure, we can use physical force to pick up a child and carry her away, or to take away one of her chucked toys, but you sure as hell can't make a child swallow pea soup. For the child, it's a sure win. Your kid is undefeatable. But here's the thing: kids seek and find these power-hungry behaviors only when they live in a world that they perceive keeps them in a one-down position.

SOLUTIONS

Until you stop caring so much about what your child eats, every bite becomes a measure of who is winning and who is losing the food fight. The rule with power struggles (and a food strike is a doozy) is don't win and don't lose. Instead DROP the rope in this tug-of-war with your child. A big fat reminder to you power-monger types: You can't "act" like you don't care; instead, you have to really let go of this concern. I can't tell you how many people I have worked with who initially faltered with this advice, only to have immediate success the moment they threw their hands up and said, "Whatever!" It's at exactly that moment that your little hunger striker will say to herself: "Crap. She's out. She's not invested in changing me anymore. I'm not gonna miss out on chicken and go hungry for nothing!" Up until that moment, the child in the power struggle has been honor-bound to refuse food.

DROP the Rope

Let's break down how to DROP the rope in a power struggle:

> **D: Determine whether you are in a power struggle.** You feel totally defeated by your child's unwillingness to eat and your inability to get food into her! You find your insistence over time has led to even more resistance.

> **R: Reassess the situation.** What do the Needs of the Situation (NOTS) call for? If she can get the food to her mouth, eating is her job, not yours. Stop micromanaging her business. If she is truly starving, it's off to the hospital for intravenous nutrition. If not, mind your own business.

> **O: Offer an olive branch.** Listen and call "truce." Let your child know you get it, that you've listened to what she's been trying

to tell you through her behavior: you've been overly concerned with her eating and that from now on you'll be more respectful toward her and her right to decide for herself what she eats. Below are sample lines to try out.

Zingy One-Liners:

"You know your body best."

"You really know how to manage your body all by yourself!"

"Looks like you're listening to your tummy."

"I am sure you know when you're full and how much you need."

"You decide for you."

P: Plow on positively. Make healthy meals, serve them at predictable times, don't look at what your kid is eating or not eating, don't talk about what she eats or doesn't eat. Just enjoy the meal and some pleasant table conversation. Let the proverbial chips fall where they may.

After a few days (or weeks or months), hunger will motivate any living creature to eat—but only if it's no longer a political statement, with eating viewed as defeat. *You* control that perceptional change. If you decide it's *not* your business to change your child's eating choices, she is freed of your tyranny and can choose for herself without the psychic repercussion of feeling manipulated by you.

Long-Term Strategy
Help your child find positive power in mealtimes. Here are some ideas:

- Could it be time to move from a high chair to a booster?
- Can your child practice cutting her own pancakes?
- Could she pour her own syrup if you put it in a little non-breakable cream pitcher?
- Is it time to retire the bib?

- Could she wipe her own face?
- Can she serve her own portions from the communal serving bowls?
- Is she a teen who needs you to step just that much farther back from analyzing and controlling her eating choices?

Involve your child in menu planning and preparation. Assure your child that you do understand that different people have different preferences. Explain that if she would like to make choices about what she'd like to eat (from a reasonable range of choices), you'd be more than happy to accommodate her requests (respect for child)—but at the appropriate time (respect for order). That means that you are not willing to whip up spaghetti *after* you've spent an hour preparing stew (respect for self). However, you can put meal choices on the agenda for the family meeting.

Remember, in a democracy you always have a say, but you don't always get your way. The important part is being invited to influence food choices, at the appropriate time and place. Don't fret that your five year old is going to demand sour keys for supper now that it's on the agenda.

• •

Basic "How-Tos" of Family Meetings

You'll hear me talk quite a bit about family meetings in this book. That's because family meetings are a principal way to ensure that the democratic process is alive and well in your family. This is the time when the family decides on family business together. I dedicated an entire chapter to family meetings in *Honey, I Wrecked the Kids* to teach the "how-tos" of holding these meetings. I suggest you read that chapter when you can. However, for now, here are the basics to get you going:

- Hold short weekly meetings (10 to 30 minutes max).
- Make meeting attendance voluntary, but be clear that whatever is decided applies to all.
- Post an agenda that all can add items to during the week.
- Assign a scribe and chairperson (rotate roles).

- Follow an easy, routine format:
  - ° Compliments: "What I liked about this week in our family . . ."
  - ° Old business: How did last week's solutions work? Tweak if necessary.
  - ° New business: discuss items on the posted agenda:
    - · State the problem,
    - · Brainstorm solutions,
    - · Narrow solutions,
    - · Decide (using consensus, not voting) which idea you'll try for one week.
  - ° Planning: sync family calendars with the upcoming week's activities, menu planning, transportation planning.
  - ° Dispensing of allowances.
  - ° Adjourn (confirm time of next meeting).

Take Time for Training (TTFT). Use this as an opportunity to educate. Young children can learn about the various food groups and help pick something from each food group for dinner. Our doctor's office had a nice poster of the food groups, so I asked for a copy and posted it on the fridge. When it was time for meal planning I let my children help choose the elements of the meal: "Let's pick a protein for supper. Where is that on the chart? Okay, now we need a few fruits and vegetables, which would you like?" At the grocery store, I would hold up items and ask: "Is a cucumber a fruit or a vegetable?"

But What If . . .

My son is fine with dinner, but it's the snacking and junk food before that we wage war over.

See this as an opportunity to *empower*, not *overpower*, your child. Open up some choices. I promise you, you'll be pleasantly surprised.

Below are sample scripts for the junk-food lover who wants more say in their eating independence.

Sample Limited Choice Script

"Looks like you *love* potato chips. They are yummy aren't they? I like them too. It's okay to have treats like that occasionally, but not every day. Let's decide how many times a week we should have chip treats, and I'll leave you to decide when in the week you would like them."

Sample Freedoms and Responsibilities Script

"I am worried that if you eat those chips too close to supper you won't have room for the good, healthy food. However, it sounds like you know your body and you feel you do have room for both. How about you make that choice for yourself? If I see that snacks are interfering with eating a healthy dinner and you're not able to manage that responsibility yourself, then I'll have to take over that job again."

OVEREATING

How chubby is too chubby? You hear so much about kids being unhealthy, but we are also not supposed to make them vain and teach them superficial beauty ideals. It's confusing.

If you are worried your child is overeating, get it checked out and get your concern validated or put to rest:

1. Make an appointment with your child's doctor. Physicians follow children's growth on a personal-growth chart. So long as the child follows the expected trajectory over time, he's fine. Some children will always be in the lowest fifth percentile, others will always be in the top fifth percentile. So long as they stay on their curve, it's all good.

2. If you are still worried, increase the number of times you see the doctor and give yourself permission to not fret between appointments. Stay focused on objective data instead of subjective worries.

3.   If there is an issue that needs addressing, the child is more apt to respond positively if he hears it from an authority figure other than his own parents. "Doctor's orders" are more likely to be followed without a power struggle.

What I am hoping to help you avoid is fanning the flames of an eating-related disorder. Food can take on meanings other than health and sustenance. Eating can fire up the reward center in the brain, especially now that so much of the standard American diet is laden with sugar and fat, which can lead to a psychological dependence and addiction. Here we are all worried about our kids smoking, drinking and doing drugs, but we're killing them quietly with our fast-food-nation lifestyles.

UNDERSTANDING THE PROBLEM

Food can be a boredom buster, a habit associated with watching TV. A "social activity" is walking to the corner store with friends and buying a four hundred-calorie chocolate bar. Putting on weight can create a wall and make us inaccessible, or purposely make us unattractive if we don't want to attract sexual attention. There are so many ways food and our minds can get interwoven in ways that are unhelpful.

Often eating is a shortcut for avoiding, rather than dealing with, negative emotions. Kids can have poor coping mechanisms, or lack problem-solving skills, and they turn to shortcut solutions, masking pain by eating and getting a short-lived jolt of feel-good pleasure instead.

• •

Democratic parenting techniques—such as encouragement instead of praise, logical consequences instead of punishment and family meetings that teach children vital problem-solving skills will help children cope with stresses in all areas of their lives.

• •

SOLUTIONS

What you want to *avoid* is the automatic assessment that the child is a poor decision maker or somehow lacks control. That thinking just invites parents to take the reins. It's a classic control maneuver (managing children's eating and imposing rules, like food lockdown). This approach usually invites a rebellion, as the children feel controlled and demeaned. If you hide the snacks, they start to sneak them into their rooms and gain great satisfaction in triumphing over you and your plot. In fact, even if they are not hungry for a snack, they will feel compelled to outwit your tactics just to overcome their feelings of being your puppet.

Instead we have to respect that the food problem is theirs, not ours. We are available to them should they want our support in tackling this issue.

So, if you have to talk to your child about eating issues, here is what you can do to help ensure it's a productive conversation.

Use an I-message to relay your concern. I-messages are aimed at disclosing something about *you*. A you-message, on the other hand, points the finger, assigns blame and is busy with fault-finding— putting the recipient on the defensive.

Sample I-Message Script
"I am feeling a growing concern about some of the eating habits you might be developing. I am worried that you're not getting enough of the good nutrients in your body."

Be a team. Rather than posing yourself as the authority who knows better, share information and resources with your child as a way to build an alliance, to be a team facing a problem together.

Sample Script
"I am feeling some concern about your eating habits. After reading this article in the paper on xyz, I thought it was something you should know about too. Are you interested in reading it? Or do you want me to tell you what I learned?" (Notice: I'm asking for permission to share information, I am not pushing my agenda.)

Remember to *always* show your child unconditional love. No matter what he looks like, how he is feeling, in sickness and in health, he needs to know you care; that you have his back, that there is no problem so great you can't tackle it together (as Barbara Coloroso would say).

Find out if something stressful is going on. And seek help if necessary. Is your child being bullied? Failing math? Believing that his new teacher hates him? Your child may need to speak to a counselor.

THE PICKY EATER

"Picky eater" is a derogatory label that paints a child into a corner. Try to find the positives of this quality. Why not think of your picky eater as a discriminating eater instead? You have a child who knows her preferences and is not afraid to express them; is loyal to favorite things; will never get poisoned by stopping to eat unidentified mushrooms on a hike. There's the upside.

UNDERSTANDING THE PROBLEM

Everyone is different. Some kids have issues with texture: eggs make them gag; the gooey seeds in okra and tomato are a turnoff. Of course, there is the classic childhood distaste of the bitter cruciferous vegetables (e.g., Brussels sprouts, broccoli). Turns out that genetics plays a part in whether the taste buds can detect the compound responsible for making these veggies taste bitter. So, in fact, *not* everyone does taste the bitterness of these vegetables. Genetics can be blamed for people who are "super sensors," having tongues with twice the density of taste bud receptors as a "normal" tongue. They have a more intense experience of tastes, so maybe olives and blue cheese and hot peppers aren't gonna be their thing.

Solutions

So how do you parent around all this?

Show respect. Respect the human differences that make us all wonderfully unique, making the family a place all people can be made to feel at home and honored. (Don't force a child to eat something she doesn't want to eat, or argue that "it's not *thaaaat* bad.")

Do not unduly burden any person in the family. This includes the cook. It is reasonable to leave the spaghetti sauce off the noodles, but it not reasonable to expect mom to cook a separate serving of chicken fingers when everyone else is eating spaghetti. The child with the discriminating palate must learn how to fit into a larger world and to cope with foods she doesn't particularly like. What will she do when she is at a birthday party? Or eventually a business lunch?

Expand the food repertoire. Develop your child's taste by:

- *Repeating exposure:* never give up on presenting a food, just because they "never eat it."
- *Being creative and fun:* carrots and bell pepper strips placed on a plate to look like a house are more likely to get eaten. Carrots called "X-ray vision carrots" are more likely to get eaten too.
- *Making it easy for your child to succeed:* a child is more likely to successfully consume two carrots if only two are placed on the plate; a pile of 25 is overwhelming and *none* will get eaten.
- *Serving food buffet style or in serving bowls:* make it possible for people to serve their own amounts and selections. Make sure to include something in every meal that the picky (oops, I mean discriminating) eater will like—and yes, that may mean that the sole food item on her plate is cucumber slices,

but the optics are that everyone is sharing the same meal. That's inclusive. There's no special service, and yet you are respecting differences.

- *Empathizing*: Try saying something like, "It must be hard to only like a few foods, since they are not always available. But I know you'll work it out. You always manage to find a way to look after yourself." (Again, you are setting up lovely expectations for coping and success.)

By implementing these strategies, we show the child that we respect her, but we don't give her special service, which can lead to a pampered attitude in life. The child makes accommodations to fit into the greater social order. *That* is cooperation.

. . . .

No ticker-tape parades, please. If your child does decide to eat a piece of pizza that has mushrooms (gasp!) on it, let's not make a huge fuss over the matter. Keep it on the down low if you want to encourage her to be exploratory.

. . . .

But What If . . .

What if her picky eating is compromising her health?

In this case, I suggest you get your suspicion confirmed by a doctor and work with his or her advice. The doctor may recommend a special supplement. The doctors I've talked to confirm that only in the most severe cases do they have to intervene. Mostly it's a case of managing the relationship between the parent and child, plus being patient and creative. Some children will eat vegetables if they are pureed into tomato sauce or grated into a muffin, for example. Experiment with hot, cold, cooked, canned, frozen—you get the picture.

WILL EAT ONLY IF IN FRONT OF THE TV

Fear. That is the problem, isn't it? I know the thinking pattern: "If I don't distract her with TV while I shovel this stuff in, she'll never eat." Or, "He gets down so quickly from the table, like he has ADHD and just has to move. But if I paralyze him in front of the TV, he'll get a full meal into his belly instead of a few bites."

UNDERSTANDING THE PROBLEM

The intentions are noble. Mom is trying to solve the problem of getting her fidgety child to eat a proper meal—at any cost. But, the "at any cost" alternative is actually sustaining the problem. The child has no motivation to act in any other way. He is actually able to evade his responsibility of eating at the table with the rest of the family. Instead, mother is bending the rules to accommodate the child.

SOLUTIONS

Our job as parents is to establish routines, and the child's job is to fit into that routine. That is how we begin to train our child for cooperation and social living. Without that training, children run the risk of developing a self-centered perspective.

Here's how to change it up.

Be firm and friendly. If the family culture you want to establish is that meals are eaten together at the family table, make it so. Invite your child to the table to partake in the family meal, and excuse him when he's done. If he gets down off his chair, that's his choice—but be clear that the next time food is available is at the next scheduled mealtime It's just like boarding school, camp, or a stay in the hospital. In group settings, children get that this is the system they have to learn to adapt to—and they do.

Firm: don't waiver on this arrangement by allowing your child to eat at other locations or by offering food during non-meal/snack times. That just confuses. Yes, he may eat less while he figures this new system out, but there will be no health costs to this short phase of adjustment.

Friendly: stay cheery and don't cast any aspersions. I know it feels really bloody cathartic to say, "Well, I told you so" or "If you ate when you were supposed to, you wouldn't be hungry." But that authoritative tone comes at a cost—typically, a backlash.

Instead, if your child comes to you complaining of hunger, simply be empathetic.

Sample Script

"Oh dear, you left the dinner table before you ate enough to make it through till supper. Rub your belly. You'll make it! Dinner is in 45 minutes and I know you'll manage it! You're just learning how to run your body and know how much it needs to hold it over between meals. You'll figure it out! Hang in there."

Keep it pure. Stay out of it. Let Mother Nature and natural consequences do the teaching here. If you are really worried, visit your doctor to make sure your child is healthy.

Natural Consequences

What motivates our children to stay at the table and eat their fill is the same thing that keeps us at the table. Hunger. The natural consequence of not eating enough is that we feel hungry—and it's not pleasant. Your fears that your children will starve if you don't force-feed them is inaccurate. (And I hope I have shown you the opposite is true.) The more you force, the more they shut down eating. The more you back off and leave it to them, the better they are at figuring out how much they need to eat and getting down to business about it.

BUT WHAT IF . . .

What if he has a tantrum?

Sure, he is no doubt upset. You've been inconsistent all these years and now you read this book and decide to enforce the rules. What the heck? As your consistency improves and the child learns where the boundaries actually are, tantrums about the issue will subside. Till then, turn to chapter 2 to read about how to handle tantrums.

Bees to Honey
Rather than insisting on attendance at the family table, which engages you in nagging and repels them, try instead to attract them! Make the family dinner table a special place. As social animals, the sharing of a meal holds huge significance. We're wired to want to participate in this social ritual, to feel included and like we belong. Keep your family meals fun, engaging, interactive and positive. Your children will want to be a part of them. Don't force; attract!

GAGS OR SPITS FOOD OUT

One teaspoon of sweet potato looks like a lot more when its sprayed all over you . . . Tired of getting what you're serving back atcha from a tot who spits out supper?

Understanding the Problem

What can I tell ya? "No means no." You have to trust your child. If she is spitting it out, she's done. (In fact, it is not suggested that you introduce your child to solids until she can turn her head away from the spoon and have enough tongue control to spit it out.)

Solutions

It's Logical Consequence time: Eat and you get more food, spit it out and that tells me you're done. Ta da!

Simply say, "All done," then wipe her down and mealtime is over. For now. You can offer up little meals every couple of hours and see if you get a better response. They'll connect the dots that if they want to keep eating they need to not sputter and spit it out.

Different moods make food okay one day and unacceptable the next. Our job is to respect what our children reject, but to continue exposure and opportunities to adapt to new tastes and textures. Gradually increasing the size of the chunks, the thickness of the cereals, the ratio of solids to purees helps move children along a gradual continuum. However, we should never create pressure or go against their will. Keep food and eating fun and be patient. Any worries about nutrition should be brought up with your doctor. Just know that you have human evolution on your side and things generally work out. It's better for the species to eat and survive.

WON'T GIVE UP THE BOTTLE

You ask me: "How do I get my toddler to give up the bottle?"

I ask you: "Who's his supplier? Is he smuggling bottles in behind your back?"

Basically, the scenario boils down to the same salient points. You offer a sippy cup, he protests. When he refuses the alternative, you worry he'll dehydrate and you go back to the bottle.

You learn: He won't give up the bottle.

He learns: Mom is a pushover; protest till you get your way.

Win the battle of the bottle.

Understanding the Problem

As parents, it's our job to teach our children skills and to move them from dependence toward independence. When we infantilize them, it can lead to feelings of inferiority. The sooner children are able to mature and overcome inferiorities, the better. So moving from baby bottle to regular cup is another opportunity to graduate them to joining the traditions of others in the family. It feels inclusive! Yet, some children need more encouraging than others. They may not be so eager to give up their old ways. Some don't like change of any kind. Some have a special relationship with their bottles, the way others do with their blankets or pacifiers. (Sucking can be a source of soothing—it happens even in utero.) I am not telling you *when* to give up bottles, I am only giving you a beacon to steer toward and tactics to use when you're ready.

Just know that in our culture children often *like* being a baby because they see that in our modern families, there is a lot more importance paid to those who "can't" than those who "can." Being helpless seems to keep adults really involved.

I hope that makes you feel better about your decision to move forward with bottle weaning.

SOLUTIONS

Here are empowering ways to make the transition.

Set limits that allow for choice. Here are three limits you can try setting. See what you think will work for your tot:

1. *Limit how* many *bottles in a day:* Prepare two bottles for your toddler and put them in the fridge. Let your child know that those are his bottles for today, but when they are done, that is all there is until tomorrow. (He can have them anytime he wants.) You control how much, the child controls when.
2. *Limit when he has his bottle:* Alternatively, you can control the amount by tying it to a specific time of day. For example: "Yes, you may have a bottle; we have those at bedtime."
3. *Limit what is in the bottle:* Only offer bottles filled with water. Some children will not want their bottle if they can't have milk in it.

Set up the "Final Bottle". Have the child help you pick a "last bottle day"—maybe a birthday or some other special day. Mark it on the calendar and have him help you pack up the bottles for a friend's new baby or the garbage. Some children like the act of generosity, and being a part of the process is empowering for them. Having it marked on the calendar allows your child to get his head around it, to prepare for it. Meanwhile, you stay firm on the arrangements.

Or—more elusive but also effective—tell him: "This is the last nipple that I am buying. When it wears out, I am not buying a new one." Ergo, last bottle.

And then, *stick with your plan.* Say what you mean, mean what you say, and follow through, firm and friendly. That's effective parenting.

● ●

Can't or Won't?

I had a mom ask me for help with her eight-year-old son, who still required everything he ate to be pureed in a blender. I asked if he had a phobia about choking or any throat disorders in the past. Nope.

I asked if he had managed to swallow anything solid yet. Yup. Potato chips and brownies.

I went back to first principles: he had the right to eat food pureed, but she had the right to refuse the extra burden of pureeing his dinners. Therefore, she needed to teach him how to use the blender.

I am sure that sounds extreme, but it's a good example of the slippery slope we can all go down. Where is the boundary? When can you clearly separate out the developmental (can't do) from the behavioral (won't do)?

I think my questions clarified that the boy "wouldn't"—rather than "couldn't." Again, mother's fear of his *not* eating clouds the issues and creates more problems than it solves. A hungry child will eat.

● ●

CHAPTER 6

FROM TROUGH TO TABLE— THE DEMOCRATIC APPROACH TO TABLE MANNERS

Won't Set the Table When It's Their Job · Won't Come to the Table When Called · Gets Up and Down from the Table · Who Invited Tom Foolery to the Table? · Talks with Mouth Full · Refuses to Clear Plate · Toys at the Table

Table manners. Is that an oxymoron? The family dinner table is a good barometer of how democratically a family is operating. Does dad sit at the head of the table unaware that he is holding up patriarchal traditions? Does mom run back and forth from kitchen to table delivering the forgotten salt shaker, a request for a refill of milk or second servings of lasagna? Sure, she's a trial lawyer from 7 a.m. to 6 p.m., but at home she slips on her invisible apron and becomes caregiver to the family. Do the kids bicker? Is most of the conversation about behavior? ("Did you wash your hands?" "Did you even try it?" "Watch your milk." "Leave your sister alone.") The entire family dynamic can often be seen in this one little snapshot of family life.

As menacing as mealtimes can be, the family meal is actually at risk for extinction in modern family life. Research from the Vanier Institute of the Family shows that Canadian families eat only about

50 percent of their meals together. I mean, lunch and breakfast are next to impossible, but supper? Our minivans are becoming the dining tables of the twenty-first century, with 40 percent of our daily calories consumed in cars via drive-through windows. Well, how else ya gonna feed 'em when you have to shuttle kids from after-school tutoring to evening hockey practices?

What a missed opportunity. There's something really sacred about coming together to eat. The breaking of bread, the celebration of the harvest, the coming together as a community to share food—it's magical. It contributes to our feeling of connectedness. We forge bonds over food. We have deep emotional memories about eating rituals. Ask children and they will say, "It's the *one* time that my whole family is together at the same time," and our children want (and need!) more of it. Teens especially—even while they moan about it. What teens don't tell you is that they miss talking to you. Statistically, where's the mostly likely place to find adults and teens talking? Yup, over the supper table.

So, that's my sorry tale. I want to inspire you to revamp your thinking about the family meal. We need to reclaim supper. Let's revitalize the ritual that is fundamental to the family institution. To that end, I am offering up solutions to the major problems that, parents report, cause friction.

WON'T SET THE TABLE WHEN IT'S THEIR JOB

So, here is the first fight—the one that sets the tone for the whole meal. Why does getting kids to set the table have to be such a battle? You don't have this headache doing the drive-through at Taco Bell. But don't grab your car keys just yet.

UNDERSTANDING THE PROBLEM

I can understand the child's resistance to being told to set the table. It's the same feeling men have when women bark at them to cut the grass, or how women feel when their partners yell, "Iron my shirt, I have a meeting this morning." No one likes to be ordered, commanded or pushed around. And I don't want a kid who is okay with being pushed around, do you?

How we approach chores impacts whether our children (or spouses) feel reduced to mere slaves forced to perform free labor or if they feel like equal team players who are doing their parts to help run Team Family. Team players are more willing to set the table. Well, duh!

Solutions

If we are to change up our goal from making children mind our orders (obedience) to making them *want* to do something (cooperation), we have to create the conditions that foster cooperation. What are those, you ask?

1. Being in a mutually respectful egalitarian relationship, where neither feels like a tyrant or a slave to the other.
2. Feeling a sense of belonging, affiliation and connectedness to the group, team or family.

Okay, easy to write, but how do we actually pull that off? Here are strategies that should improve matters.

Involve your kids. Ask yourself, "Who created the family chore list? Who decided which child was responsible for what task?" If you did—time to change that up. Bring up the topic of chores at the family meeting and see if you can amp up the kids' involvement by asking them to sign up for jobs, or create new jobs they'd like to do to help the family.

Shake things up. No kid wants a life sentence as the table setter or kitty-litter-box cleaner. Discuss how often people would like to rotate chores. Maybe a week of table setting has led to task-boredom and it's time to shake it up.

Create teams. My children liked signing up to do chores together, or teaming up with a parent. Many hands make for a light load, right?

Now instead of being banished from the TV room to the Siberia of the kitchen, forced to set the family table alone, the chore becomes special "Daddy and Daniel time."

Let natural consequences unfold. Go ahead and make supper as usual, but when it's done, just put it on simmer. Pour a glass of wine and start reading the paper. Eventually someone (other than the authority figures in the house) will complain, "I'm hungry. When are we eating?" You can say, "When the table is set." After all, you have completed your job. You cooked the meal. Hunger will motivate *someone* to set the table, even if it is not his or her turn to do it.

Show your appreciation. Instead of complaining when the child *isn't* doing his job, show your appreciation for his help when he *does*. This tells him just how important his job is to everyone. After all, "without the table set, we can't eat. It is a big help to everyone. Go Daniel! What a helper!"

Let siblings help. Perhaps a famished sibling offers to do the table-setting job for dawdling Daniel, who is the official table setter that week. Let the sibling help her brother out and recognize this act of kindness. After all, we are a team, and it's nice to know we have each other's backs. But, a word of caution here: if the sib's sole motivation is simply to make herself look better by making Daniel look bad, either don't make a big deal of her contribution, or dissuade her from doing the job by saying something like, "That's okay, Daniel is capable of managing his responsibilities." Don't take the "Look at me, I'm the hero, Daniel is a putz" bait.

Bite your tongue. Another way you might let this play out is to serve the meal, call the family to the table and . . . bite your tongue! The necessity for the table being set will quickly become apparent to the errant table setter. Without being nagged or reminded, Daniel will recognize the needs of the situation on his own, and that is far superior to a lecture. By reaching his own conclusions from natural consequences (life teaches the lessons, not you), children are less likely to moan and rebel—which is usually the fallout from being told, reminded, scolded and generally coerced into a job.

But What If . . .

What if both kids are supposed to set the table together, but that leads to fighting and a child complaining, "Moooom, Brianne is not doing her part! She never pulls her weight."

Zingy One-Liner: "I am sorry you are having trouble motivating your sister; I am sure you two can work it out."

This one-liner is an example of putting your children in the same boat and not getting involved in their sibling squabbles. Brianne may be much smaller than her big brother Daniel, but she is able to hold her own by withholding her help. Daniel may have used his sister's bike that day without asking, and while you might have thought that was unfair because she is smaller, weaker and supposedly helpless to get her bike back, she now has the ability to conquer her brother by refusing to help him. When children are left to deal with each other independently, they'll both eventually realize that it's not advantageous to tick one another off. This lesson is lost if parents get involved in siblings' conflicts.

But What If . . .

Respectfully, Alyson, I really don't think my kids can do this. I see one child always getting their way over the other, and I can't sit by and idly watch that injustice.

If your children can't solve the problem between them, put it on the family meeting agenda (see, p. 71). It's okay to help children find solutions so long as it is not during the time of conflict.

Just to be clear here: there is no right or wrong way to manage the distribution of labor in your house. Table setting doesn't even have to be a kid's job. What matters is the process of involving everyone and creating a system that brings harmony and works for your situation. There have been times in my family life when the entire household ran more smoothly if I did all the time-sensitive food-management jobs and left the children to do their chores on the weekends instead. Find the solution that fits your family.

- -

It Worked for Us

At the Connelley's family meeting, the agenda item was difficulty getting people to set the table in a timely manner. Mom explained she didn't want to feel like a nag, or to have to be the table-setting police. Was there a way to do it better?

The youngest child, Sean, spoke up: "I hate setting the table for dinner because everyone else gets to watch the end of the show and I have to leave just when it's getting good."

Ah. Turns out that dinner was always served at 5:30 p.m. and that meant that daily at 5:20, someone was called away from the favorite after-school show. And he or she wants to know how it ends!

The family brainstormed a few options: If the table had to be ready for 5:30, it could be set at *any time* before that, for example, right after school at 3:30, or a little bit at a time during commercials. Or the family could move the family mealtime to 5:40. They decided to try starting meals 10 minutes later for one week. At the next family meeting during "old business," they discussed how it worked. Everyone agreed the problem was solved.

Solutions, not discipline. The team worked together to be responsive to everyone's needs and meet the needs of the situation.

- -

WON'T COME TO THE TABLE WHEN CALLED

Ah, yes, it seems like we should be able to just call our children and they come hither. Well, we can dream, can't we?

Let's step into the world of the child and see what, potentially, the problem could be.

UNDERSTANDING THE PROBLEM

It could be that dinnertime is inconveniently called near the end of a TV show. (How fast would you run to the table if I called you five minutes before the end of *Grey's Anatomy* or *Desperate Housewives*?)

Or it could be that, in the age of social networking and texting, your wired children are actually in the middle of conversations with about 10 friends. Expecting them to push back from the keyboard immediately and come to the table is actually as rude as hanging up the phone without so much as a good-bye. We need to respect that they are in the middle of something and need time to wrap up. They should be commended for their manners, not chastised for being late.

If you're convinced that none of these is the culprit and it's just good old-fashioned "driving your parents nuts" behavior, then we're looking at dawdling—a wonderful form of passive power. It's a child's creative method of *not* giving you cooperation. In fact, somehow, moving right along and coming to the table promptly feels to them like being a puppet to your commands. Mom says "jump!" and they ask, "How high"? Dad says, "Come to the table, it's dinnertime," and they say, "Sir, yes sir. Permission to log off, sir!" When you're a kid getting little directions like this all day long, day after day, it becomes irksome. Even, dare I say, oppressive.

Solutions

Share information instead of giving marching orders. The idea is that we are aiming to control the social order, not the child. So, instead of ordering, "Turn off the TV—it's dinner," share information instead: "It's suppertime." Notice, no instruction. The child is free to choose for himself. Let the natural consequences unfold.

- -

True Story

Ben liked to watch TV in the basement before dinner, but getting him to the table was always a chore. The problem was so pervasive that mom and dad got very terse and insistent as soon as the clock's hands hit 6 p.m., assuming, "Here we go again!" From Ben's perspective it meant being treated rudely for no reason. He believed they had no faith in him to do what was needed. Every night they barked, "Get up here right now, mister!" When Ben's parents took my advice about *not* urging Ben to the table but instead just announcing the meal, he arrived immediately the first day, declaring, "See! I do come to the table; you just never gave me a chance to show you."

- -

Ben was expressing a frustration many children feel. When we remind children, they lose the satisfaction of showing us they know how to be self-directed. Instead, be patient, add that paaaaaaause that allows them to be successful in managing their lives and honor their abilities instead. It's another chance to be more encouraging.

The principle we're tapping into here is the ole *attracting bees with honey*. The more you urge children's speed, the more they slow down, so instead we'll draw them to the table using the power of our social attractiveness. See p. 71 for more on this principle.

• •

Natural Consequences, Life's Best Teacher
There are natural benefits to being at the table punctually:

- The food is hot.
- There is more of the food the child likes still left.
- The child gets his choice of seats at the table.
- The child gets more time with the family.
- The child gets his parents' undivided attention.

He'll figure it out.

• •

GETS UP AND DOWN FROM THE TABLE

Is your dinner table a veritable feeding trough? Nothing more than a fancy repository for chicken nuggets? Do your kids take a bite, run around playing for a bit, mosey over for another gulp, then take off again, french fries hanging out of their mouths?

Hmm. How do you like that as your family custom? Do you want to have grandma and grandpa over for holiday dinner and have that going on? Of course not! Perhaps you're worried that your little Charlie is hyperactive or maybe you and your partner have been arguing over whether he is just too little to be expected to sit still at the table. Well, if you've flipped to this section of the book, what must have crossed your mind is, "When, when, when do I enforce the rule of staying at the table to eat?" (Oh, and there's also the issue of the how.)

My answer: Now. I mean, for Pete's sake, even if he is the kind of kid who has the Ferrari brain of a kid with ADD, or the energy of Jim Carrey or Robin Williams, he is *not* excused from the responsibility of being cooperative.

UNDERSTANDING THE PROBLEM

Here is how I conceptualize the situation: freedoms and responsibilities go hand in hand. As soon as your toddler moves from a high chair to a booster without a strap, he is able to get up and down on his own. Yeh, celebration! That is an important move toward autonomy and self-directedness. I suggest you make this move as early as possible. However, being free of straps and restraints doesn't mean he gets to bring havoc to everyone else's mealtime. We need to train for both autonomy *and* social integration. This is exactly the stuff of child-guidance. We need to teach children our culture's table customs.

It's every child's job to discover the new limits and boundaries, and to road test them to make sure they are true boundaries. Expect your child to be a good explorer, and be prepared to be an effective parent ready with the child-guidance principles in hand.

I know so many people who leave their children in seat restraints simply because they don't know how to train them to be self-motivated enough to sit down without being strapped in.

Ta da! Here is how.

SOLUTIONS

We want to teach our children that, in our culture, we sit at the table for the duration of the meal and leave only when we are done. To teach them this social norm, we must provide an experience (rather than flapping our lips about the rules) that demonstrates this.

Demonstrate logical consequences. I suggest you teach this social custom through the use of a logical consequence (LC). Every LC must meet the 3R criteria:

Reasonable

Related

Revealed in advance

If your rule is missing any one of the three Rs, it's a punishment.

A logical consequence of your child's leaving the table is that his opportunity for eating is over. He is, in essence, excusing himself. Therefore, his plate is removed. That is reasonable and related, and so your child will understand the logic to your actions and won't perceive your removal of the plate as punishment, exerting your great personal power over him to sabotage him for leaving the table.

To satisfy that last R requirement, we need to reveal the rule in advance.

- -

Sample Script

"We sit for the meal. When you get up from the table, that tells us you're done, and we'll remove your plate."

When your child gets down, you remove his plate from his place setting. Moving it to the middle of the table, or off to the side, is fine; you don't want to make a big, grand statement that comes off as, "See, now look what you've done!" Instead, quietly and gently move the plate aside and calmly state: "I see you are done." Then, continue your meal.

If he scrambles back to his chair and says, "No, I am not done yet!" (which he will the first time), you can reply: "I am sorry. You decided to get down. You can choose differently next time."

- -

And that's it—don't say anything else. There is no need for negotiation or reminding him of the rules. He gets it. It's simple reality. The more you talk and explain and reassure or moralize, the more it becomes about *you*. Don't distract your child from the learning:

> Stay at table = food to eat
>
> Leave table = no food to eat

I know, I know, you have always wanted to do that, but what held you back is that you know your child will have a total meltdown. You've tried to prevent the tantrum by caving. Sure, in the short run you short-circuited a tantrum, but the mess you've created is worse: now he gets up and down from his seat at the table *and* threatens you with tantrums for anything he wants. Gotta get off that crazy horse.

So, here is the big pill to swallow: yes, he may freak out. Sure, he doesn't know you were suddenly going to be firm about something, ya big pushover. It really doesn't help your child when you are inconsistent because he never knows if you really mean what you say. So when you do really mean it, it throws him for a loop. He's thinking: "Wow, she is never firm on this one. Why is she today? That is so unfair." It's that feeling of being treated unfairly that prompts the tantrum. (Turn to chapter 2 to learn more about dealing with tantrums.)

The first time you impose the rule it's hard for everyone. You hate that your child is responding to a sudden change in the way things play out in your home and is upset that you are not doing what you usually do, which is to cave to his demands. Alas, all this turmoil is proof that you are doing something effective. The child is experiencing the consequence of his personal choice and is disappointed with the outcome. This bodes well for him choosing differently in the future.

But What If . . .

What if they don't care if you remove their food?

What can I say? Sorry, they are not hungry. You certainly don't want to force them to eat. Only they can monitor their tummies and their appetites. Sometimes children have growth spurts and eat a ton. Other times they are not feeling so great and so they eat less. If we leave them to self-monitor, they'll manage just fine. I find that most parents seem to want to scrutinize suppertime as the indicator of how well their child is eating. But by suppertime, children have usually consumed most of their daily calories. For children, dinner is the smallest meal of the day. And that is good. The body is almost done all its activities for the day. It's on its way to resting for the night. It doesn't need energy now.

● ●

"Eat breakfast like a king, lunch like a queen and dinner like a pauper."

—Adelle Davis

● ●

- -

Tactical Tip

Be sure not to alter the timing or quantity of the next meal. If Jamie got down from the lunch table at 12:02 p.m. and his snack is not usually served until 3 p.m., don't move the snack any earlier or make it any bigger to compensate for Jamie's uneaten lunch. Lots of kids learn to turn up their noses at the chicken breast served at lunch if they know they can push away and get a snack of bagel with cream cheese in an hour. Instead of you altering the patterns to meet the children's preferences, it is the children's job to adapt their eating to fit into the family mealtimes.

Follow Up: If you continue with this tactical tip and you don't get upset or preachy about their choices, by day two or three the tantrums will disappear; your children won't feel taken—they have learned. They get it. They are free to make decisions for themselves, but they know that the decision to leave the table means no food till snack time.

- -

WHO INVITED TOM FOOLERY TO THE TABLE?

How can you discipline your kids for being happy and silly and for having crazy energy? After all, we do want to make the family dinner table an enticing place to be. And, a few jokes are fun. We did all laugh at Julia when she put the onion ring on her ear like an earring last night, so of course she is putting the mashed potatoes on her wrist like a watch tonight. If you want some help with this issue just pull my finger . . . Snort, snort.

Understanding the Problem

When you put a couple of siblings who have not seen their parents all day around one table, it's show time! (I even visualized the Bob Fosse "jazz hands" as I wrote that.) Children vie for the parental spotlight. Some gain their parents' attention by behaving in negative ways (pouting, whining, complaining), but they may also discover they can get you to attend to them if they disturb the proceedings in more humorous ways. Though the behaviors are (slightly) more tolerable, it's still misbehavior, um, I mean, a mistaken approach. The child is seeking undue attention or seeking power over others.

Solutions

Ignore the attention-seeking behavior. This is the first rule of thumb for children seeking undue attention. That's right: ignore the attention-seeking behavior while working to *engage* the child positively. Attention seeking tends to yield a very verbose response from parents, so aim for as little verbal correction as possible. In other words, say nothing, and use actions instead.

For example, if Jessie is bubbling his milk, don't say, "Stop that, this isn't a barn." Instead, try actions rather than words: remove the milk glass and then swiftly move on—"Is your team going to make it to the semifinals? I thought you all played really well last game."

But What If . . .

Sometimes the attention Paulie enjoys getting is not from me or my partner, but the laughs he receives from his siblings.

Watch closely: Who is reacting and responding? Who is giving social recognition to the misbehavior? If the payoff for the child is the siblings' laughter, it's gonna be a lot harder to change the dynamics.

In fact, not only does the child get attention from his sibs, but your vain attempts to stop them all from snorting and acting silly will only serve to give further payoff to yet another mistaken goal: power. The unstoppable "silly child" will defeat you by proving you are unable to get him to stop his table shenanigans. I have seen all the children gang up on the parents in an "us" against "them" war, using the sillies to defeat both parents, who lose control of the dinner table altogether.

My strategy? *Prescribe the symptoms.* Since a power struggle requires two parties in opposition, try condoning the child's behavior instead of forbidding it. I know that sounds like throwing fuel on the fire, but it has the opposite effect (once you understand that the goal is defying you). It's a way of ending power struggles by admitting defeat, in a sense. If you condone the behavior, it's no longer verboten, and what is the fun of that? You are no longer providing the required resistance. Now, take it one step farther: ask the child to perform the misbehavior. Now in order to defeat you, he'll have to *stop* misbehaving. I guess some people would call this reverse psychology. Here is what it looks like:

Sample Script

"Oh my goodness, that Paulie, he really wants us to laugh at him tonight. Seems we can't get him to wait while others talk. So let's give Paulie the floor and have him make us laugh. Go ahead, Paulie, take it away. You have your full audience assembled."

Caution: this is not meant to hurt or embarrass Paulie. It's about honoring his power by simply stating what is. If you can't beat 'em, join 'em! Test this for yourself. What usually happens is that Paulie will *not* like being made to perform and will cease his antics, if not immediately then in a few minutes when you keep asking him to do more, more!

Control yourself, not the child. With power, we can't make the child change, but we can change what we do. I can't make you sit at the table and use table manners, but I can decide the company I keep while I eat my meal. Offer choice: "Can you settle down? Or do I need to eat my meal elsewhere?" If the child persists: "Okay, I see I need to go. Let me know when things are calm." You have to be okay with the fact that the child may not want you back—maybe sibling meals are more fun and you are too strict and uptight.

Hold a family meeting. Put table manners on the agenda and bring the topic up by saying: "Our family meals are getting too silly for me sometimes. I miss talking with you guys. What can we do to strike up a balance between fun and the crazy energy that leads to bad manners?"

Engage positively. What can you do positively and proactively to engage everyone at the table? Children like connecting and being the subject matter, but too many parents use dinnertime as an opportunity to grill them about their school day—yuck! Try something more light and playful. Although I don't agree with having toys at the table, I do encourage parlor games that can be done with little to no equipment. Two-minute mysteries, 20 questions and other such games keep the fun and engagement at the table without the children having to misbehave.

TALKS WITH MOUTH FULL

I don't care how much spittle I cleaned up when my kids were small, by the time they arrived at the dinner table I was done seeing the contents of their mouths. I mean, enough already. Besides, talking with your mouth full is not going to get you invited to dinner with the Queen. Maybe they don't care about the Queen, but what about dinner with the Wiggles? Now we have their interest!

Understanding the Problem

Is talking with one's mouth full misbehavior? Or are the kids simply unaware of cultural mores like "mouth stays closed when chewing"?

It's only a misbehavior (mistaken approach) if it's a repeated pattern of interaction that gleans a predictable response from you. Translation: they keep chewing with their mouths open and you keep correcting them about it.

If you nag and remind until they finally get the message and take your correction, then it looks like you're dealing with a goal of undue attention seeking. If you're at a loss as to how to get them to listen to you, and you're feeling increasingly challenged or defeated, that means the children's goal is power.

SOLUTIONS

Disclose. Let them know why eating with their mouth open poses a problem for others. For example: "I don't like looking at your chewed food. Plus, I can't make out what you are saying when you talk with your mouth full and what you say is important to me. I want to hear you." The benefits are spelled out more clearly than simply saying "it's rude."

Signal. Your kiddo may get very excited and not notice when she's talking with her mouth open, so you can create a signal to let her know. Make up the signal together. Any signal works if you agree in advance—and some kids love having a secret code together. Takes the sting out of being verbally corrected.

Leave. Get up and leave the table, letting the child know you'll be happy to eat with her when she is able to use her manners.

Catch 'em being good. Be sure to let the child know how lovely her manners are when she does use them. You'll get more of the behaviors you notice, so notice the ones you want to see more of and downgrade the comments on the ones you'd like to see disappear.

REFUSES TO CLEAR PLATE

You do enough. You prepared the family meal, do you really have to clear the table too? How hard is it to get kids to walk their plates to the kitchen counter after a meal? I guess it is hard, because the fact is most of us just do it for our children in order to avoid another "problem." Oh Cinderella . . .

UNDERSTANDING THE PROBLEM

As soon as children have enough manual dexterity to do the task, the responsibility for taking their dirty plate from the table to the dishwasher or kitchen counter should pass from parent to child. (Invest in unbreakable dinnerware if you're worried about breakage.) So why don't they? Because experience has taught them that while you *say* it's their job, you usually do it most of the time anyway. So why bother?

Our mouth says, "That's your responsibility," but our feet say, "It's still my job." Always watch the feet!

Your kids are simply playing the odds, betting you won't pick this battle tonight. We have not been consistent and we have not established the expectation clearly. The responsibility has not *truly* been passed over to your child.

Solutions

Parenting has two goals: self-sufficiency and social integration. If you want your children to visit other people's houses and to automatically get up from the table and walk their plates to the kitchen, then you'd better have that arrangement in your own family life. You are the teacher of your customs. You have to show them how it's done, and you have to be consistent in enforcement.

Of course, the snag comes when you ask them to take their plates and they ignore your request or flat-out refuse. I've told you not to yell, not to punish, and certainly not to rob them of their responsibility. That is rescuing. So instead, here are nonpunitive alternatives to try.

One-word reminder. "Plates."

One-sentence reminder. "You've got a job to do."

Humor. "Are you going to hop back over to the table like a bunny? Or will you slither like a snake? Oh, no! How would a snake carry a plate? They don't have any arms!"

When/then statement. For the moment, leave the plates on the table. It's not your job, so don't rescue or confuse kids by doing it occasionally. Simply go about your evening, then when it's time to embark on the next activity, you can use the magic of a when/then statement: "When your job is done, then I'll know you're ready for the video."

• •

When/Then Magic

Too often we fall back into our autocratic traditions and expect children to do things simply because we say so. This is an expression of our personal power over children and is unlikely to go over well. Better to focus on the needs of the situation as dictated by the social order that has been established. Let the routines be the boss instead of you. One way to put that idea to work is in a when/then statement: "When your plate is cleared away, then I'll know you're ready for me to play."

• •

Natural consequence. If none of the above has worked, you can simply let the dishes stay on the table. When your child takes his seat at the next meal, he will find his breakfast plate. At that point you could try a when/then statement again. So after the inevitable, "I'm hungry, when is lunch?" you can say, "When I have that dirty plate in the kitchen, then I'll know you're ready for your lunch plate."

Family meetings. If clearing the table has been a long-standing issue, put it on the family meeting agenda and tackle the problem together (see p. 71). Be flexible in finding solutions. Perhaps the juniors could cook for a while, while mom tackles the table-clearing job to shake things up. Perhaps mom may want to keep the kitchen management going smoothly and agrees to clear the table herself, for her own sanity. There is no right or wrong way, but if you do go this route, be sure the children take on some of mom's other jobs to distribute labor in a way that honors everyone's commitment to making the family work without any one person feeling unduly burdened.

TOYS AT THE TABLE

Maybe it seems harmless to let your toddler bring a little toy figure to the table, but watch out: his toy choices will morph into cars with loud wheels and eventually LEGO fortresses that surround his plate.

Understanding the Problem

Ask yourself: Do you want a family dinner table where people play while they eat? It's family time, and attention should be paid to those who are with you enjoying the meal. It's your job to teach your child the expected social behaviors required for being at the family dinner table.

It's okay that life is *not* all about playing and toys. Sometimes life puts other challenges to us, like filling the time at the table with eating and family conversation, even if that is just babbling.

Solutions

It's a lot easier to never allow toys at the table than to allow them for young children only to disallow them when they are older. Begin with the end in mind.

- -

Sample Script

"It's time for supper. The toys need to go away now."

Child comes to table with toy.

"Toys are for the playroom. Can you put it away or shall I?"

Child keeps toy.

"Looks like you've decided you want me to put it away."

Mom tries to take toy, child holds tight!

"The toy needs to go away now. Can you let go or do I need to use force? You decide."

Child holds fast to the toy; you physically remove it. After all, you've given him the choice and you are simply enforcing a set limit in your house.

- -

Alternately, you can offer this choice: "Do you want to play or eat? If you want to eat, then the toy needs to go away."

This allows the child to decide for himself, but enforces the rule of no toys at the table. You have to be willing to accept that he may prefer to play. Perhaps he is not hungry.

Left to decide for himself, and using the "bees to honey" law of attraction, he may well just come along in a moment. Fight averted!

CHAPTER 7

SOCIAL SKILLS—THE DEMOCRATIC APPROACH TO SOCIALIZING YOUR LITTLE BARBARIAN

Won't Say Hello · Won't Say "Please" and "Thank-You" · Won't Kiss Grandparents · Tells Your Company to Go Home · Potty-Mouth · Curses and Swears Like a Sailor · Rude, Rude, Rude · Spitting · Gives Attitude and Tone · Doesn't Play with Friends Invited Over · You Hate Your Child's Friends · Has No Friends · You Think Your Child Is Being Bullied · Your Child Is a Bully

Human beings are social animals. We live communally, making bonds with each other, socializing with our species-mates. It is the desire of little ones to emulate and imitate the social behaviors of the bigger ones in the group. It's an innate desire hard-wired in human brains. We don't need to motivate our children to do it. We do, however, need to show them how to function in a group. And believe me, they are watching our every move. Okay—I'll stop channeling Jane Goodall and get back to real parenting speak.

So, assuming that we adults are all models of civility, we can deduce that if our children are rude or impolite, the culprit is either lack of learning (ignorance) or a perceived usefulness in *not* using the social skills they've learned. In this chapter I'll help you decipher which it is and offer solutions to your most embarrassing moments.

WON'T SAY HELLO

It's a common street scene. Mom is taking Grace out for a ride on her tricycle. Their neighbor Mr. Gervais is gardening. He breaks into a smile at the sight of the little Lancey Armstrong peddling away. He stops pulling weeds and comes to the sidewalk to say a neighborly "hello." Mom stops.

"Hello Grace!" says the kindly Mr. Gervais.

And then it happens—the talkative little gal suddenly becomes a total mute.

"Say hello to Mr. Gervais," mom urges.

Nothing.

Egads, thinks mom. How hard is it to say hello? She is nothing but nonstop chatter at home. My neighbor must think I am a bad mother for raising a kid with no basic manners. He even brings her little gifts. He just loves her, and she hasn't a simple "hello" for him? How embarrassing.

UNDERSTANDING THE PROBLEM

Is it from ignorance of the custom or choice that Grace doesn't say hello back? Let's do the rule-out:

Does she know we say "hello" when we greet people? By age three, absolutely. In fact, she says hello to other people. So it's not a training/education problem. It's a choice. Why choose *not* to say hello? Why would *not* speaking up be preferred by a child? Can you imagine the scenario from her little shoes?

This really is a very small exercise in selective mutism. It's a behavior that communicates the message "You can't make me talk." This is a form of passive power. Who is in control? The child. She'll decide whom she talks to and when, thank-you very much!

Grace knows saying hello is the "proper" thing to do, but here's the thing: kids are just less bound by social compunction than adults.

Offering a salutation to a somewhat stranger may be just more extroverted than Grace is feeling. Perhaps Grace perceives him not as the nice neighbor who gives her gifts, but as the creepy guy with a gold tooth who always pats her head or pinches her cheek. Perhaps the gardening gear mom sees as normal seems "odd" to Grace.

All behavior represents a type of movement. Socially, we either move toward or away from one another. Saying "hello" is a movement toward someone. Grace doesn't want to move toward Mr. Gervais. Instead she prefers to move away, and she achieves this social reservation by not talking.

SOLUTIONS

As with all power dynamics, we have to avoid our first tendency, which is to make 'em do what we want. *Forcing always invites resistance.* Instead, we have to gently and patiently work to improve the situation so that Grace herself feels more likely to want to move toward social closeness with people and to volunteer a genuine rather than forced "hello" at some future time.

Short-Term Strategies

Ignore. To show Grace you are not invested in her saying hello, don't give your typical urging of "Say hello, Grace." Instead, just move the conversation along. It will go something like this:

Sample Script

Mom: "Hello, Mr. Gervais."

Mr. Gervais: "Hello! And hi there, Grace!"

[Nothing.]

Mom: "Your garden is coming along beautifully. I see the peonies are about to bloom."

[You have modeled the appropriate behavior. Done.]

I know from working with many parents that saying nothing will just kill you! If you find it's important to say something to demonstrate that you are not being an ignorant parent, try this:

Zingy One-Liner: "We're still working on our hellos."

Enough said.

Catch the child being good. Next time you see Grace saying hello or using her social skills, you can comment: "Grace, you always make people feel so welcome with your cheery hello!" Or, "You use such lovely manners. People often mention your politeness to me."

Let the child overhear a compliment. Children love hearing about themselves. Next time you are on the phone and Grace is within earshot, say something like: "That granddaughter of yours is polite. She says big hellos to people when she meets them. She really makes their faces light up."

Long-Term Strategies

As Grace's confidence improves, she will find it easier and easier to stick her neck out in more tense situations—like saying hello to a wider range of people. Work on building up her self-confidence through encouragement; reinforce the message that "hello" is a gift she gives others, rather than something she does to be good or to follow a command.

WON'T SAY "PLEASE" AND "THANK-YOU"

"Can I have a juice?"

"What do you say?"

"Pleeeease."

Are you wondering how many bloody years you'll have to give this prompt? This is Manners 101. Why are kids so resistant to offering up such a basic respectful exchange?

UNDERSTANDING THE PROBLEM

The resistance to saying "please" and "thank-you" is children's response to feeling pestered. Let's face it, we use those reminder prompts so many times a day (on top of a hundred other little mini-instructions about the minutiae of their lives). They get fed up! Especially if the relationship feels more up-down in nature than egalitarian. Suddenly, it doesn't feel like a respectful exchange of pleasant manners. To a child who feels like a social inferior, it feels a tad more like groveling. (Think: You want a juice? Well, you'd better thank the higher powers that be.)

And also remember that we adults ask for things all the time without saying "please." It's just implied when you trust that someone has manners. When you ask a salesclerk at Walmart, "Which aisle are the batteries in?" you don't use the word "please." But because the sentence is uttered by an adult, the absence of "please" goes unnoticed. Children, however, are held to a higher standard. It's as if we assume they are innately inconsiderate, and that assumption is just another example of the low opinion we hold of children. And here's the thing: that implied low opinion is part of what maintains their feelings of being socially inferior.

Solutions

Model manners. Keep up your own good manners. They'll catch on.

Practice dramatic play. Practice manners in a fun setting. Host a tea party for the teddy bears and dolls. Kids eat this up. Wear white gloves and make up menus. Take it over the top. It's a great way to teach without being preachy.

Change up your *dance steps.* Remember that children choose their (mis)behaviors because they expect them to elicit a predictable response from you. Your first impulse, your typical reaction or reply, is the payoff, and so while you are no doubt tempted to prompt, "What do you say?" that is exactly the response expected. Do *anything* other than your knee-jerk response. If you do your part of the dance differently, the kids can't dance the same pas de deux with you anymore. You changed the dance. Translation: don't require the *pleases* and *thank-yous* for a bit, and you'll find that after a time they start to come voluntarily.

Catch 'em being good. When kids *do* say "please," let them know you like feeling appreciated for your efforts.

Hear the tone, not the words. Sometimes the "thank-you" is implied; you're just not hearing it. Don't be a nitpicker; we want children who understand the value of courtesy, rather than merely parroting meaningless etiquette for your benefit.

Tactical Tip

It's hard to say nothing when your child clams up right when he is supposed to be offering the socially appropriate "thank-you." It's embarrassing for parents. Instead of the usual prompt, try this:

Zingy One-Liner: "I can see by Josh's face that he just loves that wonderful present! Thank-you."

Or,

Zingy One-Liner: "You're a lucky boy to be getting juice and cookies from Mrs. Carmichael. Thank-you, Mrs. Carmichael."

It's a small point, but in both cases, mom offers her *own* gratitude, rather than speaking on behalf of her son.

Increase the P's and C's

"P" and "C" stand for participation and contribution. These magic bullets help a child feel belonging and equality in the family.

Most children have probably been the recipients of constant ongoing parental services. They may not have experienced the joys of being the givers. The more your children become competent and share their talents with the family, the more they'll be in a position to hear someone say, "Thank-you for the lovely table setting" or "What great pancakes this morning, Tatum. Thank-you!" They'll come to see how nice it feels to give to others, and their interest in participating in these social mores will increase too.

WON'T KISS GRANDPARENTS

Poor grandpa comes all the way from Tulsa to see his beloved grand-kids and they refuse to go near him for a hug or a kiss.

UNDERSTANDING THE PROBLEM

Well, it's pure and simple really: They just don't want to. Period.

Regardless of how much they like, dislike, love or adore their grandpa, kissing and hugging is still an act of intimacy. Children have a sense of personal space and develop their own boundaries about how much touching they are willing to do with certain people. This is a good thing. It varies from child to child and over time. Some kids will kiss anybody, while some won't kiss even their parents.

SOLUTIONS

Respect children's choices. No means no. If they don't feel like kissing, they absolutely should not be made to kiss. Think about the message you are sending them about choices regarding their bodies and intimate contact. If you override their own inner voice that says no, you are inadvertently training them to submit and ignore that important voice. We could unwittingly be teaching them that adults rule their bodies (wrong) and even if it doesn't feel right, they should follow orders (really wrong).

Sadly, almost all sexual abuse comes from a well-known adult in the family or circle of "trusted" friends. If children learn one *must* kiss grandpa even if it feels wrong, then one must also have to kiss Uncle Pedophile. Yikes. We want our children to resist when it feels wrong. Let's encourage that response.

So grandpa is arriving tomorrow and now I have you freaked out about pedophiles. That's rotten. This will get you through the awkward moment:

Zingy One-Liner: "Sorry, Grandpa, she is not up for kisses today."

If grandpa protests (and you know he will), you can lighten the mood by offering some humor: "Oh, Grandpa, no need to beg! *I'll* give you an extra hug if you need one." Later, you might take him aside and key him in to your strategy.

TELLS YOUR COMPANY TO GO HOME

There's nothing like having friends over for dinner to do a little adult socializing (for a change), only to have your child send them away partway through the visit.

"Why me? Why now?" you ask yourself. No doubt you're flustered. It's hard to be eloquent and gracious when you're waiting for the floor to open up and swallow you.

UNDERSTANDING THE PROBLEM

Looks like your child is being very clear about not wanting company. Why might that be? Children often go from one extreme treatment (the center of parental attention) to the other (totally pushed aside and ignored when company visits). The trick is to moderate those extremes.

SOLUTIONS

First, we need to *include* our kids. (Are you now envisioning your eight year old sitting out on the deck smoking a stogie or sipping a martini? That's not what I mean.) The point is, you have the right to entertain in your home. However, it is also your child's home and she too is "having company." Instead of pretending you never had progeny, find a proper way of balancing the event.

Involve. What could you do to increase your child's feeling of being a part of the host family? Here are some of my ideas (you'll think of more):

- Have your child write or decorate invitations.
- Have your child write the date on the family calendar.
- Ask your child if she would like to help you prepare something for the meal (arrange the cheese on the cheese platter, shuck the corn).

- Ask your child if she'd like to take coats, or to walk around with the chip bowl.
- If your friends are bringing their kids, put your children in charge of a kids' corner or kids' meal.

Plan. Help calibrate expectations by running through in advance what the night will look like (see the "Sample Party Plan" example below).

Treat. Make something fun and different for your child to look forward to while you're partying with your pals (e.g., a special movie or dessert).

Sample Party Plan

In advance of the party, mom explains that the adults will be eating later, without the kids. (Plan)

Jules helps mom fold and place fancy napkins on the table so they look like fun little fans. (Involve)

Jules has volunteered in advance to be the "coat check boy," ferrying coats up to mom and dad's bed. (Plan, involve)

Kids need upfront involvements, so instead of waiting till after dinner, *start* the party with Jules giving a tour of his room, or something that he is proud of and wants to show off. (Involve)

If you want an adult-only meal, make something fun and special so your child is also experiencing his own special occasion. Maybe it's his favorite mac and cheese eaten on a TV tray while watching a favorite show. A later bedtime or sleeping out in a tent in the family room while you visit in the living room. (Treat)

If you didn't have the plan all worked out, and immediately after Emily Post arrived your child told her in no uncertain terms to "go home," you need to take this one straight on. State firmly the proper limits and boundaries.

Zingy One-Liner: "These are my guests. You can join us or find something to do on your own."

Now you have clearly established it's not the child's place to decide who comes and goes from your house, and you have respectfully reinforced her right to participate or decline.

POTTY-MOUTH

Poo-poo head. Penis breath. Farty fart master (I just made that up, but go ahead, you can use it). Potty-mouth is all good fun, until he lets one out in a quiet movie theater, or at the crowded Hanukkah table.

UNDERSTANDING THE PROBLEM

Oh, to be a kid again. Yes, potty-mouth should be on the developmental charts sometime after learning to walk and continuing until well past the 12-year molars. There is a universal love of the verboten, and in most cultures that includes anything to do with toileting. Seems to strike a chord with the young lads more than the young ladies.

Learning body-part slang and then using it out loud is sure to stir giggles. It's silly. And that silliness tends to irritate parents, who find it infantile and irritating. Somehow, our request to drop the potty-mouth just reinforces the naughtiness that makes it so appealing. Besides, our constant reminders to "keep it clean" keeps the child in the limelight and our frustration over our failed attempts gives him the power to defeat us.

SOLUTIONS

Spit in the soup. No, not literally. I mean spoil the fun of the behavior, in this case the attention-getting power of potty-mouth, by revealing the child's goal to him: "I guess it still amazes you that bodies make farts and poops. You seem to like to impress others with your newfound knowledge. I don't find it shocking news anymore." (And then be nonplussed when he lets one slip.)

Be consistent. If you laugh at your child's silly language during a tickle fight, only to reprimand him another time, that one laugh you gave him will keep 'em trying.

If you can't beat 'em, join 'em. Children hate when parents misbehave. So explain that if they can use potty-mouth, you want to exercise the same right. Hearing mom say "fart face" may disgust them. You can then make an agreement that either everyone talks like that or no one does.

State what you are willing to do. You can let your kid know that you don't like listening to potty-mouth. Let him know that you'll be happy to come back and resume playing when the language is cleaned up. You can't make him stop, but you can stop listening.

Teach discretion. Most of us speak two languages: the language you use with your boss, and the one you reserve for good friends. Now might be a good time to teach your kids the difference. So, if they choose to use silly language with their peers and no one is offended, that is between them, but that language is not okay when grandma is over, or the family is dining at a restaurant. Sometimes when we give kids an appropriate place to get their sillies out, they are more likely to be cooperative about *not* misusing the language when it really matters to you.

CURSES AND SWEARS LIKE A SAILOR

One day, your sweet little child is going to learn words that have much more power than "poo-poo head." Kids with older siblings will be exposed to these words earlier and learn quickly they are "bad" words, which means powerful words.

UNDERSTANDING THE PROBLEM

Knowing swear words is something akin to getting into a secret club, proving your maturity and adding a little toughness—which is especially valued in "boy code."

SOLUTIONS

Get philosophical. Notice I didn't write "preachy"? Instead of getting all up in their grill, which will just block communication, get curious *with* them:

"Why do people like to say the a-word?"

"Did you know that brain research proves that when we swear after hitting our thumb with a hammer it actually reduces the pain? Why is that I wonder?"

"Why do we have so many words that subjugate women?"

"Why are there soooo many nicknames for penis but none for elbow?"

Also discuss the idea that the words themselves are only as powerful as people allow them to be. The biggest swear word in Quebec defames the church. It's cultural. The power of the offense comes from us, not the word. But mostly we want to dig into the goal again. Our words can be used to impress peers, but they can also be weapons if the intent is to intimidate or hurt.

Come to mutual agreements. You will not stop your child from learning swear words. Did you hear that? It's inevitable. Knowing that, what are acceptable parameters? Is it okay to swear at home? Do you swear at home? (I suspect a double standard is not going to be acceptable.) We all let one slip occasionally, but together the family can set the bar of acceptability. At a family meeting you can discuss how the family wants to operate (see p. 71). Our family uses the term "level three" when the bar has been breached and people are slipping into swearing when it's not needed.

Spit in the soup. My mother was an art teacher and impressed upon us the value of creativity. She viewed swearing as being the lazy out, lacking in creativity. Somehow that took the power out of swearing; it no long seemed "bad" so much as uncreative.

Listen to the meaning, not the words. No doubt some of the swearing is directed at you, usually in the course of a fight. (The F-bomb, as in "fuck you," comes to mind.) The child is conveying her anger. She wants to hurt you. Don't get distracted by the impropriety of the swearing; instead, key into the fact that the child is so upset with you that she wants to hurt you. The method is not as important as the goal. Children and young adults with the goal of revenge must be handled sensitively. Children never seek revenge first. That means they are letting you know, "I want to hurt you as I perceive you have hurt me." It takes a keen parent to pick up on this and see it for what it is. The best tool for the goal of revenge is to listen—discover the hurts. Receive the message.

Sample Script

"You must be really, really hurt to tell me to F—off. You are important to me. How you feel is important to me. I want to understand. I don't think either of us can talk very well about this when we're this upset. Let's both take some time apart and come back to this when we're calmer."

When you reconvene, don't discuss the curse. It's the symptom of a much more troubling pain, and when the hurt is healed the swearing will no longer be an issue.

Tactical Tip

Remember Eleanor Roosevelt's famous line, "No one can make you feel inferior without your consent"? When parenting, we can protect ourselves from attacks by adopting this attitude, but we must still address the child's goal: revenge. Something serious is up. We have a relationship issue with our child.

BUT WHAT ABOUT . . .

Hey Alyson, how about a swearing jar?

Lots of people have told me that they have a swearing jar (when someone swears, they have to pay a fine to the communal jar). I don't like the idea myself. It feels demeaning to me. I wouldn't have liked it as a kid, and I sure would hate it as an adult. Being "docked" would feel punitive and, frankly, if I was so mad I felt I wanted to swear, I'd happily throw 20 bucks in the pot anyway! In the end, language is a social agreement, and people will choose if they want to adhere to the social contract. They'll be more willing to do this if the relationship is healthy and egalitarian. Keep up all the other long-term strategies you are working on in this book to achieve that state and this gimmick will not be needed.

RUDE, RUDE, RUDE

Maybe I've bitten off more than I can chew creating just one category of "rude" because rude can look so many ways. Barking orders is rude, but so is pushing the plate away during dinner and saying "Yuck!" Each behavior is different, but there are commonalities.

Understanding the Problem

There are codes of conduct that are socially acceptable in every culture. Every child needs to learn these. For example, you don't want to be taking food from the communal pot in India with your left hand. The left hand is reserved for wiping duties, the right hand is for eating and shaking hands. How would you know that unless someone taught you?

If it's considered polite to hold the door for others, ya gotta teach all that simple stuff. Children are not born with this knowledge. That is where the old TFTT (Take Time for Training) comes in. Instead of constantly correcting or criticizing behaviors, spend some time showing children the correct behaviors we'd like to see. Again, use dramatic play, teach manners and behavioral expectations in a causal way at home—not in the actual moment the behavior is required.

• •

"You'll spend more time correcting a child than training them properly in the first place."

—Dr. Rudolf Dreikurs

• •

Imagine for a moment, then, that someone who *knows* the custom uses his *left* hand to eat out of *your* food dish. Or closes the door in your face. That is purposeful behavior. The offender *knows* he is acting rudely. He doesn't want to treat you respectfully. Why?

In hierarchal relationships, respect flows only one way: upward. Traditionally, parents would make children show their elders or superiors respect, while the elders proceeded to belittle children, keeping them in a one-down position. That may have been tolerated by children in the past, when children understood that their lot in life was to be at the bottom of the social pecking order. But thankfully the world our children were born into is different. An African-American is running the most powerful nation in the world, and moms and dads are in egalitarian relationships. Many in this generation of children don't really see a pecking-order world anymore. The new world appears pretty much socially flat.

So when we treat children in disrespectful ways, they won't tolerate it. They don't perceive themselves as being one down, and they know they deserve to be treated with respect and dignity. It's tit for tat with this generation. If you are rude to me, I'll be rude to you. We're equals!

Parents are often unaware of their own rudeness toward their children. I suggest for one day you listen to *everything* you say to your child, and ask yourself if you would talk like this to a peer, spouse or friend. Probably not. We've all become so accustomed to treating children rudely that we don't even *notice* it anymore. We just think it's what parenting looks like.

Solutions

Stop being disrespectful. Become aware of your tone, language and tactics. Ask yourself if you would talk to a friend like this, and if the answer is "no," stop.

Signal. Ask your child to help you become more aware by creating a private signal used when she feels you are being disrespectful to her.

Repair the relationship. If you've been harsh to one another for a while, you'll need to do some relationship repair. Find some way to spend special time together so you can put "deposits" in the emotional bank account.

Abide by the rules. Some children come to believe that the rules don't apply to them. This belief may have come about from excessive pampering. Perhaps the parents always bent the rules for their child, always made special exceptions for their "little munchkin." The child (erroneously) concludes that she is excused from the general rules, that she's above them. People who hold this belief in adulthood are at risk for illegal and corrupt behavior. It's one thing for a child with allergies to require a snack different from the one offered at day care, but if your child doesn't like the school offerings and gets a snack from home while all the other kids eat the standard snack, we've got a problem Houston.

Use an I-message. Your child may not know she is being disrespectful to you, and you need to let her know with an I-message: I feel _____ when you _____ because _____. I'd rather _____.

For example: "I feel disrespected when you stick your gum under the kitchen table, because you're damaging our family property. I'd rather you put your gum in wax paper for later, or in a tissue for the garbage.

● ●

"The proper way of treating a child is precisely the same as how you treat your fellow man."

—Dr. Rudolf Dreikurs

● ●

SPITTING

Have you got the spittle master in your house? Everything is peachy until he doesn't get his way and then *patooooo*, he lets loose a loogie. Gross! Talk about packing a weapon. Some kids have tantrums, yours has salivary glands. At least it's quieter.

UNDERSTANDING THE PROBLEM

In times of conflict, parents typically yell, shame, punish or take away loved possessions or privileges. And what can kids do to fight back? Scream, shout, hit and, oh yes, spit. It's a great form of one-upmanship: "You might be able to take away my toy, but I can top that. I'll spit at you. Ha! So there."

SOLUTIONS

Practice active listening. Children are communicating with you through their spitting behavior. What are they trying to say to you? Can you let them know you hear them?

Examples:

"You must be very angry with me."
"You want me to know this is *not* okay with you."
"You want to get back at me for what I've done."
"I see you're spitting mad." (literally)

It's affirming to know your parents get you even when they don't agree with you. Such blowups mean they're unhappy about something, and the more we learn to listen and problem solve with our children, the better. But times of conflict are not good times for problem solving. So if the spit was a rebuttal for turning off the TV for bedtime, you can say, "I see you're angry and don't like our bedtime routines. Can I write that down on the family meeting agenda for you?" (See p. 188 for more details on how to be an active listener.)

Redirect. For example: "Spitting is for toilets—here is where we go to spit." Walk the child gently to the toilet bowl. (Your calm manner is key here.) I know that sounds lame and on first flush sounds like it won't work, but the idea is to not be ruffled by the child's attempts to fight with you and to then move on to the long-term strategy.

Long-Term Strategy

The trick is to revisit what the conflict was really about in the first place. Somehow, the child perceived your actions to be unfair or unreasonable. Just to be clear, it's the child's perception of the events that matter. Her feelings are her facts. We have to try to see the world through her eyes.

Many times parents feel justified in their actions but usually they are falling into one of the three common power-parent pitfalls: they're suffering what I like to call "a parental TIA."

1. *Tone.* Are you being snarly or snarky? Do you know the difference? Just how aware are you of your communication nuances? A terse tone or stony body language can ruin your efforts because unwittingly you are coming off as overpowering and inviting your child into a fight. Keep it light and gentle. Humor, warm smiles, humming and lots of gentle touching can keep things going smoothly as you correct, discipline or enforce limits and boundaries.

2. *Inconsistency.* If bedtime is 8 p.m. but you sometimes let it slip to 8:30 or 9:00, your child will find it "unfair" when you do enforce 8 p.m. You'll argue that bedtime has *always* been 8 p.m., but come on, really? Has it? The conflict will be resolved if you maintain consistency in bedtimes—even on nights you'd enjoy having them stay up later.

3. *Arbitrariness.* Are the rules and agreements clear and understood by the child? When you say, "No, you can't have a cookie," does the child perceive your judgment to be arbitrary ("Because I said so") rather than stemming from a more established and consistently enforced rule ("Only two treats a day" or "Not before supper")?

GIVES ATTITUDE AND TONE

You announce it's time to get outside and rake the leaves. Your daughter slams down the remote, rolls her eyes at you and says, "Whatever..." You say, "Pardon me, young lady!" To which she pulls a face and says, "Chill out! I'm coooooming. Gawd."

UNDERSTANDING THE PROBLEM

Children can find creative ways to show their protest. When people feel they are in an inferior position, they may comply to avoid punishment but will use "that tone" as a form of protest that keeps their own sense of dignity intact. Tone and attitude accomplishes this. It behaviorally announces: "If I am going to be unhappy, you can suffer the wrath of my mood too." Misery loves company.

Children may have picked up this technique from watching their parents' methods. How is your tone? We are all a little guilty of using the adult equivalent of "Whatever!" Generally, adults in our society talk down to children and it's mostly accomplished through tone and attitude.

Being "in a mood" also serves a purpose. It announces to people that you are feeling off and that they had better tiptoe around you. It announces that the world had better back off and not put demands on you. Great aversion tactic: "Don't ask Jen to set the table; she's in a mood."

SOLUTIONS

Watch your tone. Need I say more?

Ignore the child's tone. Don't take the bait and get all up in arms. That will only serve to help the child achieve her goal.

Address the content of the child's speech rather than the delivery. If she announces she finds the meatloaf disgusting, you can reply chirpily, "Sorry you don't like what's for supper tonight. That's a bummer. I hope there is enough other stuff to fill you up."

See what's up. Find out if something is upsetting your child.

Long-Term Strategies

Continue to work on improving relations. Are you spending some time together in meaningful ways? Are you staying in touch with the kid underneath all that attitude?

Continue to work on distributing the power democratically. This way, the family operates less top-down. Are you holding family meetings regularly and using consensus in your decision making? See p. 71 for more on family meetings.

Keep the lines of communication open. Even when your inclination is to tune out that one, don't. The content may still be important. See if you can find a safe time to talk about how life is going for the child and if something has come up in her life she might want to talk about.

DOESN'T PLAY WITH FRIENDS INVITED OVER

Kayla asked to invite Ella over for a playdate. Mom peers in and sees Ella bored to tears, picking her navel lint, while Kalya is fully engrossed in her own little world working away on her leapfrog game. What is the point of having a playdate if the children don't actually play together?

UNDERSTANDING THE PROBLEM

There are a few things that might be contributing to this issue.

Age. Preschoolers engage in parallel play as a bridge to learning collaborative play. Each plays his or her own activity beside a friend before learning to interact in each other's play. They may not know *how* to play with each other yet.

Birth order. If your child is an only child, he may have a higher need for alone time. A playdate may sound like fun for a little bit, but he may want to retreat to his comfortable play style after a while.

Interpersonal issues. Perhaps during earlier play something happened that made your child decide the playdate was over.

Who picked the playdate, anyway? Did you set up the playdate with someone *you* wanted to have over? Maybe your child isn't keen on that kid. Maybe your child thought he'd like to play with this friend but, on closer inspection, changed his mind. (Like that has never happened to an adult.)

Time. There is no right or wrong amount of time for a playdate, but for littler kids, two hours is plenty. You may just have exhausted their playdate socializing energies.

Solutions

Take the lead. If the kids need help getting play initiated, you might step in and take the lead. You can be Julie of *The Love Boat.* Structured activities like shuffleboard, uh, I mean board games, will be easier than dress-up or dramatic play.

Plan activities. If it's a relatively long playdate, consider having a few planned activities that offer variety, and see what flies. Baking cookies with you, doing a craft, riding toys on the driveway. But also build downtime or a break into the schedule and maybe plug in a movie. This play stuff is a lot more work for them than you'd imagine. Give them time to slow down and reboot.

Manage expectations. Manage your own expectations about how social your child is. Whose problem is this, anyway? If having one best friend and only seeing him every other week is good by your child, who are you to say differently? Not all kids need a lot of action and social time. If you are extroverted, you may worry your child is deficient socially, when in fact he is simply more introverted in his style.

YOU HATE YOUR CHILD'S FRIENDS

Do you hate your child's choice of playmates? Why does your child always have to pick the worst kids to befriend? Do you worry that her friends will be a bad influence? Maybe she acts badly when they're together, or shortly after they leave.

UNDERSTANDING THE PROBLEM

Childhood is a time for learning. Navigating friendships and peer relationships is a big part of the work of childhood. As children grow, they'll experiment with different sorts of friends, they'll try on different personas. Some you'll like, some you won't. Often the child with a lot of social status is the one every kid is jonesing to be friends with. Being friends with the "star" raises one's social status. Even if the "star" is somewhat of a jerk.

The important thing to keep in mind is that this is *your* problem. Your child isn't complaining about her friends. It's *you* who doesn't like them, not your kid.

SOLUTIONS

Mind your own business. It is *not* your job to match-make or pick your child's friends.

Guide and discipline. You *are* responsible for the guidance of your own child and disciplining him if he is acting badly. If nasty-boy Dylan is over for a playdate with your little lovable Larry and they start running around the pool deck—which *never* happens when Dylan isn't over—you can't blame Dylan, and you can't excuse Larry. You can, however, be an effective disciplinarian and take action. If the rule is no running, you must enforce that rule. Period. If Larry tries running after Dylan is gone, the solution is not to stop Dylan from coming over but to enforce the rule of no running with Larry each and every time he tests this behavior.

Reflect. Hold a mirror up to your child. Tell him that you notice he gets into more trouble, or is rougher, when he plays with a particular friend. Ask him if he enjoys that time. Reflect on the qualities he has enjoyed in previous friendships. While you can't pick your child's friends, you can discuss what good and difficult friendships look like.

Educate with books. There are lots of children's books that have friendships as a theme. Ask your librarian to help you find some titles and use the books as discussion starters.

Ask yourself who the role model is. Why do we always think that "bad" children will unduly influence our children and as a "bad" role model lead them to sin? If we accept that children influence one another, why not reverse the situation and realize *your* child might be a *positive* influence? We need children like yours to reach out to the children who could use a pal. Don't further isolate the child who is struggling. It takes a village to raise a child, and perhaps this is your child's opportunity to play a vital role.

HAS NO FRIENDS

When parents tell me that their child has no friends, I put on my detective hat. Typically, what I sleuth out is that "no friends" isn't really the case. Usually, the child has one little pal, or had a really good friend back at the old school. It's a critical distinction because it tells me the child *can* make friends. It takes only one friendship to prove she has the ability, and it takes only one friendship to provide the psychological connection that is recognized as a protective factor in maintaining mental health.

UNDERSTANDING THE PROBLEM

Learning to make friends is a social skill children develop over time. Some seem to come by this with ease, for others it's harder. If your child is struggling, maybe she's simply more discriminating about who she befriends, so it's slimmer pickings; or maybe she just doesn't require as much social engagement as others. Some children have a social awkwardness that can slow their acceptance into a group. But if they have the capacity to make even one friend, we know they are capable and have the "wiring" for friendship.

SOLUTIONS

Ask an expert. If you are concerned your child may have a social deficit that is extreme, you may want to seek professional help. Ask your physician for a referral.

Expand options. If your gut says your child is just discriminating and hasn't found a friend on the block or in her class, see if you can find an extracurricular group that suits your child. If she is into reading, maybe she would like to join a book club, or if she's technically minded, a robotics club might be ideal. Bottom line: expand the child's current social sphere.

Enlist help at the school. Enlist the help of the child's teachers. "Make a friend" isn't a task to be put on a homework sheet—and recess or free play can be challenging for some. Imagine walking into a cocktail party not knowing anyone. Who do you approach? What will you talk about? What if they don't accept you? It's stressful for many. That is what playtime is like for children. It's *much* easier for children to be social when they are given a structured task. The teacher might know of someone in the class who is social and inclusive. She could put your child in that kid's desk group. The teacher can team the two up to go bang chalkboard brushes outside. (Oops, I guess they dust the electronic whiteboard now.) The point is, when the teacher teams them up to do work on a task, the social roles are more easily understood than in free play and it makes for a more comfortable starting point.

Encourage. Whatever you do, don't pity your child. That sends the message that you don't believe she can handle the situation. Instead, have faith—even when she may not have it herself.

Zingy One-Liner: "I think I am a pretty good judge of character and I think you make a great friend; it will work out—honest."

It Worked for Us

I had my daughter in a day care near our home. She hated it. I mean H-A-T-E-D it. She cried all morning. I had never seen her like this. She was a social, happy, outgoing kid who loved to play, and I never had separation issues leaving her with a babysitter or on a playdate.

I knew the woman who ran the day care. She was a former teacher and had been a mainstay of the community for over 15 years. Her facility was so well regarded it had a long wait list. Everyone loved her. So what was my kid's problem?

It turned out the problem was not the caregiver, or the facility. It was that my daughter didn't have any friends in the class. I thought the best thing was to keep her home with me whenever possible, so I started her late in the year and I enrolled her for only a few days per week. All the other children started in September and went five mornings a week. She was really a bit of an outsider. In your words, she wasn't "socially integrated." She had not found her place in the group, or sense of belonging in the classroom. I was thinking of sending her *less,* and you suggested sending her *more.*

On the next tearful day, I sent her to day care with cupcakes for the group to ice and decorate. I included a bunch of different candy toppings so there was an activity for the entire group. The other children loved it! My daughter got to demonstrate how to use a piping bag to ice the treat and everyone was involved in putting sprinkles and gumdrops on their cupcakes. After that day she couldn't wait to get to day care in the mornings. This event was the icebreaker that got her engaged with others and now she is socially on her way! What a difference being connected makes. I am so glad I stuck it out and took your advice.

YOU THINK YOUR CHILD IS BEING BULLIED

I want parents to take bullying very seriously. But (there's always a "but," isn't there?) sometimes "bullying" is not really bullying. I get *a lot* of calls from worried parents about children being bullied when in fact they are just not being treated very nicely. Childhood comes with negative experiences—growing pains if you will—that aren't necessarily bullying. It may make you feel somewhat better to know that even bad experiences can shape us positively.

So how do you know if your child is being bullied for real? Since children don't necessarily come right out and tell their parents, keep an eye out for these possibly telling signs:

- Not wanting to go to school or participate in extracurricular activities
- Anxious, fearful or over-reactive
- Exhibits low self-esteem and makes negative comments about himself or herself
- Headaches and stomach aches
- Lower interest and performance in school
- Loses things, needs money, reports being hungry after school
- Injuries, bruising, damaged clothing, broken belongings
- Unhappy, irritable, little interest in activities
- Trouble sleeping, nightmares, bed-wetting
- Threatens to hurt himself or herself or others

UNDERSTANDING THE PROBLEM

Children who are shy, anxious, insecure or struggle socially are often targets. Children who are viewed as different in race or physical characteristics (weight issues or having a disability) are also more prone to being targeted.

If it turns out your child is being bullied, here's what you can do.

SOLUTIONS

Bullying demands change at multiple levels. It is not just a problem for the victim, it's a community problem. Be sure to notify the school, the bus driver and the lunch-room supervisor. If your child's school doesn't have a bullying prevention program in place, take up the cause and spearhead a taskforce to get one in place.

Until then, your child needs to be protected. The reason many kids don't talk to their parents about their abuse is because they fear their parents' involvement will only worsen the situation with the bully. ("Had to go tell your mamma did you wuss, did ya?") And, many children feel ashamed—they believe their parents will think less of them.

If the child would like to tackle the situation by himself first, you can allow him that opportunity, but he must understand that it is your job to keep him safe, and if his attempts to stop the bullying fail, you will step in. Even if that means transferring him to a new school.

Anti-Bullying Tactics

Teach your child these anti-bullying tactics:

- Stick with a friend during the times the bully is most likely to target him. Take a pal along to the washroom or locker.
- Avoid looking upset. Practice not crying or getting red in the face. Yes, he may be faking it, but the bully has to see that the bullying is not getting anywhere.
- Try not to get angry. Parents often want their children to fight back or stand up to the bully, but this is not advised. This response only escalates the conflict.
- Remove any incentives the bully might have. If the bully wants your child's lunch money, your child can bring lunch from home; if he wants your child's ball cap, your child can choose not to wear one.
- Look distracted. Train your child to keep looking at his cell phone or reading his textbook, as if he doesn't care and didn't hear, if the bully tries to instigate verbally—to act uninterested and unconcerned.

Failing these tactics, your child needs to be removed from the situation. Bullying can have long-lasting effects. Take it seriously.

Long-Term Strategies

The parenting techniques this book teaches are all aimed at helping children develop a strong and positive sense of self. Unconditional love and acceptance along with firm and friendly discipline will all be beneficial over time. Raised with these techniques, your child is less likely to become a bully, less likely to be the target of bullying and more likely to speak up when he or she sees someone being bullied.

YOUR CHILD IS A BULLY

What if your child is the mean and bossy type? Perhaps you're worried she is on the road to becoming a bully (if she isn't already). Here are the signs you need to watch for:

- Shows little concern for other people's feelings
- Doesn't see the impact of her behavior on others
- Acts aggressively with siblings, parents, teachers, friends and even animals
- Acts bossy or manipulative in order to get her own way
- Has possessions or extra money and you don't know where they came from
- Secretive about possessions, activities, and whereabouts
- Has a generally positive attitude about aggression
- Easily frustrated or blows up quickly

UNDERSTANDING THE PROBLEM

Children who use aggression as a power tactic have learned these techniques from personal experience. They have been in relationships where they themselves were subjugated by the misuse of power. These are exactly the problematic superior-inferior or master-slave style relationships this method of parenting is aiming to replace with mutually respectful relationships. Bullying is just one negative outcome that can occur when parents use punishment as a corrective tool. (Picking up this book to learn a new, respectful style of parenting is one step in the right direction.)

You may not feel that description suits you, but just know that children who bully usually have the following in their backgrounds:

- Parents who misuse power by yelling, hitting or rejecting
- A parent who misuses power and aggression with his or her spouse
- Siblings who bully them

- Friends who bully them or are aggressive
- Social issues that prevent them from standing up to peers
- Coaches or teachers who yell, humiliate or exclude
- Few opportunities to shine or share their talents as a means of positive power

SOLUTIONS

Number one: STOP the misuse of power at home. I can't impress upon readers enough that this is a call for family counseling. Some parents are afraid to seek help—they're afraid their children will be removed by social services, or that it will add stress to an already toxic situation. Others have had bad experiences with counseling, which is a shame. I can only urge you to try again, and as a therapist I can tell you that it is always the goal of professionals to help keep families intact.

Next, take a parenting class. You will find comfort in knowing you are not alone with your issues, that they are more common than you may think. A class will give you boatloads of good ideas that will make life easier.

Finally, help your children find positive power in their lives so they don't have to go seeking power on the negative side of life. This is key. Look for opportunities to help your children excel in areas of interest or expertise. Develop their talents. Try to focus on how their talents can be used in the service of others. If they are good at music, would they like to play at a seniors' center? If they are a whiz on the computer, could they help the teacher with the school website? If they enjoy multimedia, could they make a PowerPoint presentation as a background for the school concert? You get the picture. Now get going.

• •

"The children who need encouragement the most get it the least."
—Alfred Adler

• •

Tactical Tip

Often children who have a reputation of being hard to handle are assigned to the most hard-nosed teachers or instructors. In fact, these children fare better with adults who are gentler in their approach. If they have a favorite uncle or aunt, a special relationship with a grandparent or godparent, see if you can increase their exposure to this positive role model in their lives.

CHAPTER 8

HEALTH, HYGIENE AND HIGH FASHION—THE DEMOCRATIC APPROACH TO MANAGING ONE'S BODY

Won't Brush Teeth · Refuses Hair Brushing · You Can Never Get the Ponytails Right · Hates Water and Getting in the Tub · Will Only Wear One Favorite Pair of Pants—and They're Dirty · Refuses to Wear Socks · Won't Take Medicine · Sticks Hands in Dirty Diapers · Disagreements about Wardrobe · Won't Get Dressed · Won't Put on Pajamas at Bedtime

Babies are totally dependent on their parents for care. But as our children grow, they need to learn about all the many things we need to do to care for our bodies (and they need to practice—which implies the inevitability of mistakes). As with all areas of competence and self-reliance, the sooner the better.

There seems to be a varying range of interest in this topic. Some children seem obsessed with hygiene and their appearance as pre-schoolers, while some kids make it a low priority—somewhere between memorizing the flags of the world and famous eighteenth-century composers' middles names. I don't know what kind of chick you hatched, but you have to work with what you've got—without creating problems along the way. In this chapter, I'll cover the most common issues that cause parents difficulty. Hopefully, we'll have you on the way to a well-polished, lice-free child soon.

WON'T BRUSH TEETH

I have yet to meet a parent who hasn't fought the battle of brushing teeth at some point. You are trying to get tuck-ins done and over so that you can watch *Grey's Anatomy* and instead you're held hostage in the bathroom with a kid who won't open his mouth!

UNDERSTANDING THE PROBLEM

I love the minty fresh taste of just-brushed teeth. Why don't kids? I have a few explanations:

1. Kids don't mind their own halitosis. In fact, if they just finished a glass of orange juice, toothpaste is going to make it curdle.
2. Brushing is the last stop before going to bed, and the longer you can hold off on that, the later your bedtime!
3. Some toothpaste can sting kids' mouths.
4. Having a brush rammed down your throat by someone else sets off the gag reflex and is unpleasant at best.
5. Children have little or no appreciation for why we do this silly task, as they have never had a cavity, gingivitis or a root canal.
6. It's a great way to exert power over your parent and win. It's like playing rock-paper-scissors—a locked, closed mouth beats an eager parent with a toothbrush. If a child is looking for ways to one-up you, this works.

SOLUTIONS

Here are my suggestions for trauma-free tooth brushing.

Apply logical consequences. One gift we can give our children is the understanding that in life, freedoms and responsibilities go together. Applying logical consequences teaches children this connection.

In order for a logical consequence to be effective (and not punitive) it must meet our 3R requirements:

- **R**easonable
- **R**elated (to the freedom or right)
- **R**evealed in advance (to the child so he is able to decide and make his own choices that preserve his power)

Children would like to have the freedom to eat sugar and sweets. That freedom comes with the responsibility of caring for their teeth by removing the sugar that causes tooth decay. Eating sweets and tooth brushing are a package deal: if you want sugar, ya gotta brush. You don't want to brush, you forfeit the sugar. Simple.

Here's how that's going to play out . . .

Let your child know that as long as you see him being responsible in caring for his teeth, you are happy to allow him to have sugar (in the form of juice, milk, candy, cookies or other favorite things).

However, should he choose *not* to care for his teeth, you'll understand that he is choosing not to have sugar (or other tooth-rotting substances) and you'll feed him a "tooth-friendly diet" of good, wholesome fresh foods instead.

When your child refuses to brush, say: "I see you are choosing not to have sugar," and then move right along to the next activity (tuck-ins or leaving for school). Don't fight, force or lecture; simply drop the subject.

Don't worry about the effects of one or two days (or even a week) of missed tooth brushing while you are training your child to understand the connection between this freedom and responsibility. Cavities won't happen in that short a period. Focus on the long-term goal of developing good oral hygiene for life.

Testing Phase

Expect your child to test out the option of not brushing. Don't be disappointed with his choices. Don't be interested in his choice at all. Just know brushing = sugar, no brushing = no sugar. Be focused on what you, the parent, need to be doing. If the child perceives that you want him to brush, and that this is subtle manipulation rather than free choice, he will not want to pick the option *you* want—that will feel like you've won and he has lost. The goal is to prove to the child that you are not trying to control him.

Follow Through

If the child chooses not to brush, you must do your part and follow up with the consequence: remove the sugar you are feeding your child. This is the hardest part for parents, but this is where the experiential learning happens. When the child has demonstrated he can brush as required, he can have sugar.

> "Children do not learn from the threat of a consequence—they learn from experiencing the consequence."
>
> —Dr. Rudolf Dreikurs

Tactical Tip

Keep a firm and friendly attitude. Don't say anything negative or judgmental like, "If you had brushed like I told you to" or "See, I knew you'd be mad." Those comments are hurtful and send the message "I was right, you were wrong."

Solutions

Use a when/then statement. I find great success with this tool. If your child requests a juice in the morning, say, "Yes, you may have a juice. *When* the old sugar bugs are brushed off your teeth, *then* I'll know you are ready for some." The immediacy of this seems to work well with little kids. You'll find, over the course of 24 hours, you can have them brushing three times a day, albeit it at unconventional times. Who cares? Dentists tell me three times a day is great. Once you have dissolved the power struggle over brushing, kids are more apt to begin brushing at more conventional times, like before bed and after breakfast.

Problem solve. The NOTS (needs of the situation) call for getting the pesky plaque off. If your child hates the taste of toothpaste or has a strong gag reflex, there are other ways to solve the plaque-removal problem:

- Try dental gum, which is designed to help clean teeth.
- Try oral rinse and flossing sticks, which may be less irritating than a brush.
- Use baking soda applied with the tip of the finger.
- Let the child hold the brush. The more control the child has over the brush in his mouth, the less overpowering it will feel. Don't believe me? Have your child brush your teeth and see how much you feel you are at his mercy. The more control kids have, the better the experience and sensation.

But What If . . .

My dentist says kids aren't skilled enough to brush their own teeth until they are at least seven years old.

Your dentist knows best, and I agree that until kids gain the necessary manual dexterity, you've still got to get in their mouths and lend a trained hand. So here are some creative ways to win mouth access, without triggering resistance.

Perform quality control. I suggest you let your child brush on their own for a week or so while the bad feelings of the brushing battle subside and they enjoy their independence. Then, when it feels like you could up your involvement again without stirring up old problems, ask if you could be the "tooth checker." Go in after with the tooth brush and while brushing say in a kind of "hide and seek" or "detective looking for clues" type way: "Let's take a look and see how you did . . . any bugs up here? Nope, you got all those. Let me see at the back here . . . (brushing your way to the back), nope! My goodness did you leave *any* for me? You got them all, buddy! Good brushing!" (meanwhile, you've rebrushed every tooth surface while "searching").

Use humor. Instead of being insistent and serious, try a little jingle to lighten the mood and decrease fighting. "Up like a rocket, down like the rain, back and forth like a choo-choo train" was the one I used.

Call in the experts. With power issues, parents always seem to come off as the authority. In the case of teeth, the authority figure is the dentist. Why not let him or her share the news? You don't always have to be the bad guy. Children listen to almost anybody other than their parents, so have the dentist give the instructions.

Schedule more check-ups. If you are really, really concerned about your child's teeth, don't use your worry to fuel your fight; go for more regular cleanings. It may be more expensive, but so is having bad teeth.

REFUSES HAIR BRUSHING

Bath time is over, the conditioner is on and the detangler spray bottle is set out. Let the torture begin! It's tough work brushing through matted and tangled mops of hair—and it can be painful for the child. We've all heard our kids shout "It hurts!" Perhaps your child just flat-out refuses to let you even come near her with a brush.

Understanding the Problem

Detangling hair hurts. Kids don't like it. They will avoid it at any cost.

Solutions

Cut the hair. Having hair that is long enough to tangle requires brushing. This is another example of freedom and responsibility going together: if you want long(er) hair, you must do the care and detangling. If you don't like the detangling, that is fine—you just need to cut the hair shorter. Having longer hair and *not* looking after it, however, is not an option.

Often it is parents themselves who love their children's locks and prefer them to have long hair. Sorry folks, but it's not your choice to make. Hair is an accessory, not a health issue. This is about the right to exercise one's personal preferences. A child is not chattel, and kids have the right to pick their own hairstyles. Think of this as good practice for when your teenagers want Mohawks or purple hair—it's their personal style, and as parents we have to reinforce that we love their insides and that the outer stuff is just superficial and is really of no importance.

Problem solve together. If your child doesn't want a haircut, work together to figure out what would make the situation more sufferable. Perhaps wearing it in braids more often? Perhaps watching a movie while detangling, or separating the hair into a few sections, with short breaks in between, would help. If you ask your child to work on ideas with you, she'll feel more invested in the solutions chosen and give you less grief. Of course, most kids like their suggestions best, so try to go with those for the best success. Also, parents can ask the true authority—the child's hairdresser—for tips on brushing. Ripping it from the root down is painful; instead, work from the hair tips up to the scalp bit by bit. Ask for recommendations on equipment and products next time you take your child for a haircut so your child hears this information too.

Take Time for Training (TTFT). The sooner kids can brush and comb their own hair, the better. Like learning to tooth brush, you may let them take a turn first and then do a final once-through yourself to make sure no tangles were missed.

YOU CAN NEVER GET THE PONYTAILS RIGHT

Higher, lower, too tight, they're uneven! Seems no matter how hard you work on ponytails, it turns into a pitched battle.

Understanding the Problem

Trust me—it's not about your talents as a hairdresser. That's just a red herring. Children can gain a sense of power by undermining your efforts with something that is so subjective you can't ever possibly get it right. The child commands the situation and you are unable to succeed: that feels satisfying to a child who is seeking power over her parent. Look at you squirm. Look at you fail. This is a common situation; it reverses the roles for a child who usually experiences a sense of futility in her efforts.

Solutions

This is another situation that can be resolved by changing the overall power structure in the family. The more mom and dad can push power down to the children, and the more they can move away from punishments and rewards, the less children will be impressed with power. They will make fewer bids for power in uncooperative ways.

In the meantime, you've got a dance recital to go to and the ponytails must be in. So here are ideas to get through the immediate situation.

State what you are willing to do. For example: "I am happy to put your ponytails in, but you'll have to help me by letting me know where they go, since I always seem to get it wrong." "I am willing to try one more time, but if they are not to your liking, you will have to try on your own or ask someone else—maybe Dad or your dance teacher—to help you."

Reflect feelings without fighting. For example: "I am sorry I can't seem to make your vision of what ponytails should look like actually happen. That must be frustrating when you see in your mind exactly where they should be. I wish I could help more. Maybe someone else will have better luck."

But What If . . .

Alyson, if I try once and then refuse to try to get her ponytails right a second time it will lead to a total meltdown.

Yes, it might. Read up on how to deal with meltdowns in chapter 2. Because behavior is goal-oriented, you have just thwarted the child's ability to reach her goal of being in the position of power over you. That upsets kids: the old method isn't working. They see change is afoot. When they scream, "No, no—just try again, just try again—it will be fine, you'll see!" stick to your original promise: "I said I would do them once. I am sorry it didn't work out. I will try again for you tomorrow. I am sorry you're upset with me."

When the next night comes, you can accept the invitation to do your child's ponytails, and she will know that if they don't turn out right, you'll live by your one-try rule. Undoubtedly, to maintain her own position of power and control, she'll agree that they look just fine.

HATES WATER AND GETTING IN THE TUB

Is every bath night a nightmare? Do you think bathing a cat would be less dangerous? Does it take two mighty parents strapping a kid to the ground to strip him of his clothing? There has to be a better way.

UNDERSTANDING THE PROBLEM

Some children do have a real fear of water. Kids don't like how it can unexpectedly splash into their face or eyes. Some children associate bath time with hair-washing time and may have had the painful experience of getting shampoo in their eyes.

For the majority of families, however, fear of the water is not the explanation. Many children are defying the order to bathe. It's a contest of wills. The refusal to bathe is just another statement of "You can't make me."

SOLUTIONS

As with all power struggles, we have to DROP the rope. Let's review.

DROP the Rope

D: Determine whether you are in a power struggle. Are you angry? Feeling provoked or defeated? Does the situation escalate? Hmm. Yes.

R: Reassess the situation. What are your roles and responsibilities? What are the child's? What do the NOTS (needs of the situation) dictate? (See "Tactical Tip" below.)

O: Offer an olive branch. This step in dissolving power struggles is all about the messages we send that say we are not engaging in conflict, and that we come in peace. Often, our body language, tone and choice of words make it appear to the child that we are preparing to fight with him, and it triggers him to fight back. Instead, show in your words and actions that you are offering a truce, *not* inviting a fight. Show your peaceful intentions by making a joke. I mean, you can't be joking and fighting at the same time, right? Instead of announcing that it's time to bathe, try something funny and creative. For example, tickle the child and say, "Hey, giggle boy, are you ticklish? Do you want a tickle fight? Am I sticking my fingers in your dirty armpits—ahhh, nooo—armpit smells, ahhh, nooo—*tickle tickle*—my fingers are melting. We'd better tickle you to the tub!"

Or surprise him with the unexpected: "Let's see if we can slither up the stairs like water snakes do and slither into the bath," then lie on the floor and start to writhe. Do *anything* but the same old marching orders he is accustomed to.

P: Plow on positively. Focus on your action rather than the child's, and keep your attitude positive. What do *you* need to be doing? Offering choices? Tickling? Setting up a sponge bath? Moving along to something else? If you stay invested in getting him into the tub, he will stay invested in *not* going there. You can only control your actions. That is where you have your power. Let go of the notion of "making them" do something. Keep your focus on dissolving the power struggle that is creating the problem, rather than winning.

- -

Tactical Tip

Remember, in order to reassess roles and responsibilities, you must look at the NOTS (needs of the situation). What does the situation dictate must happen, rather than what do *I* want to happen *my* way? Here is a breakdown:

Parents' roles: we have the responsibility of keeping our children healthy, not squeaky-clean. We bathe way more in our society than in many others, and doctors will tell you we bathe kids more than required. A sponge bath at the sink is often sufficient.

Children's roles: to begin to manage their own bodies and to exercise some choice about the how and when. Parents can move some of the power back to the child by introducing choice: "You have to look after your body. It needs three baths a week. What nights would you like to have your baths this week?" (Have your child draw a picture of a bathtub on the calendar for those nights of the week.) "Today is one of your bath days; when do you want to fit your bath in today? In the morning? After your nap? Before family movie night?"

- -

But What If . . .

What if bath day comes and he still says no?

Point to the calendar and say, "This is the day you have chosen. You just need to pick the time now. Would you like to pick it? Or shall I?" If the child doesn't make a choice, reply: "I guess you'd like me to pick—tonight it is."

If when bath time arrives that night your child starts to put up resistance, you can say: "Our bodies need to have the dirt and germs on our skin removed to make sure we stay healthy. You can have a bath with bubbles and toys in the tub, or you can have a sponge bath at the sink—which would you prefer?"

WILL ONLY WEAR ONE FAVORITE PAIR OF PANTS—AND THEY'RE DIRTY

Washday is Wednesday, but Zack's favorite pair of sweatpants (the ones he basically lives in) are dirty and in the hamper. You offer him another pair of sweats that are almost identical, but he refuses to wear them. He's happy to wear the dirty ones. He doesn't care. He wants *his* pants.

Understanding the Problem

Let's play a game called Name That Kid.

The lovey kid. Clothing can be like a "lovey" or favorite security object. Any other pair of pants is *not* like the beloved sweats, no more than a new, soft blankie can replace the broken-in one with all the years of hugs and smells woven into its fibers.

The tactile kid. Some children are very sensitive to tactile sensations, and perhaps the sweatpants are the only item of clothing the child knows he can wear without feeling the seams, the tags or the elastics in the garment.

The self-identity kid. Some children have a special piece of clothing they wear like a uniform, believing if they aren't wearing their faded T-shirt with the dinosaurs on it, they just aren't themselves. It completes them. I know women who feel this way about wearing lipstick—"I am naked without it—I don't recognize myself."

Solutions

Regardless of their motivations, we need a solution, not a battle. I suggest you discuss how to accommodate *both* the child's limited wardrobe preferences and your laundry schedule. It's about striking up an arrangement that respects both parties. You shouldn't have to bear the burden of being a short-order laundress, and the child should be able to make clothing decisions for himself.

Brainstorm ideas. Come up with ideas like agreeing to how many times something can be worn before it needs to be washed, and determining in advance what "clothing option B" could be while the laundry is being done (kids often have a pair of jammies they like just as much). Making the rules concrete and predictable help with children who are more rigid and inflexible than others. Note: Don't problem solve during times of conflict. It's unlikely to yield great results.

Teach kids how to do their own laundry. They like being given the responsibility for using household appliances; it makes them feel like they are maturing and learning how to be independent and competent. Learning to sort laundry and operate a washing machine is easy—but you may have to get them a step stool so that they can reach the dials.

Rely on the power of peers. Their peers will let kids know if their clothes are dirty, and hearing, "Ewww! Is that yesterday's yogurt on your pants?" from a classmate is more meaningful than you saying, "You can't wear those—there's yogurt on them."

If you are concerned about what the teacher thinks, try this line:

Zingy One-Liner: "Josh is learning to care for his clothes all on his own. He has his own laundry schedule and is mastering the big machine. Isn't that awesome for an eight year old?"

REFUSES TO WEAR SOCKS

Ah, the Barefoot Contessa lives! Many children are content to slip on shoes and skip the socks—which drives some parents crazy. Interestingly, these are the same parents who tend to alphabetize their spice cabinet and date jars in their fridge.

UNDERSTANDING THE PROBLEM

Many children find socks a hassle: socks make them too hot and they either fall down or bunch up. Some kids can't stand the feel of the seams. To them, it's hogwash, this sock ritual. The truth is, socks were invented to reduce friction and to absorb perspiration, since shoes are hard to wash. Socks are a "washable layer" that we adults love.

Trouble is, a lot of kids are not yet of an age where their feet perspire. They have shoes with soft linings that don't rub and cause blisters. So the benefit of wearing socks is not yet apparent to them.

Solutions

Let's start by assessing who owns the problem here. Do your children know that socks exist? Have you taught them how to put them on? Have you invested in socks that are comfy to them (seamless socks if they have a sensory issue)? Then your good parenting work is over. It's up to them to exercise the sock option. How does whether or not your child wears socks impact you? Would you feel the same compunction to make a stranger on the street or a friend wear socks? No. It's not hurting others. It's a personal choice.

Let children experience natural consequences. Instead of telling our children about the inevitability of a blister, let them experience one. When they develop blisters or their shoes become smelly, you have something to talk about. Socratic methods work better than preaching, so ask instead of tell: it's the heart of coaching and teaching. For example: "Sounds like you don't like those nasty blisters. What could you do to prevent the rubbing? I use socks." So much more encouraging than: "What did I tell you?" or "You should have listened."

Apply logical consequences. If the child has smelly shoes or feet, *now* you have something that impacts the enjoyment of your personal space. What is the logical outcome of being odiferous? People move away from you. "I'd love to cuddle, buddy, but I can't get near those feet. When they are washed up, then I'll be able to get closer." The inherent social benefits of being sweet smelling will come faster if you don't digress into a power struggle over sock wearing.

WON'T TAKE MEDICINE

It can be difficult getting kids to swallow or chew something that tastes yucky. You think broccoli is tough, try bitter-tasting medicine. Some kids spit it up, which makes us parents apoplectic because we don't know how much of the dosage was actually ingested, and we don't want to under- or overdose our kids. Eye drops and nose sprays don't feel pleasant either. Do you want to try a better way, one that doesn't require you to learn how to put your child in a wrestling hold?

UNDERSTANDING THE PROBLEM

Parents are often so worried about the *absolute* need to get the medicine into their children that they create more problems than they solve.

Insistence and *force* are ingredients that will trigger a power struggle.

My goal, and yours, is to get the child to take their medicine. To increase the likelihood that she will actually swallow the stuff, we want to ensure that attention—and power-plays—don't throw up a roadblock. The minute the child feels that taking the medicine is losing or submitting, we're sunk.

As with all power struggles, we have to stop thinking of how we can "make 'em" and instead try to "make 'em wanna."

SOLUTIONS

First, apply the DROP model. (Flip back to the "Hates Water and Getting in the Tub" section earlier in this chapter for a refresher.) Then, consider the following solutions.

Medicine That Helps with Comfort and Symptom Relief

Let the child decide. The child's comfort is the issue, so give her the responsibility of deciding whether swallowing bitter swill is worth the relief it will bring.

"Would you like to take something for that nasty cough? It will help you sleep better. No? Okay, let me know if you change your mind." Believe me, she will be more open to trying the cough syrup if you go this route rather than if you plug her nose and force it down.

Medicine That Must Be Taken

We have to ensure it's consumed. But rather than thinking that there is no choice, we need to create ways to help the child feel more in control of the process. Here are some ideas:

Allow choice. Remember Dr. Suess's story *Green Eggs and Ham*? "Would you like it in a box? Would you like it with a fox? Would you like it here or there? Would you like it anywhere?" Try the same little choices with the meds: "It's almost time for your penicillin; would you like it now or after your snack? Would you like to take it sitting on my lap or sitting in you chair?" Or, "It's time for your eye drops; would you like me to do your left eye or your right eye first?" These seem like silly, inconsequential choices, but they give the child a modicum of control in the matter, and that helps.

Encourage involvement. For example: "This is your special medicine from the doctor. Can you show me what special place you'd like to keep it in the fridge?" "Would you like to give your teddy bear some 'pretend medicine'?" (Find an empty dropper and use water.) "You can look after teddy just like you look after yourself." "It's time for your medicine. Can you get it from the fridge?"

STICKS HANDS IN DIRTY DIAPERS

It's late afternoon and you hear stirring in the crib. You're sure it must be your little darling rousing from her nap. You walk into her room with a cheery smile and are greeted with the horror of feces-painted walls. Who knew kids were packing art supplies right in their diapers?

Understanding the Problem

The first time this happened, the child had no idea what reaction it would garner. She was just living in the moment, probably overcoming boredom. However, if it happens repeatedly, she embarks on the behavior to elicit an expected response from you, and this puts poop art in the realm of misbehavior/mistaken approach.

Given that it happens when you are not in the room, the fecal finger painting is not about getting instant attention, but if you go on about it to your friends and family, your little pooping Picasso may be enjoying hearing the stories retold. It probably evokes a pretty big emotional response from you (defacing property *and* a disgusting mess to clean up).

A devilish grin suggests that this behavior is about power. However, it could also be about revenge. Did you send the child to her room angrily? Could this be a tit-for-tat retaliation for some transgression you didn't handle well earlier in the day?

Before you can apply the appropriate solution, you'll need to figure out which of these goals most closely matches your child's.

Solutions

If the goal is attention. Keep words to a minimum when you discover the mess, and don't make the child famous for her act of silly fecal smearing. Instead, talk up her positive, helpful behaviors; tell others stories of how helpful your child has been setting the table, bringing in the recycle box, tidying toys.

If the goal is power. Don't get angry. Okay, make that, don't act angrily. One goal of power is to upset a parent. If the child sees this gets your goat, she'll try it again. Your task when power is a goal is to control the situation, not the child. When you change the child's diapers, put a piece of duct tape over the tabs to keep the diaper on, and dress her in a one-piece sleeper. Presto! Now, find ways to empower your child. How else could she be more autonomous and masterful in her life? What else could you hand over?

If the goal is revenge. Children don't employ revenge tactics first or randomly. Think back on what has transpired that could have been perceived as unfair treatment from the child's perspective. Think of alternate ways the situation could be handled if it comes up again. Apologize for not handling things well and discuss how to do things better in the future. You may not have intended to punish your child, but she *does* feel hurt. Help make amends and work on building the relationship back up with lots of positive interactions and nonpunitive corrections.

DISAGREEMENTS ABOUT WARDROBE

Wanting to control how our kids dress can cause enormous conflict. Every generation has something to say about the next. When my mother was a young teacher in the 1970s, female teachers were not allowed to wear pants in the classroom. Archaic, right? What about denim? Once a practical fabric for hard labor on the farm, it is now the pant-of-choice for Steve Jobs and other creative executives. Parents today need to be more flexible and far less serious about clothing customs than did their counterparts in past generations. Here are tips on learning how to diminish clothing conflicts within our own families.

UNDERSTANDING THE PROBLEM

We feel our children's appearance somehow reflects on us as parents. Most parents want the clean-cut kid who other conservative adults will see as acceptable. Somehow, that is supposed to confirm we have done a good job of raising the child. Perhaps we've cast our own judgments, thinking, "What mother would let her child out of the house looking like that?" and promise ourselves we'll never let that happen. We make a big deal out of clothing and try to dress our children to our tastes and rules.

Herein lies the crux of the problem: it's not our job. It is not a parent's responsibility; it's the children's—and they know it. When we usurp children's power to be self-determined about how they dress themselves, we incite rebellion.

If personal aesthetics and appearances are one of your strong personal values, you're more likely to be passionate about teaching this to your children. However, what we actually do is ram our ideas down our children's throats, desperately hoping they'll adopt our values.

Force-feeding our values produces two extreme results: the Passionate Adopter and the Passionate Rejecter. If the value is religion, you'll end up with one child who is a saint and the other a sinner. With appearance, you're likely to end up with one child who is a total neatnik fashionista and one who's a slob.

Solutions

Lighten up. Lighten up about how your children dress. This is *not* a big problem. Leukemia and poverty are big problems; tights matching the romper is not.

Don't judge a book by its cover. Your children will experiment with different personas. Stand by them in all the many inventions of themselves, without ever wavering in your unconditional love for them, regardless of how they dress. I am sure my parents didn't understand my Annie Hall layering, Madonna hair or Olivia Newton-John sweatbands. They never talked about appearances—period. Walk the talk.

Limit the number of rules. The fewer rules you have, the more likely they are to be respected. By the way, this goes for *all* rules. I recommend you forgo a rule about not wearing flip-flops in October in order to more readily gain adherence to a few important requests, like when you visit with grandma:

1. No jeans with holes or frays.
2. No visible undergarments (cover up the bra straps and tuck in the underwear bands).
3. Show camisoles, not cleavage.

Provide a clothing allowance. Start your child on a small, limited clothing allowance. When? As soon as you start fighting over purchases. My children were in Grades 7 and 8 when they got their first clothing allowances. Initially, they presented a recommendation of what they needed for their back-to-school wardrobe. They went online to find the median price for each item. I'll pay for a sweater, but I won't pay for a brand or a label. I approved the budget and off we went. Now that they are older, I roll their yearly clothing allowance into their weekly allowance, which requires more money-management skills. They shop with friends instead of with me, and I want to empower them to manage this area of responsibility in their life. It's teaching them a life skill they'll need when they leave home. Besides, the more they find positive ways to autonomy and mastery, the less likely they are to have conflicts with you! It's all good.

Take Time for Training (TTFT). However, once we teach our children the basics of dressing (seams go on the inside, labels go at the back) the rest is up to them. It's not our place to dress our children. Would you tell your husband or wife what to wear? No, because it's not your business. Timing tip: Don't teach getting dressed at 8:20 a.m. on a workday. It's much better to teach during a less time-stressed part of your day.

Make clothes accessible. Clear out the off-season clothes. Kids won't be tempted to put on a sundress in November if it's in a box labeled "summer clothes."

Downgrade mistakes. If your child picks items that don't match, or has her shirt or pants on backwards, let that go, don't criticize or correct. Instead, comment that you noticed she has on purple pants that are like the purple in her turtleneck: "Look! Same color here and here. That's called matching. You picked a matching out-fit!" If your kid wears pants under a dress, that is okay, too. Who knows, maybe she's the next Carrie Bradshaw and will set trends instead of follow them.

Let children experience natural consequences. If our children choose to wear something inappropriate for the weather, that's okay. Let them learn experientially about how suitable their clothing is. Kids learn by picking the wrong jacket or deciding not to wear mittens on cold days. Give them the power to choose (assuming it only makes them uncomfortable rather than risking frost bite) so that they can experience the outcome of various choices. Did they get cold? Or wet? That's okay. In fact, it's great. They are learning. You don't need to emphasize the lesson by going on about it: "See . . . what did I say?" or "See, if you had listened, you wouldn't be so cold." When my children were small, I would sometimes step outside myself or turn on the weather channel and share my decisions: "Oh my—it's going to be minus 5 today. I am wearing a scarf and hat."

WON'T GET DRESSED

It's 8:05 a.m. and you're sitting on the floor of the bedroom holding a pair of pants while your daughter jumps up and down on the bed. "Come on, let's just get your pants on," you say. "We're going to be late!" The clock ticks on, your blood pressure rises. How do you get kids dressed without the daily morning hassle?

UNDERSTANDING THE PROBLEM

This is dawdling, and it's a fine form of passive power. The child's behavior shouts, "You can't make me!" And the longer you sit on the floor, the more she exercises her power over you. The situation is gratifying to a child who can't seem to find the fulfilling feelings of power on the positive side of life; in modern families, most of us are not good at showing children how to find positive power. That's why I encourage you to load on the P's and C's and hold those family meetings! (See p. 110 for more on P's and C's and see p. 71 for more on family meetings.)

Often, children in our culture come to mistakenly believe that having others in your service makes you special and important and powerful, like the adults who seem to enjoy a higher social status. Servitude is how many children experience our love and feel their sense of belonging, rather than the more healthy belief that they belong through contribution, that they are not special but rather are among equals and participate in a way that benefits the group, not just themselves. No one is special or above others. These ideas are what Alfred Adler called the "ironclad logic of social living."

SOLUTIONS

Let routines be the boss. If you don't have a basic morning routine, establish one. Once you have a basic schedule in place, it is the routine that becomes the boss, replacing the perception that it's time to get dressed "because I say so" and "you must do as I say."

Use a when/then statement. Some families make it a requirement that their kids are dressed for the day before eating breakfast. If that is your established routine, you can say, "When you're dressed, then I'll know you're ready for breakfast." You decide what when/then choice works for you.

Lead, don't push. If the child is in the bathroom or watching cartoons when you announce it's dressing time, don't stand there waiting for her to initiate a move to the bedroom. Go there yourself. She is more likely to follow. If you wait, she waits. *You* make the move.

State what you are willing to do. If you are sitting on the floor and the child is still down the hall or jumping on the bed, announce what you are willing to do: "If you'd like my help, I am available now. If you are not interested in having me help, I'll get moving on to my breakfast." If the child doesn't shift gears and engage in dressing, then simply state, "I see you don't need me here. I'll see you at breakfast." Then leave.

· ·

"Watch the tongue in the shoe, not the tongue in the mouth."
—Dr. Jane Nelsen, Positive Discipline™ founder.

This means, if your child says, "I am coming, I am coming!" but he is still jumping on the bed, we determine his intent by observing his behavior rather than listening to his words. The mouth says, "I am coming!" but the feet say, "I am staying and jumping." Which do you respond to? The feet.

· ·

Offer choice. When it's just about time to go to school, give your child one more opportunity to get dressed: "It's time to go; do you want to throw on your clothes? I can help you now, or do you want to take them in a bag and get dressed at school?" It's good to let the school know in advance that you're going through this training, but you certainly don't expect the teachers to be responsible for the daily dressing of your child. Teachers understand and will support you. Ask them not to make a big scene when the child arrives in his jammies. Some kids like making an impressive entrance, and we don't want to confuse the issue by providing a new payoff for not getting dressed.

After a few mornings, your child will prefer to get changed at home rather than at school. Some kids may always do that last-minute dash. That's okay. You didn't fight. The morning is still basically on track. Consider that a success.

But What If . . .

This seems like good advice for younger children who need help dressing. Got any advice for how to speed up dressing my kids who are six and seven years old and can dress themselves but don't? I know I'm not supposed to do it for them, but we can't be late either.

For children who have just learned to dress themselves, you may want to let them know that getting dressed is their job now, but if they want company, you'll hang out with them while they get dressed. This can help those children who don't want to gain independence because they conclude the more they can do for themselves, the less mom time they'll get. These children will cling to their dependency on mom. This can be prevented by being excited about their newfound abilities and finding other productive ways to spend time together.

WON'T PUT ON PAJAMAS AT BEDTIME

You're held hostage in a bedroom with a kid who won't get his pajamas on; meanwhile, you're getting frantic because you haven't even started the work you were supposed to do that day.

UNDERSTANDING THE PROBLEM

This is another stalling tactic: aka dawdling. All dawdling is a passive power play. Part of what fuels the problem is the time sensitivities of most events. We want to be done! We've had enough of kid antics all day, and we are just aching to put our feet up and pour the merlot.

Our mood and insistence become more forceful, which invites the child to dig in her heels more. For many busy families, children only find parent face time at tuck-in time. They've spent the day with a teacher and the evening with a coach or instructor. This might be it for parent face time. No wonder they want more of it.

SOLUTIONS

Problem solve at a family meeting. For example: "Our tuck-ins are going on too long. How can we do them better? I'd like to be onto my own activities by 9 p.m., but we can discuss how to better manage what happens between dinner and 9 p.m." You'd be surprised by how many children would prefer a faster tuck-in if they know they can get in an extra board game with their parents.

State what you are willing to do. Offer to help the child get into her PJs (or keep her company if she can do this task herself), but, as per the morning dawdling, discussed above, if she continues to run and jump and dawdle, she is declining your offer, so simply move along to the next part of tuck-ins: start reading the bedtime story. She may sleep in her clothes, or change while you read or after you've tucked her in. It doesn't matter what the child decides. You only have to be concerned with doing your part: showing up, offering help, staying on schedule with reading and lights out.

CHAPTER 9

BAD HABITS—AND THE DEMOCRATIC APPROACH TO BREAKING THEM

Hair Twirling · Hair Sucking · Masturbating Tots · Nose
Picking · Thumb Sucking · Love Objects · Pacifier
Dependence · Loves Eating Glue, Playdough, Etc.

There is a difference between misbehaviors and bad habits. Parents must be able to distinguish between the two in order to deal with unwanted behaviors appropriately. Before we can figure out our course of action, we have to diagnose the problem. "Why are they doing it?" is always the first question to ask ourselves. So, how do we differentiate between a misbehavior and a bad habit?

Definition of a misbehavior: A repeated pattern of behavior that doesn't meet the needs of the situation and is aimed at eliciting a **response from another** that fulfills a goal (attention, power, revenge or avoidance).

Definition of a bad habit: A repeated pattern of behavior that doesn't meet the needs of the situation, *but*—and here's the big difference—the child's goal is **not to get a social response**. Rather, bad habits serve the child either by providing stimulation during times of low activity or as a self-soothing mechanism to reduce anxiety.

All behavior can be thought of as movement from a "felt minus" position toward a "perceived plus" position. Feeling bored or anxious is an uncomfortably negative state. By doing "something," children relieve the boredom or anxiety, which makes them feel better—a "perceived plus." It's a coping strategy.

Parenting is about helping children reduce or eliminate "felt minus" feelings. A lot of those feelings go away as they become more confident and secure in the world, by learning the world is safe and secure and that they are capable and valuable. That is why our long-term strategy of being constant encouragers who stimulate independence will pay off in our children's happiness.

While we're working on that front, we still have to deal with the pesky issues of hair twirling, thumb sucking, nail biting and all the other gems in this chapter. Read on.

HAIR TWIRLING

Is your child on the road to dreadlocks with her constant hair twirling? Have you noticed that it happens near the end of the day or close to nap time? Maybe she's even developing a bald patch.

UNDERSTANDING THE PROBLEM

The child has creatively found a way to self-soothe—and we all need ways to do that. A certain amount of life stressors are inevitable, and it's healthy to learn ways to defuse these tensions.

SOLUTIONS

You'll love this technique:

Do nothing—yup, that's right. Simply ignore it. You have nothing to worry about as kids usually just outgrow the habit and the hair grows back. If the habit is helping the child relax and is not causing bodily injury or social disruption, then let it be.

How Much Is Too Much?

Life stressors may be inevitable, but you need to keep an eye out for the red flags that indicate too much stress.

If you have an older child who is hair twirling, or you feel there is an obsessive quality about twirling or picking hair, you should intervene. By obsessive, I mean a preoccupation, something that eats up a lot of time or changes the child's regular daily living or social patterns. If she locks herself in the bedroom, for example, or declines sleepover invitations, that's a flag you might be dealing with trichotillomania (TM).

TM is a diagnosable disorder. It usually appears around puberty, though it can have roots in earlier childhood hair exploration. A compulsive hair puller spends hours grooming, checking ends and pulling specifically selected hairs. This is more than a self-soothing behavior. If you think your child may have TM, seek professional help.

HAIR SUCKING

Are you tired of seeing your child with a strand of hair in her mouth? Do you wonder if that clump of hair has ever seen a dry moment? Hopefully the shampoo is nontoxic because it's all but being eaten the way she gnashes on that rat tail.

Understanding the Problem

Babies start life with a sucking reflex that helps establish breast-feeding. The mouth has so many sensory nerve endings that as soon as they can reach and grab, any object goes in the mouth for further exploration. This oral fixation can last a long time. Once hair hits the shoulders and makes its way into the mouth, many kids find they enjoy the oral sensation of pulling a strand of hair into their mouths and sucking on it. It's soothing.

Going back to first principles, it's not really hurting the hair or causing bodily injury per se so you may decide this is something you'd rather just ignore altogether. But, for some parents, the habit is just too unhygienic and socially undesirable to watch. If you'd like to tackle a change in this behavior, I have tactics you could try.

SOLUTIONS

Rather than nagging, reminding and fighting over the hair-sucking habit (all of which give this habit an additional benefit of getting undue attention), explain to your child that it's not nice for others to look at, it makes hair stink and it grosses other people out.

Remember, we are trying to educate here, not threaten, but it's important that kids understand that the longer one has a habit, the more it becomes engrained—and that means it's harder to break when the time comes. And the time *will* come: ask your child if she sees herself sucking on her hair when she has a job or goes on a date.

If the child doesn't want to break this habit, you'll just stir up resistance if you try to make 'em stop. Instead, try these strategies.

Offer choice. For example: "You can suck your hair, but that is something others don't want to see, so would you like to stop sucking, or do you need to go somewhere private?"

If she keeps sucking, gently lead her to another room. Often that motion is enough for her to spit the hair out.

Decide for you. If the child resists moving, move *you,* not her: "I'm not interested in watching that. I'll be in the kitchen."

❧

Of course, if the child *is* interested in stopping the habit, there are ways you can be an ally and offer support:

Encouragement. Tell your child how courageous she is for tackling this challenge, how much you appreciate being entrusted with helping her and that you have faith she'll reach her goal if she works at it.

Signals. Often, children are so habituated they don't even know they are sucking their hair again, so you may have to point it out to them so they can stop. A nonverbal signal is so much gentler than being verbally reminded. Better yet, ask the child to create what that private signal will be—no one else need know it.

Change environment. Instead of focusing on the child's behavior, see if she'd be keen on wearing her hair back in ties so it's not hanging in its usual place, tempting her, or landing in her mouth without her being aware of it. Even a haircut could help if she is willing. If she can't reach it—problem solved.

Substitution. Suggest she try putting something else in her mouth. A toothpick, a drinking straw, gum—come up with some ideas together and experiment to see what helps. Work together in partnership; don't disenfranchise the child by getting too bossy with your ideas or implementation.

Distraction. Often this habit occurs in the same place, or as part of some other ritual like watching TV or reading. It might help to do other activities or change up things, to help break out of the rut and habit associations.

Acknowledgment. Notice the times the child is being successful. Every small win counts.

MASTURBATING TOTS

Lots of parents ask me what to do about their boy who seems obsessed with holding his penis, or their daughter who grinds her pelvis on her teddy bear.

Seeing their child touching or stimulating his or her genitals freaks out some parents. And let me tell you, some kids get right into it. This habit will really challenge sexually conservative parents.

They worry that if their child is enjoying it so much at four years old, what will he or she be wanting at 14?

Understanding the Problem

Have no fear: this is a normal behavior. Early interest in touching doesn't mean that kids are sexually deviant. It does mean they have discovered sensations that are pleasant—lucky them! But we're walking that fine line: teaching kids that our culture largely prefers sexual activity to be kept private *and* how to feel okay about themselves, their bodies and their early sexual feelings.

So, whether they are grinding up against the five-point-harness seatbelt or stroking their willy in their sweat pants while they watch cartoons, the message you want to convey is, yes, that feels good and is normal and people do it, but that kind of touching is private. Private versus public is what we want to teach, not good or bad.

Solutions

Hopefully, your child will save up his or her sexual energy for naptime, but if not, let me show you how to enforce a healthy boundary.

Offer choice. For example: "It looks like you need some privacy." Lead the child by the hand to the bedroom, saying, "The rest of us don't care to see that."

Decide for you. Again, if a struggle ensues, don't move the child, move yourself, saying, "I don't care to see that."

Change the environment. Try to break the connection or association that triggers the child to initiate self-touching: if it's always under a blanket in front of the TV, you can remove the blanket from the family room.

Ignore. If the child always grinds in the car seat (a common place), you can either ignore it completely (you are supposed to be watching the road, after all) or distract the child with conversation, a car game, songs. Of course, if it has become an ongoing issue, you could always pull the car over to the shoulder and say, "I see you need privacy. Let me know when I can get in the car again." Get out of the car and read a book or answer emails.

As they grow older, their sense of propriety develops further, and with these gentle tactics, you've laid a good foundation to continue building a healthy and comfortable sexual identity.

NOSE PICKING

"Oh gross! Mommy, Jaime ate his booger!"

Sure it's gross, but come on, it's not *that* bad! I don't think boogers should be added to the food pyramid, but neither should they be lumped in the same league as dioxins. No one died eating a booger. Not that a coroner has reported, anyway.

UNDERSTANDING THE PROBLEM

Children don't like the feeling of crud up their noses. They don't like the feeling of things tugging at their nose hairs. The trouble is, kids have less-developed sinuses, so mucus has nowhere to go but the nose. Children also have more exposure to various new germs and a budding immune system so they make a lot of mucus. The trouble is, they are also less socialized in the nuances of nose picking in ways that look like "we're just itching!"

SOLUTIONS

Manage the environment, not the child. Here are some ideas.

- Put a humidifier in the child's bedroom.
- Keep the child's nose lining lubricated (use Vaseline-type ointment).
- Look into nasal irrigation systems for youngsters.
- Teach the child to blow his or her nose. (Why do we parents try to keep that job so long?)
- Have tissues readily available (say, on each table in the house).

Educate. Help your kids understand that, yes, the nose makes fluid and sometimes it's thick and crusts up. Explain that it is the body's waste disposal system at work, ridding the body of things it wants out. If you eat it, you're putting it back in. And there are germs floating in that stuff.

So, the snot needs to get out of the body. They can help by blowing. If there are crusty chunks, show them how adults do it: go to the washroom for privacy and use a tissue-wrapped finger if you are going to enter the nasal passage.

The trouble with nose picking is that it can cause a nose scab. If the child picks and the spot scabs again, there is a new scab to pick. So try to keep up the lubrication until a healthy nose lining is reestablished.

❧

If the child still continues to pick in public, try one of these tactics:

Use actions, not words. Just pass the tissue box over to them; they'll get it.

Ask instead of tell. Inquire, "Do you need a Kleenex?" "Do you need a moment alone to look after your nose?" versus barking orders for the child to go blow his nose.

Decide for you. "I don't like watching that. I'm leaving."

❧

Or, consider these creative solutions (if you can pull them off properly):

Join them. Kids hate misbehaving parents. Let them know that if it is okay for them to pick, you'd like to be given the same social privilege. Why should the child be the only one? So start picking your nose whenever the child picks. He should find that upsetting—"Mom! You don't pick your nose!" Keep in mind that the idea is not to tease but to create a social learning experience.

Invite the behavior. If you feel you've been harping on the kid to stop picking his nose and now it's not just a bad habit but a way of defeating or resisting you, you can end the power struggle by inviting the behavior. For example: "James wants us to see him picking his nose. Okay, James, you have our full attention. Go ahead, we're all watching now." Again, this is not meant to be demeaning. You are admitting you can't stop him and by inviting the behavior, it's no longer defiance when he picks. The child no longer achieves his end goal.

❧

If these strategies don't work immediately, stop. You probably know how your child will respond before you begin. Some will smile and get it right away. Then it's a charm. If your child is more "sensitive," it's best to pass and move on to another strategy.

THUMB SUCKING

Ah, the beloved thumb. It's so cute when they suck their thumbs when they're little. But now that little stub of a thumb is becoming a permanent raisin, wet, wrinkled and doing God knows what damage to their bite. When do we worry? When is the right time and what is the right way to tackle thumb sucking?

UNDERSTANDING THE PROBLEM

Of the self-soothing habits, thumb sucking is among the most popular. Babies even suck their thumbs in utero. Most children outgrow these early comforting behaviors and it's no biggy. But when? Five? Six? Seven? We worry! (We're parents; it's our prerogative.)

When parents ask me about thumb sucking, I assess the situation by asking two questions:

1.   Is it causing bodily harm?
2.   Is it interfering socially?

If the child's palate is shifting, if her thumb inhibits her from talking, or if her shame of still thumb sucking is causing her to socialize less (she declines invitations to sleepovers because she only knows how to fall asleep sucking her thumb), it's time to help.

• •

"Worry is just another word for problems you don't have yet!"
—words of wisdom passed on to me by my clinical
supervisor and teacher, the late Larry Nisan

• •

SOLUTIONS

Ask an expert. Start by getting a dentist's opinion. Heck, let the dentist be the bearer of bad news. She can talk to your tot about her concern that the teeth are being moved from all the thumb sucking and explain how an overbite is now developing. Maybe the dentist even has a picture to illustrate the problem.

Just for the record, for the great majority of thumb suckers, this is not an issue. They either stop thumb sucking before the soft palate has moved or things are so transitory in the mouth that whatever bite alterations occur self-correct.

– –

Tactical Tip

Coach instead of coerce. So the dentist says, yes, the thumb sucking is creating a problem. Your job is to help your child tackle the habit. It's her problem to correct. I know, I know, it's your checkbook paying the orthodontist. But if you become a "take over Tommy," which so many task-master parents can be, you'll likely invite resistance. The fastest route to suckless is cheerleading as your child slays the thumb monkey on her back.

Help your child understand that thumb sucking is a habit. Explain that if she has been doing it for a long time, it might feel weird to stop. But anyone can break a habit—it takes about 21 days (just three weeks). Mark the calendar to celebrate the end of the 21 days. Success! She reached her goal. Maybe the dentist can arrange a phone call or brief follow-up visit to the office to help mark the special day. These are all little devices that are part of building up an accountability structure that your child might like. Be sure that your child is keen on these ideas first. She has to maintain ownership of the mission.

Encourage. Parents often rely on threats as motivational tools. It just slips out of our mouths so easily. "Dr. Copeland is going to be very upset with you when he sees you for a follow-up appointment. You don't want to let him down, do you?" These kinds of remarks instill fear (and since children are thumb sucking to reduce anxiety, adding pressure is just going to make matters worse).

Instead, encourage the child when she has setbacks: "I am glad you told me you're having a hard time sticking to your plan. That took a lot of courage."

Follow up with curious questioning: "What can I do to help you?" "What times of day are the hardest?" "What is your plan now?" "How else could you manage?" "Is there something else you want to try?"

The strategies that are most likely to work are always the ones that your children come up with for themselves. Invite them to generate ideas. If they can't seem to get the brainstorming ball rolling, invite them to sit with you to look up ideas on the Internet.

LOVE OBJECTS

I can't tell you how many dollars I've spent trying to match-make my daughters with "love objects" of my choice. No, they didn't want the little MoMA stuffed animals that were cute as hell. They got attached to potholders. How unfair is that? Instead of lugging around artisan pieces, they wanted to sleep with flame-retardant items for kitchen use. Crickey.

UNDERSTANDING THE PROBLEM

Many kids choose some kind of blanket or stuffed animal as an object of affection, to give them a sense of security. These items are highly personal and do serve an important purpose. Children are able to magically attach or connect to their love objects because it reminds them of their parents (the primary attachment relationship). Because these objects are usually soft, snuggly and smell like home, they help calm the children emotionally.

As children grow, they transition gradually from total dependence to autonomy—they begin to venture farther away from the security of mom's or dad's presence. These love objects help ease that transition.

HOW MUCH LOVE IS TOO MUCH?

So, what is wrong with having a love object? Nothing, unless it's:

1. Causing bodily harm
2. Interfering with the social order

Here are some examples:

- If the blanket or doll is filthy (and it will be, because that tattered, soiled state is part of the appeal), that is not respectful to the social order. Dirty things need to be washed. You'll have to work with your child on a plan for washday and how he'll cope without the love object for a few hours.
- If holding the blanket requires one hand, and the child can't hold hands with the child beside him at circle time, then it's interfering with social order. The blankie can be put in a cubby, left at the seat or wrapped around the child's shoulders, but right now it's hand-holding time.
- If the love object is a stuffed animal or doll that your child demands have its own chair at the dinner table—you have to set dolly a place and pour dolly milk—dolly is becoming a

burden on others' time and efforts. That's not okay. (If your child wants to serve teddy, that's fine, but demanding it of you is not.)

- Don't get me wrong, we all love to host teddy bear picnics. But when teddy becomes an invisible friend and your child demands you treat it as if it were alive, a line has been crossed.

SOLUTIONS

The more you practice the strategies outlined in my book, the more you will be giving your children a sense of autonomy and mastery. As they begin to feel they are connected, capable and courageous, they won't feel as anxious and they won't need their transition objects as much. Meanwhile, have them practice being without their love objects—especially when you are around.

Sample Script

"It's dinnertime. No blankies at the table please. Do you want to tuck him away safely somewhere while you eat? No? Sounds like you'd rather be with blankie than eat. That's okay. That's your choice to make. If you change your mind, we'll be at the table."

"Blankie needs to stay in your bedroom. He is just for sleep-time now. If you are feeling you need to cuddle blankie, you can go do that in your room."

PACIFIER DEPENDENCE

You thought pacifiers were a lifesaver when you were trying to settle your child to sleep when he was a baby, but now you're sick of seeing that plug in every picture. Your own mother is telling you to pitch the thing. But when? And how?

UNDERSTANDING THE PROBLEM

We don't call them "soothers" for nothing. Soothers really do soothe. I don't think it's cheating to use a soother, and mothers shouldn't feel they have failed at calming their infants if they resort to using one. The worst thing for a frantic baby is a frantic mother. Do what you gotta do. However, a toddler or preschooler isn't a baby anymore, and eventually that pacifier becomes more of a crutch or habit than an actual soothing agent.

Here are the questions I ponder when I'm asked, "Should I wean?"

- Is the soother causing harm to self or others?
- Is the soother disruptive to the social order?
- Does having a soother allow avoidance of life's demands?

In fact, late use of pacifiers (post-12–18 months) can impact language development. Toddlers are less apt to talk and instead will point and grunt. That qualifies as avoidance of life's demands. Or a child may try to talk with the pacifier in his mouth, which will also impact language development. It's complicated learning where the tongue needs to rest in the mouth to make certain sounds, and having a rubber object in the way is no way to learn. That qualifies as harm to self. Time to start weaning.

Solutions

Set limits. Allow the pacifier at specific times or in specific places— bedtime, car rides or when the child is winding down and soothing himself to sleep.

Allow choice. A child may have an upset that makes him so distraught he wants his soother to help him calm down. Allow that option, but let him know he has to enjoy his soother in his bedroom. This choice allows the child access to his soother without changing the limits.

Read books. Ask the librarian for children's books on saying good-bye to soothers. And begin reading these as a stepping-stone for discussions about giving it up.

Mark it on the calendar. Pick a date with your child and put it on the family calendar as the special "Give-up Soother Day."

Be creative. Here are some ideas that worked for other parents:

- "I told my daughter that, just like the tooth fairy and Easter Bunny, there was a magical soo soo fairy that collected up all the soo soos when children were old enough to cope without them. The soo soo fairy takes the pacifiers to babies who were just born."
- "My son was just crazy about garbage trucks. I told him that he could put his pacifiers *in* the garbage truck *all* on his own on garbage day. We waited at the end of the driveway on garbage day. He told the garbage truck driver he was a big boy now, and the driver smiled and let him toss the soothers in the back."
- "I put a pin-prick hole in the end of the soother so it let in air and didn't feel the same in her mouth. She didn't like the unusual shape and that was it."
- "I told my daughter this is the last one I am willing to buy and when it's gone, it's gone. She seemed to understand that, and sure enough one day it went missing and she somehow knew that was life."

But What If . . .

I like the idea of tossing the soother on a set date, but my child still really needs his soother to fall asleep. I work and am exhausted. I don't have time to deal with kids who can't sleep.

Pacifiers are a common sleep prop or sleep crutch. Often we end up replacing one sleep prop for another, so we win the battle of the pacifier weaning, only to discover we are sleeping in our toddler's bed. He's substituted you for the soother.

Instead, I suggest you brace yourself for a couple of tough nights. You can do this on the days you are not working, or during a holiday.

The child will struggle to relearn how to fall asleep without a prop, but he will. Honest.

LOVES EATING GLUE, PLAYDOUGH, ETC.

You divert your eyes for one moment and in the mouth goes the playdough. "Spit it out! Playdough is not for eating!"

Understanding the Problem

Children are naturally curious and certainly have an oral stage when anything and everything goes in their mouths. During some of their early explorations, they may have discovered that some things actually have a nice flavor or texture, though adults may not agree.

Children can also learn that when they pop certain things in their mouths it gets a reaction. Sometimes a big reaction! In fact, savvy kids learn early that if they keep putting things in their mouths, they are sure to keep their caregivers' attention, as they now must hover over them to ensure they don't do it again.

This is undue attention seeking. Parents feel annoyed or worried. They offer up constant reminders to "Stop eating that." Unlike power, the situation doesn't escalate; instead, the child responds by spitting out the playdough only to eat more or to eat something else inedible moments later. This behavior has a relapsing, remitting quality.

Solutions

Put safety first. Ask yourself if the item can be safely consumed. Find an edible playdough recipe that you can make from scratch. Now you are able to use the powerful tool of "ignoring" (see the next strategy).

Ignore the behavior. If your child eats the playdough, don't say a word. Keep doing what you were doing. Once the child sees that the behavior is no longer effective in getting your attention, he will abandon the behavior.

Long-Term Strategy

Help the child find positive connections with you so he doesn't have to use misbehaviors (which are really just mistaken approaches at finding connections with you). Join him at the playdough table and create with him. Ask him if he'd like to help you prepare lunch in the kitchen or assist you in folding laundry.

● ●

Dear Alyson,
I have twin three-year-olds. One constantly ate paper. Toilet paper off the roll, Kleenex out of the box, paper lying about the house. How could I make him stop? After reading your last book and speaking to my doctor about the contents of paper, he assured me that the little bit of chemicals used in the processing of the paper would not harm my boy if I did in fact follow through with the tactic of ignoring his paper-eating habit. After two days of not saying a word about the paper and making sure I was being more attentive when he wasn't eating paper, the whole problem resolved itself. I had been trying everything I could think of for months and months. Apparently doing "nothing" for a few days was the solution.

● ●

CHAPTER 10

BEDROOM BRAWLS—AND THE DEMOCRATIC APPROACH TO SETTLING SPACE ISSUES

Won't Make Bed in the Morning · Won't Put Clothes in the Laundry Hamper · Won't Let Sibling into Bedroom · Won't Let You in Bedroom · Destroys Bedroom during Time-Outs · Writes on Walls · Siblings Share a Room, but They're the Odd Couple

Parents pay the mortgage and have the deed to the family house, but I believe entrusting children with a place of their own is vital to developing a sense of autonomy and equality. Without this, it's easy to see how one could feel like a mere tenant, one down on the social rung. Bedrooms represent "my place," separate from "our space" for our children. Keep that in mind as you read on.

WON'T MAKE BED IN THE MORNING

The job of parenting is all about helping our children gain self-reliance and skills for social integration. It's finding that balance between autonomy and interdependence. If we aspire to have our children ever live in a dorm, or have a roommate or life partner, they'll need to know how to care for a bedroom. If they were baby ducks, we'd teach them about nest building. But they are humans, so this is how our species does it.

Solutions

Step One: Take Time for Training (TTFT)
Work beside your child to develop the necessary skills for making a bed.

Show her how to make the sheet edges line up, how to grab a corner and fold it down. Start by making the bed with her and then gradually do less and less until she is doing the entire job herself. It will look rough until she gets the fine motor skills, but that's okay. Comment on her effort and improvement, *not* the way the bed looks. Once she can make the bed herself, the responsibility becomes hers. It's no longer your job! If you want your child to fully accept that responsibility, you need to stop making the bed for her. (And certainly never go in after she is done and redo or tidy up the wrinkly job!)

* *
"Never do for a child what a child can do for themselves."
—Dr. Rudolf Dreikurs
* *

Step Two: Establish and Enforce Routine
Create and repeat a basic morning room routine. Example:

> We wake up
> We make our beds
> We put on our clothes
> We put our PJs away

When they are young, children are still enthused and joyous to be learning independence and mastery. Follow your routine every day until it becomes automatic behavior. They should say, "I just get up and make my bed, I never even think about it really, I just do it—always have."

At some point, either the novelty will start to wear off or they will become resistant. If you have been faithful in handing over the responsibility, and your child has come to understand the routine, then you can use the tool of the when/then statement: "When your bed is made, then I'll know you're ready for breakfast."

If the child refuses, follow through. She'll experience a missed breakfast. That's okay. Wait until the next request or transition in the schedule and repeat without fighting. For example: "Yes, when your job is done, then we can [go to the park, invite a friend over]."

If you remain friendly and calm, and repeat this like a broken record, the child will come to understand that *no matter what*, the job of bed-making is hers; no one does it for her. She will eventually realize that doing her job at the scheduled time is actually easiest.

Why couldn't she just do that in the first place? Because as a child ages, fitting into an imposed schedule feels too much like control. Listen up. This is your child's inner monologue: "Who are *you* to tell *me* when to do my chores? And *why*? Why make the bed? I am just getting back into it tonight. I don't care or value the look of a tidy bed at this time in my life. *You* do. I have other priorities. When do I get to decide for me?"

Once you encounter this resistance, know that this is the child's inner voice—the thoughts that she will not share out loud but will express with resistant behavior. And frankly, I think the child has a point. You've done your parenting job—you've taught the skills and handed over the responsibility. Now you have to let go of that final tether. The responsibility for the orderliness of the child's room is hers and hers alone.

But What If . . .

What if the bed continues to be unmade?

The child knows about societal orderliness, and she has the necessary skills; however, it is her personal space in the house so she has the right to keep her room in any shape she wants as long as it doesn't impact others. Simply close the door.

Meanwhile, here are other tactics to inspire, rather than coerce, a tidy room.

State what you're willing to do. Let the child know she can keep her room in whatever state she wishes, but you are only interested in being in tidy rooms that are in "company order." That means if she wants to invite you in as a guest for tuck-ins and story time, the room should be inviting. You can refuse to do tuck-ins in her room and instead have story time on the couch, kissing her good night at her bedroom door.

Promote a sense of ownership. Help the child develop a sense of pride and ownership about her room by giving her a budget and allowing her to redecorate it to suit her tastes. Older children who rebel against anything that seems orderly as a commentary about overthrowing "the man" may enjoy a cleaner room if it is painted all black and has bean bag chairs and posters up everywhere.

Catch 'em being good. The entire room could look like a bomb went off, but if the child managed to hang up one shirt on a hanger, *notice that!* (With sincerity please—sarcasm is not a parenting technique.)

Discuss room cleaning at a family meeting. Many solutions that lead to family harmony spring from problem solving together.

It Worked for Us

The Carsons were bickering about clean rooms. Sasha and Petra (8 and 10) didn't think their room needed to be cleaned every day. It took too much time. Everyone agreed to try a new solution: cleaning the room together on Sunday before dinner so that it was clean for the school week ahead. Mom agreed to come for the first five minutes of cleaning to help get them started. They planned to play music and then look forward to reading time Sunday night, since they were all reading Harry Potter together. A really good *weekly* clean instead of a sloppy tidy every day seemed to be win-win for the parents and the girls.

WON'T PUT CLOTHES IN THE LAUNDRY HAMPER

Tired of stepping over clothes strewn all over the bedroom floor? How many times a day do they need to change their clothes anyway? Some haven't even been worn, just tried on and tossed. Grrrr! Here is my thinking process and application of parenting tools for laundry.

Understanding the Problem

Picking up clothes, refolding them or throwing them in the hamper is a time-suck of a task that frankly, if left undone, usually amounts to . . . well, mom doing it for you when she gets fed up enough.

Let's see if we can make some improvements in children handling this job with some of these solutions.

Solutions

First, ask yourself: Whose job is it to put the clothes in the hamper? If it's

a.   Your job as the parent, then maybe it's time to train your child and hand the responsibility over to him.

b.   The child's job, then you may want to use one of these tactics:

- Use a when/then statement to enforce the need to respect the order you are establishing. ("When your clothes are picked up, then we'll be ready to go play.")
- Say nothing about the clothes when they are *not* put in the hamper, but recognize and appreciate when the clothes *are* put in the hamper.
- Use one word, for instance, "clothes" or "hamper." (A single word prompt can often be enough to mobilize action, and it's sure better than nagging.)
- Ask a question. For example: "Where do clothes go? You know it. High five!" (Kids love getting the right answer to any question. Try it.)
- Try humor. For example: "I am afraid Mr. Pajama is going to be lonely lying on the floor alone. Don't you think he'd like it better if he was with his friends in the hamper?"

Whichever tactic you try, I would not—repeat not—pick up those clothes and put them in the hamper. If it's not your job, doing so will only confuse the child about whose responsibility it is.

• •

Responsibility Tip

Parents often say, "That's my children's responsibility," while children will say, "Actually, my mom always does that for me." They *don't* really believe something is truly their responsibility until you *stop* making it yours.

• •

BUT WHAT IF . . .

It may be the kids' job to put the clothes in the hamper, but it's my job to do the laundry. What am I supposed to do on laundry day? You said never do for a child what a child can do for themselves, so I am stuck now.

Apply natural consequences. Let your child know that on Wednesday you'll wash any clothes that are in the hamper (but not clothes left on the floor). After a few weeks in which his favorite clothes miss washday, he may be more motivated to get dirty clothes into the hamper on Wednesdays. Simply:

Don't put clothes in hamper = they stay dirty

Put clothes in hamper = they get washed

The idea that parents need to grasp is that consequences are not some trap to make kids do things our way "or else." Instead, consequences teach. Children are given freedom of choice but also to take responsibility for the choices they make. Not picking up clothes is a choice, and with it comes not having clean clothes. That is all. Different outcomes for different choices. No hidden punishment. No need for lectures.

Take Time for Training (TTFT). If the child is old enough (nine years old or so) teach him how to do his own laundry. Show him how to use the washing machine and let him manage both his bedroom and laundry systems in his own way. Not to worry, social pressure at school will eventually motivate him to improve his skills and attentiveness. Patience.

WON'T LET SIBLING INTO BEDROOM

"No girls allowed."

"It's *my* room—now get out!"

"Mom, he's in my room again!"

"Oh, boys and girls, can't we all just stop fighting and get along?" Sure, when pigs fly, right?

Once we've established that bedrooms are a child's private space, parents are quick to jump in and enforce privacy rules. After all, didn't I open this chapter by asserting that everyone is entitled to a space of one's own? Yes, but I didn't say the room came with a security kiosk outside the door or that you had to stand guard to ensure there was no trespassing.

UNDERSTANDING THE PROBLEM

Sibling conflict is one of the toughest parts of parenting. Violating bedroom privacy is just one more example of how sibling dynamics can play out. I coach parents to extricate themselves from such sibling disagreements. However, the better parents get at not getting involved in conflicts, the more creative the siblings have to become in finding a good hook to pull you in. "Unfairness" usually ropes in a parent but good. What is more unfair than disrespecting someone's privacy? Hark! I can almost hear your collective indignation.

Even when the altercation seems "unfair," our children need to understand that their parents are not responsible for the actions of their siblings and it's not a parent's job to make sibs get along. It's their relationship to manage. They have to solve their problems together. They have to learn the fine art of cooperation. Barring the installation of locks and invisible fencing, the only way for a child to keep a sibling out of her room is to win that sibling over. She's gotta make her sib want (voluntarily) to uphold her request for privacy. She'll quickly see that if there is any bad will in the relationship, her brother or sister is not likely to uphold these little social contracts.

· ·

If you undermine the "hand-shake" agreements between siblings by using your parental power to force compliance, siblings become motivated to break the rules and get each other into trouble.

· ·

If a child comes to you tattling on her trespassing sibling and you step in and try to use your position of power to remove the sibling (verbally or physically), you are:

- Robbing the child of an opportunity to own the problem and learn the necessary problem-solving skills.
- Inadvertently taking sides by acting as the security guard to one child's bedroom.

Solutions

When the child comes seeking your help, try one of these strategies.

Be empathetic. For example: "I am sorry you're having trouble with your sister" or "I am sorry things are not going well between you and your sister."

Help the child identify proper problem-ownership. For example: "Staying out of each other's room is a problem between the two of you. It doesn't involve me."

The child will rebut, of course: "You're the parent. You're supposed to stop her!" Again, correct the misperception: "Yes, I am the parent, but it's not my job to control your sister's behavior toward you. You'll have to find some way to make her want to cooperate with you."

Encourage. For example: "I am sure you two can work it out. You are very good at getting along when you choose to."

Emphasize self-efficacy. Emphasize "you have the power" instead of blame. Children often erroneously learn to play helpless in order to elicit help from others. They can be quick to assign blame to others instead of understanding their role in the conflict. We can help them understand that *every* person can influence a situation by deciding what they can do themselves.

My Pappy used to always say: "What are you willing to do?" That was his pat answer whenever I came complaining of an injustice. Given that you can't control other people, given that you can't make anyone do anything, you can control only yourself—your choices, your reactions, your attitudes. It's a powerful life lesson. Start young!

If the children really can't seem to find a solution, you can offer to talk about it at a family meeting. (See p. 71 for more on family meetings.) Problem solving at the time of conflict is rarely effective since most fighting serves the goal of engaging you and getting parental attention.

WON'T LET YOU IN BEDROOM

If your child won't let you in his room, fine. Great! Go have a coffee—you've just been taken off the clock.

UNDERSTANDING THE PROBLEM

For most kids, it's nice to be able to have a parent-free zone, their own little clubhouse to retreat to. And frankly, it feels empowering to be able to say "Keep out" to your parents. How many limits have you imposed on them? Now they have an opportunity to set and enforce a personal boundary in the world—good for them! Especially if the adult doesn't break down the door but instead respects the child's right to privacy.

Don't erode the trust you've built by sneaking around them. I have heard too many stories of parents who "found" things when they were "just putting away socks." Sounds mighty suspect. Don't fabricate a rationale for poking around. Finding "evidence" by searching without warrant is not respectful. It's a violation of your child's privacy and the child will indeed feel violated.

If you have reasons to suspect your child might be using drugs, say, don't try to find the stash or catch him using. Instead, talk to your child about the reasons you're suspicious in the first place. Discuss changes in his behavior that have prompted you to think that maybe something is going on. Example: "I am worried about the change I've seen in your sleep habits (eating, weight, activities, choices of friends, school attendance, attitude) . . ."

Don't let your fears cause you to breach trust and mutual respect. If your child is doing drugs, violation of his trust will only make matters worse.

BUT WHAT IF . . .

I have to go in his room to clean. I need to collect laundry and vacuum.

If your kid doesn't want you in there, respect that. If he would like his laundry done, he can put it in the hall for you on laundry day. No laundry in the hall, no laundry for you to do. Carry on.

If he wants his room to be the recipient of vacuuming services, he can demonstrate that by having his room in "vacuum order"—clothes and clutter picked up off the floor so the carpet is accessible. If he doesn't want cleaning services, he can leave a note on his door indicating that he passes on cleaning that week.

DESTROYS BEDROOM DURING TIME-OUTS

You thought you were taking swift and decisive action when you put your child in her room for a time-out, but 15 minutes later when you come back to check on her you discover she has not used the cool-down time to "think about it" but has instead trashed the room.

UNDERSTANDING THE PROBLEM

This is a further escalation of the fight. The child is put in what really amounts to forced confinement, and he revolts and retaliates to further escalate the fight by destroying property. "Oh ya? Take THAT!" is what he's saying with his behavior.

But now what to do?

Solutions

First, I'll give you the really quick answer and tell you to simply make a remark tying freedoms and responsibilities: "Looks like you have a job to do." (You're free to throw stuff around, but you are also responsible for cleaning it up afterward.)

I can also tell you to hold your child accountable to doing the cleanup by using a when/then statement: "When your room is cleaned up, then I'll know you're ready for snack." (Or whatever the schedule dictates happens next.)

Lastly, I can share that if this is the outcome of removing them to their room for time-outs, then you need to retire the tool of "time-outs." Instead, try moving YOU away from them. For example, if they are throwing things or being rude, calmly offer choice:

"Can you calm yourself? Or do I need to go?" If they continue, walk away. Go to your office or bedroom or bathroom and close the door. Let them know you'll come back out when they are calm again. Removing yourself is less likely to escalate the fight. So try that, and things should improve. A "positive time-out" for children in distress should focus on helping them regain a sense of calm, emotional composure, not further agitate them by entrapment. They should have a comfy chair, maybe calming music, a blanket and book or comic—all geared to helping them return to a relaxed state.

Even with these improved responses, parents are still missing the deeper issue at hand. You have a child that is so, so hopping mad she wants to ruin property, destroy things, lash out against you. *That* is the problem. Damaged books are no biggy compared to damaged feelings.

What if, just if (work with me now), the child was actually justified in her rage? Forget her young age, forget excuses about impulse control or inability to emotionally regulate and all the other things we do to dismiss a child's anger. Think back to a time you were furious, you were outraged. Anger is a secondary emotion. It erupts from feeling violated, feeling your rights were removed, feeling unjustly treated.

When has that happened to you? Have you ever been wrongly accused? Blamed for something that wasn't your fault? Felt trapped by a situation? In those moments, what would have helped you?

Practice active listening. When we are so upset that we desire revenge, the best response is for the other party to listen. In fact, not simply listen but really *hear*, to feel our feelings with us. Being empathetic to the hurt person, seeing that person's perspective even when you don't agree with it, works miracles.

Active listening makes our loved one feel worthy. We have to learn to be good active listeners. Here's how:

1. *Find a comfortable position at eye level with your child.* You don't necessarily have to look into your child's eyes—in fact, that may be too intense for some children. Walking and talking or lying on a bed looking up at the ceiling may be less threatening. However, avoid towering over your child.

2. *Get rid of external distractions.* Turn off the radio or the TV. Don't look at your BlackBerry when it pings. You need to be fully present.

3. *Respond with interest.* Nod; say, "hmm, okay" to show you are following; prompt for more: "Then what happened? What did that feel like? Can you tell me more about that?"

4. *Focus only on what the speaker is saying.* Usually we stop listening and begin preparing our defense. Don't let your mind wander in this direction. Fight off these thoughts and stay focused on the speaker. It's like learning to meditate. It will take time and practice.

5. *Keep an open mind.* Don't decide if you agree or disagree until after the speaker has finished. I told you this was a tough skill to master!

6. *Avoid advising.* The speaker wants to be heard and understood, not instructed on how to do something better or told how you would have handled the situation. Avoid giving advice, and simply give the child the space to share with you without fear of being judged or criticized.

7. *Paraphrase.* Be sure to echo back what you understood the child to be saying. The important part is his emotional state, not the facts: "So you felt embarrassed when I grabbed your hand in front of your friends?" "You seem to be saying that you feel judged when I make comments on your homework, is that right?"

When we use the power of active listening, we discover a lot about how our child experiences life in the family. If we allow ourselves to be learners instead of litigators—who have a high need to defend or be right—we'll be in a better position to find solutions. Learning to be a good listener also teaches our children how to listen to others—including us.

WRITES ON WALLS

There are at least a couple reasons to write on the wall. People seemed to like it when Michelangelo did the ceiling of the Sistine Chapel. Not so much when Talia took a ballpoint pen to the walls in her bedroom.

UNDERSTANDING THE PROBLEM

Maybe Michelangelo's goal was beautifying, but probably not so for Talia. She's defacing property in order to reach some mistaken goal. Is it attention? Power? Revenge? Avoidance? Let's see if you can tell as we tackle suggested solutions together.

SOLUTIONS

If your two year old "beautified" the wall, you need to let her know, "That's not okay. Markers and crayons are for paper." Then, show your tot how to clean the wall with a spray bottle and paper towel. If the markings don't come off, let the child clean the wall as best she can so she sees what permanent ink is all about firsthand.

This is *all* you need to do and say. I know you might want to embellish and amplify the lesson by adding your own lecture. I can just hear you: "See, it doesn't come off does it? Look what you have done. You have ruined the wall. That makes me sad. You had a beautiful room and now it's ugly." Eck. None of that is helpful. Actually, those words just make matters worse by turning the cleaning event into a punishment. Our goal is to teach, not punish. It's hard to learn when you are upset. Now the child is not attending to learning cause and effect because she is too busy being defensive, blaming you for her hurt feelings and making a victim of herself.

Now, apply logical consequences (see p. 6). The bedroom is no longer a place for markers and crayons. Keep those in the craft area. The child can try markers in the bedroom later, next week maybe, or next month.

However, if our Talia is old enough to know not to write on walls, and then she does anyway, that is intentional defacing of property. She is seeking revenge. Her actions say, "You hurt me and I'll hurt you back by ruining your house." I am not as concerned with the walls as I am Talia's feelings. Gosh, what has happened that she is so hurt that she needs to lash out? That is where we need to focus our parenting attention.

- -

Sample Script
"Talia, you've marked the walls of your room. You must be very angry with me. What have I done to make you want to lash out like that?"

- -

When asked, some will spill the beans and let you know in no uncertain terms what they are thinking and feeling. Others, however, will give you stony silence. Here are ideas to get your kids to open up:

- Continue to practice your active listening skills (see the section "Destroys Bedroom during Time-Outs" on p. 186). The child will be more inclined to open up and share if she is met with listening instead of defensiveness.

- Instead of giving up and walking away, see if you can stay and maybe see if she will let you rub her back till she feels better. Kids often start talking after a little bit. Your continued presence says you care, even if they never talk.

- See if the child will draw you a picture of how she is feeling and then have her tell you about the picture.

- My kids like to IM, text or email rather than talk face to face when the topic is really difficult for them. That is totally fine. Whatever it takes to get the communication flowing. It's also nice to have some time to compose your own replies.

- If communications are at a standstill, seek family counseling. Unhealed hurts will continue to fester.

- Adults have a mistaken idea that youth rebel against and hate limits. If you have a mutually respectful relationship and you work together to establish reasonable limits and boundaries, enforcing them respectfully should not cause hurt or retaliation.

But What If. . .

Who is going to fix the wall that was defaced?

After you have squared things away with your Talia and healed whatever hurt her in the first place, she is still accountable for her actions.

Here's my advice: *Ask instead of tell.* It might sound something like this: "I'm glad things between us are better, and that we have found a new way of handling this problem in the future. Now that we're good, what do you think should happen with that wall?" See what she says—you'll be surprised how responsible and accountable kids are willing to be.

SIBLINGS SHARE A ROOM, BUT THEY'RE THE ODD COUPLE

Do you have Felix and Oscar sharing a room in your house? You can see how they will be extra challenged in sharing a space. But if the Americans and the Russians could get along on space station Mir, your kids can handle a shared space on Earth. They have to figure out the reality of two different people working toward some common ground. Or maybe their lesson is to not let things bother them. What great life lessons our children learn in preparation for getting along in the workplace, in marriages, in future families.

Solutions

Don't pity them. If you feel sorry for one child because he has a sibling who is a pill, you're taking sides and sending discouraging messages about the other child. More conflict will ensue, not less.

Offer empathy and encouragement. Let them know you understand how tough it can be, but also tell them that you trust them to manage the situation successfully.

Help them create some private space within their room. Bunk beds or book shelves placed in the middle of the room to create alcoves of space, or folding screens will work wonders.

Don't interfere in their fights. They have to learn to win the cooperation of the other on their own. If they fight and you step in to "help," you will be inadvertently taking sides. This phenomenon is expanded on in *Breaking the Good Mom Myth.* Your children will continue to keep the conflict alive if they think they can get parental involvement in the fight. They enjoy the undue attention and getting each other in trouble. However, left mano a mano, they'll quickly learn it's more enjoyable to get along than fight, so they'll strive to work things out between them.

Take it to a family meeting. It's hard to solve problems in the heat of the moment. So, suggest they put the issue on the family meeting agenda (see p. 71). In this way, our children feel they are being supported and that we are not abandoning them unfairly.

CHAPTER 11

THE PLUGGED-IN KID—THE DEMOCRATIC APPROACH TO MANAGING THE WIRED WORLD

Inappropriate TV viewing · Addicted to
Gaming · Acts Aggressively after Watching Violence
· Controlling Screen Time · Wants a Cell Phone

Kids today are born totally immersed and comfortable operating in a digital world. They enjoy having the upper hand over their parents in this domain. In fact, they are ROTFLMAO when they text POS.

Digitally speaking, parents are more likely to be "late adopters" and are apt to be afraid of the "big unknown." They often catastrophize, given the media alerts they read. And there are things to be concerned about for sure. Children have the potential to be exposed to more dangerous images and messages now more than ever before.

Parents often resort to draconian measures—total lockdown—to secure their own feelings of control over their children's lives and activities. I think Prohibition taught us that zero-tolerance methods and building higher walls just invites people to crawl higher, dig under or go around.

I come from the position that the best approach is to be wide-eyed and alert. I recommend education and ongoing dialogues with our children. More than ever they have to trust our advice, respect our limits and be willing to come to us when things are amiss. Too often children say they didn't tell their parents when they saw a bad image, or were being texted by a stranger or bullied online, because they were afraid of getting in trouble. If we parent with punishment, we are putting our children at risk.

So, step over Elmer the safety elephant—*we* have to help teach our children a new kind of safety; we have to be informed parents who know how to establish limits and boundaries that our children willingly adhere to.

"Prepare Instead of Shelter" is the motto. You can't change the world, but you can equip your child to navigate safely through it. Let's tackle that now.

INAPPROPRIATE TV VIEWING

You walk into the family room to announce bedtime only to find your nine year old's eyes glued to the TV set, watching the mob slaughter scene from *The Godfather* on the movie network. "Hey! I thought you were watching the basketball game!" Let's face it, violence, sex, coarse language and adult subject matter is a click away. What's a parent to do?

Understanding the Problem

Curiosity and peer pressure is going to have our children checking out content that will make our adult heads spin. Boys, in particular, faced with the pressure of meeting the so-called male code will feel they must watch violence and sexual absurdity as initiation into manhood. Boys inoculate themselves against fear by watching gore and violence. This is a way to earn one's bravery badge and impress peers.

Girls will feel left out of the conversation at school if they don't know what happened last night on *Jersey Shore*. Peer acceptance is riding on this. But does a 14 year old really need to get her dating and sex education from these characters? Scary thought. But before you go wagging the finger, why exactly are you watching *The Bachelor*? Pot, kettle. Just saying.

Banning TV, or getting angry and yelling about your children's disobedience to the TV rules, will do little except persuade them to hide their viewing from you. It's a missed parenting opportunity, and that opportunity is crucial parenting because without an adult to help kids make sense of what they see, they may be traumatized by the images, develop fears or come to think the real world operates the way it does in movies and reality shows. We have an active role to play here, and just putting our foot down is not enough.

Solutions

Be firm and friendly. For younger children, you can simply say, "that show is not okay" and change the channel. They know they were watching something outside the acceptable parameters and you've enforced the limits.

Tie freedoms to responsibilities. For younger children, remind them if they want the freedom to watch TV, they must accept the responsibility of watching shows you've pre-approved. If they deviate from those shows, they will lose the freedom of watching TV unsupervised.

For older children, it may be time to revisit the selection of shows they can watch and expand their repertoire. Here is how to parent through the *Godfather* debacle:

Don't get angry. Let your child know you saw he was watching something for older audiences that he is not allowed to watch and realize he must be curious and interested in it. This gentle statement sets the tone for not fighting about the infraction but instead invites conversation and understanding.

Use an I-message. Instead of sending "you" messages, as in, "You shouldn't watch that. You'll have nightmares," "You're not old enough," try sending an I-message. Remember, they are constructed like this:

> "I am feeling _____ (your emotion) when you _____(the child's behavior) because _____ (the reason or explanation). I'd rather _____ (the alternate behavior you'd like to see)."

So here goes: "I'm afraid that when you watch violent shows on TV you might get scared and have nightmares or feel anxious. I am also worried you might get the wrong ideas from shows like that. TV and movies are made to look real, but truthfully they don't really show how the world works. I'd rather you come talk to me so we can decide together if a show is appropriate or watch it together."

The conversation is likely to unfold from there. "Did you know that what you just saw is just one gruesome scene. It's from an award-winning movie about a Mafia family. Do you know what the Mafia is?" Your child may say, "Ya, there's this kid Dominic in our school and his family is in the Mafia." Bingo! Teaching moment. The movie opened the conversation to correcting your child's understanding of the Mafia. "Being Italian does not mean you are in the Mafia. When people say that, it's a way of insulting the boy and his Italian heritage. The Mafia is . . ."

Enforce the TV limits but explain that it's your issue. For example: "I guess you feel you are ready to watch shows like that, but *I'm not* ready for that yet." This can feel less controlling to the child and win her cooperation since you are not saying she can't manage, you're saying *you* can't—it's your shortcoming.

Offer to revisit the limit. For example: "If you'd like to watch some-thing like that, can I watch with you so we can talk about it together? Maybe this one is too extreme, but we could try another less violent show and see how it goes." This offer to accommodate and participate shows your willingness to be reasonable and cooperate. You may need to increase the child's range of TV viewing, but request that it comes with the added responsibility of doing it with adult guidance and supervision. At least now it's not becoming the forbidden fruit.

❧

When we let TV teach values, we miss the opportunity to teach our own. Let the TV show be the springboard for conversations on violence, male stereotyping, sexualization of females, product placement, gender roles, how power impresses, the misuse of power and a million other topics that make up "media literacy." Still confused about what you might say? Google media literacy and find resources for parents.

• •

General TV-Viewing Guidelines

Establish your family culture, expectations and guidelines around TV viewing while your child is still young. Here are my recommendations:

1. When no one is watching, turn the TV off.

2. Model good TV viewing habits yourself. How many adults have a nightly routine of crashing after dinner in front of the TV and spending the balance of the night until bedtime passively consuming TV? What else do your kids see you do with your evening? Anything?

3. Suggest non-TV activities to do with your children, like reading together, or some great family games like charades, Pictionary or The Settlers of Catan. Given an alternate choice, children would rather play with you than watch TV.

4. No TVs in bedrooms (including the master). Bedrooms are for sleeping (and, you know . . .). Instead, watch TV together in the family room. If you peered into the average family's house on any given night, you'd see everybody is home, but each is watching a different TV program in different rooms of the house. That is isolating and disconnecting.

5. TV viewing should be a planned activity. Check listings for appropriate quality viewing, and turn off the TV when your show is done instead of surfing mindlessly.

6. If your youngster is going to watch TV unsupervised, have him watch a show you are familiar with, or at least stay and watch the beginning of anything you don't know and check in periodically.

7. Learn the rating systems. Each TV show has to put up its rating at the beginning of the show. You can point to the rating and say, "This show is rated for 14+. I am sorry, choose something else." (The rating sets the limit, not mom.)

8. For young children you may want to use blocking software so they can access only certain channels and prevent an accidental slip of the converter from *The Backyardigans* to *Band of Brothers.*

• •

ADDICTED TO GAMING

It's 2 a.m. and you see light coming from under your son's bedroom door. You go check and find he is still up playing EverQuest. Has he been playing all night? Is he an addict?

Understanding the Problem

People do get addicted to gaming. It's as serious a problem as any other addiction. While it may not have the harmful bodily effects of, say, being addicted to a substance, addictive behaviors like gaming and gambling still ruin lives.

All addictions work on the same principles, and their warning signs and symptoms share the same quality.

Addictions are a method of escaping or finding a false "buzz," "joy," "pleasure," "up" or "hit" in a life that is otherwise devoid of those things. This is especially true for interactive fantasy games where players interact with others online, assuming a persona in the game that may gain them status that they can't find in reality.

The addict needs more more more to get the same effect over time (one hour of playing builds up to playing almost 24–7). The addiction is interfering with functioning (up all night, skipping school to play, losing friends and relationships over the time spent on gaming). The addict gets irritated and upset if he can't practice his addiction. The addict dwells on thoughts of his addiction even when not engaged in it.

SOLUTIONS

Discuss your concerns. Share with your child what you're noticing:

> "You've only been to school two days this week."

> "You haven't been out with your friend Josh in over a month."

> "You've only been sleeping a few hours a night."

> "You got fired from your part-time job for not showing up."

Cap the playing time. Together, see if you can come up with a set amount of time for the game and see if the child can downgrade his playing without getting upset about it. If he can't, share that this also gives you reason to be concerned that the gaming may have gone from passion to addiction.

Encourage the child to research. The addict is often in denial about the problem, especially with gaming because it seems innocent, like play—how is it harming anyone? But their playing is costing them. Ask the child to do some of his own research so he sees that it's not just your opinion but, rather, a psychological problem that does actually exist for many people. Your concerns come from a place of love and caring, not anger and lack of understanding.

Seek treatment. Treatment may ultimately involve enrolment in a professional program. Hopefully if you take the steps above to address the addiction, the child is more likely to hear your concerns. If you are aggressive or oppositional in your approach, he is more likely to dismiss your concerns and refuse your influence.

Remember that addiction ultimately is a way to avoid confronting the challenges of life. If your child has trouble with self-esteem and struggles socially, try to address the problem head-on. Help your child find excitement and social connection offline through constructive relationships.

ACTS AGGRESSIVELY AFTER WATCHING VIOLENCE

Okay, Spiderman, what's the deal? Why is it every time your kid watches a movie with super heroes in battle you are subjected to karate kicks, grunting noises, surly faces and a dukes-up kid the rest of the day? What happened to playing quietly with dinosaurs and reading books?

Understanding the Problem

We know TV viewing does increase acts of aggression in some age groups more than others. All people are social creatures trying to belong and make sense of their world and their place in it. Gender rules are learned or reinforced from watching TV, and often it's the male characters that are inciting aggressive acts. The message that to be a boy is to be tough, strong and independent is alive and well in TV-land. Boys will emulate and imitate their TV role models.

Solutions

Don't excuse the behavior. Just because a show stirred up the child's inner karate kid doesn't mean you "understand" and lower the bar on expectations for his behavior.

Enforce the boundaries and state your values. For example: "This is a nonviolent house. If you want to play rough like that, take it outside please." Or alternately: "I don't feel safe when you play that way. I am going elsewhere."

Explain that freedoms and responsibilities go together. For example: "If you can't watch that TV show and be calm afterward, then I guess we'll have to stop watching that show. If you can show me you can watch that show *and* still play safely and respectfully afterward, then it's okay to watch. We'll try again another time."

Help to find constructive outlets. If you have a high-energy boy with testosterone surges and you're a quiet subdued parent, you may find his energy abrasive. Instead of trying to make the child something he is not (still and quiet), channel his great energy into positive activities. These kids will need to get outside to run and burn energy for hours every day.

DISREGARDS SCREEN-TIME LIMITS

"Harrison, get off the computer [DS/PlayStation/Wii/Xbox, insert your screen of choice]. Your time is up."

"Harrison, you said after this level and it's been 10 minutes. Get off right now."

"Harrison, I've had it. I'm pulling the plug."

You know what happens next, right? Harrison screams and pushes over his chair, and may go so far as to spit, swear or strike his mother. This upset can go on for some time. Remind me why we buy these damn electronics?

UNDERSTANDING THE PROBLEM

When a child explodes the first time you enforce a boundary, you recognize that he is upset with the limit. But if the tantrums, explosive behaviors and anger occur each and every time you enforce the same screen-time limit, something is up. Why is the child so angry?

Anger is the emotion that we generate to protect ourselves when we feel a perceived threat. Your child's anger signals an underlying deeper feeling—basically, he feels he's been wronged. Anger is an appropriate response to being wronged. Standing up for yourself is actually self-respecting behavior. I want my children to speak up when they've been wronged, but, gulp, I don't want it to be me who "wronged" them, and I don't want them to use attack tactics as their response, either. Let's look at what we've done unknowingly since children can't seem to put words to it.

1. *Arbitrary limits.* Harrison sees no rhyme or reason for getting kicked off the computer right then. Apparently, mom just feels like it's been long enough. In essence she is saying: "Get off because I say so. I get to decide this for you." He resents this power mom has over him. It's the powerlessness that makes him angry.

2. *Imposed limits.* Perhaps mom did have a "one hour of screen time only" rule that Harrison knew about and that she was enforcing. But who decided the limit? Probably mom alone, and Harrison feels it's an unfair limit, so every time mom enforces her imposed limit, he feels wronged by her constraints.

3. *Consistency.* Harrison may know that the limit is supposed to be one hour, but when they go for dinner or Harrison is stuck waiting while mom is picking tiles for the backsplash, she is the first to suggest he play his DS to pass the time. In reality it still comes down to mom saying yea or nay. When she does claim "an hour is up, you know the rules," it still feels arbitrary. Why does she have to be strict today? Harrison takes this to be mom being mean to him, rather than seeing the extra time as being nice.

Let's face it. Parents still lord power over their kids by manipulating their screen time. There always seems to be strings attached that parents can pull. If the children misbehave, parents take away their games as a form of punishment. We say if they can play and for how long. Children feel this ever-present control over them. It will lead to explosive backlashes.

Let's see if we can improve things.

SOLUTIONS

Before I give you pragmatic advice, let me toss a big thought out for you to chew on.

Some kids love *love* their electronics, right? That freaks parents out. If our kid was hanging his head over a chessboard for hours on end, we'd think we had a Bobby Fischer on our hands, brag to friends and send him to chess camp. If it was soccer, we'd be thrilled to see him outside kicking a ball around for hours, and would go to all his games. But God forbid you have a geek kid! Parents often view the passion for electronics as somehow being a mindless waste. It's really rather biased, don't you think? Just because it's not your cuppa tea, there is still a lot of learning, skill building and problem solving happening. And regardless, it's the child's joy.

I think setting limits on screen time has to be revisited again by the experts. We are a wired world. In the old days your day may have started something like this: read the newspaper, check the TV for the weather report, listen to the traffic report on the radio, balance your checkbook at the kitchen table, pay your bills at the bank, write your friend a letter, call your coworker on the phone. Now, I do all that online through websites, Skype, emails, IMing, online banking and so on. Is that too much screen time when the activities are so diverse?

My children use their computers to play games and chat with friends, but they also check the weather; do their homework assignments, research for projects, word processing and PowerPoint for presentations; learn chords and songs for their guitar and piano; edit videos they've recorded, IM with their grandma and cousins, build a website for their upcoming trip to Kenya, check their bank balances and more.

If I were to limit my kids' screen time, what would they cut out? How would I monitor how long they spent on each task? They're multitasking masters. That seems too onerous, and I don't see the point of it, frankly.

I think screen-time limits are a parent solution to a problem. What exactly is the problem? Is it ensuring the kids get their homework completed? Is it a way to ensure face time with the family? Is it a way of trying to get them to be physical instead of sitting passively? And, just for the record, when you tell kids to stop screen time, they usually don't go out and play physically; instead, they just move to another passive activity. Sorry.

It helps if we think in terms of the actual root problems rather than jumping right to the solution of limiting screen time.

There. Thanks for indulging me. Had to share that. So regardless, we need solutions.

Problem solve at a family meeting. Use your weekly family meeting time to discuss these problems and seek solutions together (see p. 71 for more on family meetings). Remember, any solution you come up with together, by consensus, is likely to work better than any parent-imposed solution. Because you meet weekly, your children only have to adhere to the agreement for one week. You'll find they are more cooperative when it's only a week, because if they don't like the standing agreement, they know they can revisit the arrangement at the next meeting. Assure them, you'll keep tweaking it week after week until you find a solution that works for everyone. How affirming! What a great way to share power and allow your children to have a say in matters that affect them.

Create a "fail-safe." When you come to your agreement, ask your children what should happen if they don't uphold it. Now they are participating in creating the consequence (or what I call a fail-safe). By asking our children to create the consequence, two things happen:

1. They are less likely to break the agreement.
2. They aren't upset when you implement the fail-safe since they had a say in its creation.

Be consistent. Since your consistency in enforcing agreements can be an issue, discuss *that* problem with your children at the meeting too. It's okay to say, "I don't want to be the timekeeper in all this. How else can we do it so it's consistent, but I am not constantly watching over your shoulder or watching the clock?" See what your kids come up with. You may want to research software designed for this purpose. Some track usage, have alerts, visual time clocks to count down time remaining so your kids know when they're nearing the end of their sessions. Some freeze the keyboard instead of powering down so the child doesn't lose their work or score. Programmable power switches can be set to turn off power at a set time. I've never needed to use these, but maybe that will help your family. It's the *process* that matters. These are issues of control and power we're solving here.

Introduce an outside authority. Instead of you being "all knowing" about seemingly everything, share the research you've read with your children. Bring an article to the meeting. "I just read this article in the paper about children and screen time. It made some good points. I thought we should talk about some of them." They might not read the article, but they see that you are being informed by an expert and it's not just your personal perspective.

Learn more about their games, hobbies and interests. If you play Super Mario Kart with them, IM with them, have your own Facebook page, they're more likely to be influenced by your opinions. It's easy to dismiss parents as "not knowing what they're talking about." Besides, you may find playing Rock Band with your children is as interactive and fun a family night as a board game.

WANTS A CELL PHONE

Tired of hearing your 7th grader whine, beg and plead for you to buy her a cell phone? Does your child complain that *everyone* else has one, why are you the only parent on the face of the planet that thinks they're still too young for a cell phone?

UNDERSTANDING THE PROBLEM

I think the argument "You're too young" for a cell phone will probably backfire on parents because kids take that as a vote of nonconfidence, and will be offended. Instead, have your child present you with a persuasive argument. Say, "I am open-minded. Convince me!"

My two thoughts on this are:

1. Parents need to provide for the child things they "need," but "wants" are discretionary.
2. There isn't anything inherently wrong with cell phones, but the issues seem to come down to:
    *   Responsibility for care (not losing it or breaking it)
    *   Responsibility for cost (initial, monthly and extra charges)
    *   Responsibility for proper use/etiquette
    *   Responsibility for safety

SOLUTIONS

If you share your four concerns with your child, you can work with her to overcome them.

Responsibility for care. Emphasize your concern.

Sample Script
"I would be okay with you having a cell phone, but I am concerned it might get broken or lost. I understand mistakes happen, but it's a skill to be able to remember where you put your possessions and to treat them with care. Maybe when I see you're looking after your other possessions that cost less, like your camera, we can see about giving you things that are more expensive and work up to a cell phone."

Responsibility for cost. Share what your budget is. For some families, there simply is no money in the budget for cell phones, but if the child wants to pay for it herself, with her babysitting money, this obstacle has been resolved. You'll have to be clear about *all* the costs, including the ongoing fees. Some families pay for the base cost and the child pays for usage. You decide. There is no right or wrong. Just be clear about expectations up front.

Responsibility for proper use/etiquette. Having a phone also comes with the responsibility of knowing phone etiquette. That means education and setting expectations for phone use, such as:

- Not talking on the phone or texting during school.
- Not talking on the phone or texting during family time, for example, at the dinner table.
- Holding a short conversation only or putting the phone in silence mode when in the car or at a restaurant, where talking would be disruptive to others.
- Putting a lock on the keypad so others don't take the phone and send fake messages or make long-distance calls.
- Returning your calls. Kids often get cell phones so that their parents can reach them when they are out and about, but kids see their parents calling and ignore the ring, knowing it's home calling. Be clear that they need to respond to your calls, and also agree you won't call every five minutes.

Okay, I just gave you my list, but imagine how much more empowering and educational it would be to instead ask your child to do their own research and present to you their own suggested phone etiquette rules that they themselves have come up with as part of the "convince" package. They'll feel more committed to sticking to those rules than ones you research and impose on them.

Responsibility for safety. Your children need to be educated about basic safety too:

- Don't answer calls from numbers they don't recognize.
- Don't say where they are going, how much money they have, or anything else that someone overhearing could use to seek them out and cause them harm.

- Never believe a voice is that of—or a text is from—anyone it claims to be unless they know that person personally. Hang up.
- Your family should have a password that only your family knows. If your child gets a call from an adult who wants to pick her up or drive her somewhere, that adult *must* know the family password. Even if the adult says, "Your mom is in the hospital—she couldn't tell me the password. Quick, I have to take you to her!" Hang up. Don't ever go with someone who doesn't know the password.
- Avoid silliness. Your children need to be aware that just like online, people on cell phones are more apt to make lapses in judgment or act in ways that are outside their normal code of conduct. Being rude, bullying or poking fun is more likely over these devices and can really hurt people. Be sure your children don't fall into that trap. Be sure they understand that people can confuse communications more easily. If they wouldn't say it to their face, don't say it or text it on the phone.

Phones that surf the net need the same safety guidelines as the home computer.

Camera Phones

Phones that take photos make it easy for kids to snap and post inappropriate photos—like pictures from change rooms, pictures of kids drinking, smoking, necking. Once taken and posted, it's all out there on the net forever. Teach your child to be photo wise, both as the subject and the photographer.

You may even ask for a written agreement between parent and child, so things are very clear. If the child writes this up and presents it to you, she is more likely to internalize the issues. Include in the agreement the fail-safe for misuse as described in the section above on screen-time limits.

SCHOOL 101—THE DEMOCRATIC APPROACH TO ACADEMIC AND SOCIAL ISSUES AT SCHOOL

Has Poor Grades · Doesn't Pay Attention in Class ·
Homework Hell · Doesn't Care about School or the Subject
Matter · Hates the Teacher · Always Late for School ·
Switching Schools · They're Autocratic—We're Democratic

School is a child's first job. It's an important developmental step, one in which the child is growing her social sphere and responsibilities. The school community has rules separate from family rules, and the child's role in the classroom is separate from her role in the family. She has to be industrious, has to work alone, has to work cooperatively in groups (just like in the workforce). The teachers and principals are the new authority figures, eclipsing mom and dad.

We want (dare I say need?) our children's school years to be positive—and it's *not* just the factoids of the curriculum that are important. We want our children to develop confidence in their ability to learn and get along outside the home. We want them to become adept problem solvers (and I don't just mean in math class).

As parents, we should focus on helping our children understand that learning is their responsibility, allowing them to take ownership of the process. Only then can they feel pride in their achievements.

If we misplace the emphasis, children can become put off by learning—feeling it's our agenda being forced upon them and quickly lose interest. *We want to foster a sense of pride that comes from them, not us.*

The biggest hurdle, of course, is discouragement. Children will continue to try only when there is hope of succeeding. Once they lose sight of that possibility, all is lost. They abandon trying altogether.

In this chapter we'll look at some of the common school problems that face children and their families and offer solutions so you can avoid early discouragement.

HAS POOR GRADES

It's every parent's worst nightmare: the baaaaaad report card. How could it be? Please Almighty One, take my right arm and a kidney, but please don't let my child be a poor student.

We are a sad and desperate lot, aren't we?

UNDERSTANDING THE PROBLEM

Somehow, parents believe that if they handle schooling correctly, their child should get As in every subject, every year. That is worrisome.

Remember that an A means *above* grade expectation. Really, we should be aiming for Bs—*meeting* the learning expectations. (In recent years, our curriculum expectations have been pushed to the absolute extreme. Many educators will agree it's bloody unreasonable, but let's not get into politics here.)

A C grade, therefore, is not a fail. It is a yellow flag informing the student they are struggling in an area of learning, alerting them to a need for additional support.

We have to face the fact that education for the most part is still rather old school (pardon the pun) and uses a fairly cookie-cutter approach; but our children's learning styles and abilities vary greatly. What are we as parents to do?

Solutions

Early (and often small) interventions prevent our children from becoming discouraged and making the erroneous assumption they are "stupid." *That* is hard to undo. But struggling academically can have so many root causes, it's hard to know what tack to take. Here's what parents need to keep in mind first and foremost:

Don't fret. Take a deep breath. Don't let fear of your child's failure or fear of other's judgment cloud your thinking. And don't for a minute let your child think that you love her less or that her worth as a beautiful human being is related to a report card.

Dig to find the root cause. Focus on uncovering the issues that are holding the child back (more on that below).

Keep solution-oriented. Work collaboratively with your child and your child's teacher to find solutions, not point fingers and blame.

Become a master encourager. Home needs to be the safe, open arms you fall into after a tough day at school. Children are black-and-white thinkers and will perceive you are either *for* them or *against* them. They have to feel parents (and their teachers) have their back as they tackle their own learning goals.

> You can lead a child to school, but you can't make her learn. That is her responsibility. We play only a supporting role in the task of learning.

A Game Plan for Change

Keeping in mind that learning is always the child's responsibility, we can support their learning in the following ways:

Rule out potential danger. Book a medical checkup to ensure your child has good hearing and vision. Determine if there is a learning style or disability that should be addressed. Schools often have limited budgets and long waiting lists, so you may consider paying for a private assessment.

Ultimately, you have to advocate for your child, but that doesn't mean you need to go in with fists swinging. Work collaboratively. The more people you have on your team, the better.

Schedule student/teacher meetings. For children struggling academically, scheduling regular meetings with the teacher can be helpful. Too often we wait for report cards and correspond only by notes in an agenda. Face-to-face meetings are much better for communication, identifying problems and working toward solutions. Don't hijack the teacher at the door. Schedule a meeting to discuss concerns and be sure to include your child in every meeting. Otherwise, it's really talking behind her back, now isn't it? Address short-range goals and be specific. See the box below for powerful questions to coach your child toward setting her own goals.

· ·

Powerful Questions for Coaching Our Children toward Their Goals

"What mark do you want to get on this assignment?"

"What do you need to do to get that mark?"

"What is your plan?"

"What do you need from me?"

"What would you like me to do if I see you're not sticking to the plan you've made for yourself?"

· ·

Creating a Study Plan

Here is a sample study plan that could result from coaching:

- I'll read over chapter 8 on Monday and write up study notes.
- The teacher has agreed to review them with me Tuesday in class to see if I got all the most important points.

The teacher also said she could help me weigh which areas are more important than others since we discovered that one problem I have is that I sometimes study the wrong things.

- I'll study on my own Wednesday night after hockey practice.
- Mom agreed to quiz me on Thursday.
- The teacher suggested I might have better success if I read the entire test over before beginning and to answer the questions that I know first.

The teacher also said I can put up my hand and ask her for help if I don't understand a question on the test. I find that really embarrassing to do, but I think I will try to be brave enough to do it this time. I really want to get at least a 70 percent on this.

Wow—now that sounds like a plan! I'm cheering for this kid too.

Of course, the power of having regular meetings is that when the test results come in, the team can meet again so the student can reflect back on what worked and what didn't. This will help the child make another study plan for the next test. Focus on what is working and do more of that. Chip away at solving more study problems and keep at it. They're on their way. Things are improving! You can't get to a 75 percent without passing through 70 percent, so steady on. With hope restored and effort actually producing results, the student's motivation will be restored.

Seek extra help. If needed, hire a tutor or get peer support in the classroom. I don't recommend parents take on the dual role of being your child's parent *and* tutor. It backfires for the vast majority of families. Don't you have enough "dynamics" without going all Dr. Henry Higgins on your kid?

DOESN'T PAY ATTENTION IN CLASS

Your child studies so well at home but is too busy disturbing his neighbors and basically doing anything other than his desk work in class. How do you get your child to pay attention in class during lesson time?

UNDERSTANDING THE PROBLEM

Remember learning CPR? They teach you the order "A-B-C": first airway, and then breathing, finally cardiac. Similarly, Abraham Maslow outlined the human hierarchy of needs that dictates first we must meet our survival needs of hunger and thirst, then security and protection, followed by social belonging and status. Only once we feel integrated and accepted by our social groups can we attend to fluffier matters like self-actualization and learning the elements of the periodic table. If you're cold and starving do you really want to be wasting energy memorizing the atomic weight of oxygen?

Students won't be able to engage in learning if they have not yet found social security among their fellow students. Misbehaviors will abound until that task is well in hand. Instead of coaching around approaches to learning, the focus instead should be on resolving the student's feelings of social insecurity. He needs to feel he belongs and is accepted by his peers and teacher.

SOLUTIONS

Here are strategies you could recommend the teacher try:

Team building. Build more team-building exercises into the curriculum, especially at the start of the school year, each day and especially in advance of seat work or instruction time. Have extended circle times, morning meetings or class meetings depending on the grade. There are lots of resources for teachers at www.responsiveclassroom. org that you could point your child's teacher toward. Teachers often feel they don't have time for these "soft activities" but, the fact is, teachers can spend up to 60 percent of classroom instruction time dealing with behavioral issues. The teacher will easily gain this time back by having a classroom that has succeeded in achieving social cohesion.

Purpose. Find ways for your child to have a role in the classroom. (Give him jobs—feeding fish, handing out materials, taking attendance, managing equipment during gym, etc.)

Notice strengths. Each child has some strength that can be drawn forward. Teachers should be talent scouts looking for these strengths and finding ways each child can use his or her strengths to benefit others and the entire classroom. Talkative children could do the morning announcements, artistic students could be in charge of decorating the bulletin boards, techie kids could help update the classroom websites and so on.

Notice improvements. Your child may have bugged her desk partner halfway through the math lesson, but the teacher can comment on the first three minutes in which she was focused! This is core to encouragement.

Stop reporting negatives. Teachers often report back to parents via notes in the student's agenda saying, "Piper had a bad day today. . ." Or they simply draw a frownie face. No more. Stop these practices immediately and switch to "love notes" instead (see later in the chapter, p. 221) or make an appointment to talk face to face.

HOMEWORK HELL

It's 7 p.m. and you know what that means: homework hell. You're chained to the kitchen table, sitting on top of your kid, frustrated with her attitude, screeching at her to focus. Grrr!

UNDERSTANDING THE PROBLEM

Okay, just to fully disclose my bias. I hate homework. In a nutshell, it's ruining family life, and research proves most of the stuff is actually *hindering* learning. (Read Alfie Kohn's *The Homework Myth: Why Our Kids Get Too Much of a Bad Thing* or Daniel Pink's *Drive: The Surprising Truth About What Motivates Us* for more on that.)

However, for now, I am a mother of two kids in the public school system, so we still have to deal, right?

Here is some pragmatic help for the current dilemma: getting Hunter and Harriet to tackle their homework.

Solutions

I have already advised you to always look for the root cause. It all boils down to discouragement. But it comes in different flavors. Here are the three biggies to watch for.

Three Common Sources of Homework Discouragement

1. Volume, Volume, Volume

My daughter was rolling around the kitchen table, moaning, head down on her math worksheet, complaining, "I can't do it." Instead of placating her—"Oh, yes you can"—I asked a curiosity question instead: "What makes you believe you can't do this?" Her reply was: "It's too much. I only have three done, and this *whole* sheet is due tomorrow." I recognized that it was the size of the task, not the concepts, that was the source of her discouragement. I helped her break the assignment into more manageable chunks. I took the math sheet and cut (yes, with scissors) one strip of questions off the sheet. "Do you think you could do this row before dinner?" Yes, she could. After supper I cut off another row. You get the point. Seeing one row at a time made the task manageable for her.

Is there a way you could help chop the task down so it seems more doable and less overwhelming?

2. Doesn't Understand the Concept

Imagine being asked to do something you had no clue how to do? I seem to recall this feeling recently myself when I was reading instructions on how to install new taps in my kitchen. The instructions probably would have made sense to a plumber. I saw all the parts, all the terms, and inside my head I could hear my little inner gremlin saying, "You can't do this—you'll never do this, this is going to be a disaster, you're going to fail, you're going to embarrass yourself."

Imagine you're a child. Get inside her shoes. Try to imagine her thoughts and feelings. Imagine looking down at the page and the inner gremlin starts to speak up: "You don't know this. You don't understand this. You are stupid. You are going to fail."

Those inner thoughts and beliefs create anxiety. The child perceives herself to be in the "perceived minus" position. She wants to get to a "perceived plus." (See Chapter 9 for more on these concepts.) But if the child can't solve the problems, if she doesn't understand the concepts, then she will use mistaken approaches (misbehavior) to get to a position of perceived plus.

Maybe she tries procrastination (Lord knows I do!), or complains, doodles, does another task, looks out the window, starts to play. She evades the task altogether in order to avoid those anxiety feelings. It's a shortcut to feeling better in the moment: if you are not "trying," you are protecting your ego at least in the short term.

If you are asked to do something you are not competent at, you are facing your weaknesses and your inabilities, and your inferiority feelings are going to skyrocket. For the insecure child, the one not sure of her worth, this is high stress.

So it's *not* going to help the child to bark out, "If you'd just concentrate, you'd be done by now." We have to address those gremlins, those fears, those feelings of stupidity. We have to calm the psychic stress that says every minute you "try" you are revealing your inadequacies.

When we can show the child success, some success, *any* success, she begins to feel differently. This is why early interventions help so much. If we can help the child detach her own worth as a human from her ability to name the parts of the mitochondria, we'll be making headway.

When your child is stuck on a concept, it's okay for her to write on her homework sheet: "I don't understand this question." Now the teacher knows they need to revisit this concept with the student. If all parents did that, the teacher might find out that she went too quickly and lost half the students in her lesson; she'd circle back and review the concept. Instead, too many parents write in the answer or try to teach the concept. Not usually a good idea. The concepts typically build one on the other, and if the curriculum keeps demanding more, our children are certainly going to begin to tune out with discouragement.

3.   Learning Environment

Historically, we were taught that to get children to focus we should have them sit still and face forward. However, research is proving our old ideas are just plain wrong. Children who fidget are actually doing something, subconsciously, that aids learning. The new adage is "Learning loves movement." When the body is in motion, the pathways between the right and left hemispheres of the brain are opened, so *more* information flows. Some schools have capitalized on this knowledge by allowing children to stand at their desks. Some have had success with putting Velcro strips inside the desk that the children can run their fingers along to create movement and tactile sensations during quiet instruction times. Some schools allow gum chewing during exams and this improves performance. There is still a lot to be learned, and it takes time for new findings to trickle down into the average classroom. But if you think your child needs to be in an isolation chamber chained to a desk (instead of squatting on a kitchen chair working with music on), you're wrong.

Parents also think "work before play" and expect children to do homework right after school and before they play ball hockey or video games. But actually, those video games help children move their brains into a state called "flow," which is a state similar to meditation. It allows them to de-stress after a day of learning.

The bottom line is: Keep an open mind and read up on the new findings. Don't knock your child for being lazy. Learning is natural if we find the right conditions.

DOESN'T CARE ABOUT SCHOOL OR THE SUBJECT MATTER

Understanding the Problem

A child who protests strongly with "I don't care" is usually saying, "I care very much and I don't want you to know it." It's easier, psychologically speaking, to decide you don't care or don't like something when you are doing poorly at it. The child has come up with a creative way to solve the dilemma of feeling badly about not succeeding: If I don't care, then it will hurt less when I fail.

Solutions

This is a sign of discouragement, not a poor attitude. Encouragement is always the universal salve to remedy these feelings. Let's look at how we help the child restore his sense of hope of succeeding so he can get back in the learning game.

Acknowledge feelings and look to other goals. If the child *really* doesn't like the current unit, let him know you understand. There are lots of things on the curriculum that may not appeal to everyone's interests. Instead of telling him to "buck up, you can do better" say, "I know it's tough, let's just try to get you through it."

Then, appeal to other goals he has, like what mark he wants to get. For example: "I know you aren't interested in knowing about the parts of the plant, but I also know you like your report card to be something you're proud of. What mark do you want to get on the test to keep your grade point average where you like it?" "How can we help you get through the stuff that is not that interesting, but still help you hit your goals for getting the report card you'd like to see at the end of the term?" When we allow the child some wiggle room, when we understand that it's a long-term goal of years of academia, we're more apt to keep him encouraged. Sometimes we have to accept "good enough" work so that he doesn't stop altogether. "Working below potential" occasionally is humane, given children in the current education system have little to no say in the areas they are expected to study.

● ●

Encouraged students face the challenges of learning, and get on with doing what's required. Discouraged students evade, rebel, avoid, stop or find ways around the demands.

● ●

HATES THE TEACHER

Brianna comes in from the bus, throws her bag on the floor, screams, "I hate Mrs. Hutchinson" and storms to her room. Uh, oh. What to do?

UNDERSTANDING THE PROBLEM

Interpersonal problems (among adults and children alike) are bound to come up. The rule of thumb is to be empathetic and comforting while minding your own business. Avoid the pitfall of triangulating the problem by involving yourself in the dynamic. Instead, equip your children with strategies to deal with conflict. The exception to this rule is when the power differential between adult and child is too great.

SOLUTIONS

Listen without advising. Sometimes kids have a bad day at school and they just need to let off some steam. They are not looking for your wisdom ("Did you tell the teacher that Jacqueline pushed you first?") or your admonishment ("Well, if you weren't fooling around in line, Mrs. Hutchinson wouldn't have had to yell"). That will shut down communication now and in the future. Instead, think of your job as creating a safe place where they can let it all out.

Reflect back what you have heard and offer support. For example: "Sounds like an awfully tough day. You thought you were wrongly accused and that your teacher was out to get you. That would just stink! Can I give you a hug?"

Show faith without rescuing. "I'll bet you'll work through this with Mrs. Hutchinson. You always seem to know how to get things back on track. Let me know if you need anything from me." If the child says, "Can you talk to her?"—decline. "No, I think that's your job, but if you want to write a note or practice what you are going to say, I could help you with that." It's important for our children to understand that in life they will have to deal with people they don't like, or who don't like them. It's an inevitable part of life. But we learn lessons about getting along from bad interactions, too.

Get involved. If you feel that your child is not able to function in the classroom because of her relationship with the teacher, and your coaching and encouragement have not helped, it's time to amp up your involvement. Ask for a meeting *for the three of you* to sit down and discuss the concerns. If matters don't improve, you may need to take it to the next step and involve the principal. But always start with direct communication with the teacher first.

Powerful Little Love Notes

Besides class size, the number-one predictor of academic success is the child's perception that her teacher likes her.

Many teachers don't know about the art of encouragement, so you might suggest the teacher learn about "love notes." A love note is a letter from the teacher to the child, given at the end of every day, sharing with the child the things she noticed and appreciated about that child in the class that day.

Example:

"Brianna, I really appreciated your help cleaning up the art station this afternoon. I noticed how you asked your friend Peter for a turn with the red paint, and he seemed really keen to want to share and paint with you. I enjoy our time together and want to hear more about your new puppy at carpet time tomorrow!"

—Mrs. Hutchinson

I have recommended love notes to many people. You will be amazed at how powerful they are in bringing about positive changes.

ALWAYS LATE FOR SCHOOL

Every morning it's the same fight—"Let's go! Get up! Get Dressed! Eat, EAAAT—we're going to be late . . . Again!" What a tough way to start the day. The secretaries at the school office know you by name and have your child's pink late slip pre-filled out when you arrive. It's humiliating, infuriating and exhausting.

UNDERSTANDING THE PROBLEM

Kids' morning dawdling is a form of a passive power struggle. The more insistent we are to make them MOOOOOVE along, the more they dig their heels in to resist our control.

SOLUTIONS

The basic idea is to pull instead of push. The trick is to focus more on what we need to be doing and less on what our children are supposed to be doing (and aren't). If we keep ourselves on schedule doing the jobs we are responsible for, and quit trying to keep the kids on that schedule, we'll actually have better success. I know—sounds backwards. Parents think if they let off their kids would not move at all but, in fact, the opposite is true. Control is slowing them down, freedom will speed them up.

My morning routine system is similar to catching a plane. You're the pilot. The pilot announces time for boarding and time for departure—then takes flight at the scheduled time. The passengers are responsible for getting themselves on the plane or they miss their flight. After missing a few flights, passengers learn to leave for the airport earlier. The passenger makes an adjustment to fit into the flight schedule. Your children, like the passengers, will learn to make adjustments to their morning routines independently if you just keep acting in the role of pilot following the flight path and departure time yourself, without any need for anger, reminders, etc.

Here are the steps to pull that off:

Step 1: Make a plan with the kids (not for them). At a family meeting, discuss that mornings are not working well for anyone. You don't like yelling and they probably don't like to be yelled at. Ask them for input on how to do the morning routine better. If you involve them in establishing a new routine they're more likely to be cooperative. That alone won't be enough, but it sets the tone for the idea that things are going to be different and allows you to discuss what they're responsible for doing in the morning and what your jobs are. The more ideas they come up with and you implement—the better.

Step 2: Take Time for Training (TTFT). Are there things you do for your children that they could be doing on their own if you taught them? Could they learn to get their own cereal bowl out of the cupboard? Could they learn how to toast a bagel in the toaster? Could they learn how to check for all the items that need to go in their backpack for school? If so, work on improving these skills as they lead to autonomy and mastery. STOP doing things for them that they can do for themselves.

Step 3: Plan to be late. Because this change in the family routine will take a week or so to establish, I suspect you'll be late or slower than usual until everyone gets their groove on, so *plan* for that. Don't book meetings at work for 9 a.m. In fact, you could ask to use vacation time and plan to come in for 10 a.m. each day that first week. If you don't have that flexibility, then add the time buffer at home into your schedule. If you have to be out the door for 8:30 a.m., aim to be out the door by 8:10.

Sample Morning Plan

With power struggles, we need to avoid urging, insisting and micromanaging. Instead, we get on with our responsibilities and leave the child to manage hers—but still hold her accountable. I've broken the routine down into a few hot spots that usually snag parents so you can see exactly how that looks.

Getting dressed. Depending on her age, you may still be needed for help with dressing. Arrive smiling, ready to do your job of helping her. If she ignores you, or keeps playing, running around or jumping on the bed, she is stalling, showing you that you can't make her get dressed. Here is how you keep the motion moving forward without fighting:

> "I am here to help you get dressed." She keeps jumping.
>
> "Okay—I see you aren't interested in my help. I am going downstairs to get breakfast, see you down there."
>
> You have offered your services and she has declined—move along!
>
> Often, once you start moving she will say: "Okay, okay, I am ready." If this happens, stay and help. You'll do your job if she is cooperative. If she doesn't want your help—don't force it, exit instead.

Eating breakfast. Set breakfast on the table and call "breakfast time" to alert the children. Then, sit down at the table to enjoy your breakfast alone—keep your attitude positive, and no nagging or reminding. You have done your job of getting food ready; they have the job of coming to the table and eating. If you feel you HAVE to say something, make it an I-message:

> "I am worried that you'll miss breakfast and be hungry at school."

If they don't come, they've declined to eat—move along! I suggest you set an alarm on the stove indicating when breakfast is over. When the timer rings, clear the table. They may indeed miss breakfast or only arrive in time to have one bite of toast. After a few mornings they'll discover you're not holding up the meal for them anymore and hunger will motivate them to come eat, so long as they don't perceive coming to the table as losing a fight with you. You gotta keep your own demeanor calm and friendly (*think like a pilot, think like a pilot*) so they know you are not fighting with them, or being quietly manipulative. You have to prove you're not invested in what choices or decisions they make for themselves regarding breakfast. This ultimately gives them the autonomy and self-direction they are looking for.

Brushing teeth. Don't fight over brushing teeth. Again, walk to the washroom and state, "I am available for tooth brushing if anyone would like help." If no one shows up in a moment—move along. They don't want your help. If they refuse to brush or skip it, let it go for now. However, when they do ask you for something that has sugar in it, like milk or juice or a granola bar, you can use a when/then statement:

"*When* you get the old sugar and plaque off your teeth, *then* I'll know you're ready for the new sugar." This will intrinsically motivate them to want to brush and it ties freedoms and responsibilities together (if you want sugar—ya gotta care for your teeth).

I doubt they'll brush during the usual times initially, probably opting instead to brush just before they get that beloved yogurt tube, but without a fight and over time, they'll decide to brush during more traditional times.

Moving along now to the next part of the schedule.

Putting coats on. If it's time to get coats on and they are still not dressed, offer choice:

"Hey little buddy—it's time to go, are you going to get dressed quick like a bunny or should we take your clothes in a bag?"

If they get dressed—great. If not, pop the clothes in a bag and let them change at school.

These choices are meant for little kids that don't feel embarrassed about wearing jammies to school. It should not be an act of humiliation! For older children, they may choose to change in the car in the school parking lot—or simply skip this step and proceed to the next step suggested.

Start getting yourself ready for the trip to school. Put on your coat. You can give another simple time mark: "Time for coats." If they whine that they can't do it or moan for you to do it, don't. Here are some replies you can try:

- "You think you can't do it—but I know you can."
- "That's your job to do."
- "You're so capable—you'll figure it out."

Then just keep getting yourself ready. Try a little humor, like putting your boots on your hands like mittens or something that shows you are acting silly and not fighting. They really want you to put up your dukes, so if you continue to show you are not fighting material they are more likely to move along peacefully.

Leave the house. Once your coat is on, announce you're ready to go, and you'll meet them outside or in the car. It's really important in the "pull/pilot" model that you keep moving along without fighting. Staying in the foyer to ensure they keep getting ready actually slows them down further as your presence provides an audience to their displays of flaying on the hall floor, not putting on their boots. The longer you stay, the longer the show. Go outside and shovel snow, deadhead the flowers or sit in the car with a coffee and listen to the radio. Show's over, they should come along shortly now, but give it 10 or 20 minutes.

If they don't come along, and you are at your drop-dead time:

Go back in and announce it's time to leave. Then ask, "Can you come on your own or do I need to carry you?" If they don't come along, it's carry time. If they fuss, put them down and say, "Oh, I see you'd like to walk—great!"

For older children who can't be carried, but who are too young to stay home alone, say "last call for a ride to school." If they don't come willingly, you need to carry on with your typical day, despite the child being at home. If you work from home, let them know you've got to get on with your work and so you assume they are declining a ride to school. Start working and let them stay home—don't change your day one iota. They don't have to be banished to their rooms—they can play. But you're not available to help or play or serve them. The TV rules remain unchanged.

If you have to go to work, plan in advance with a neighbor or nanny or grandparent to come watch them. I know that is a HUGE undertaking, and potentially costly, but remember, you will only have to execute this a few times in that Take Time for Training week. One tough week now during the Take Time for Training period will buy you morning harmony for years to come. Totally worth the investment. But of course you need to have this prearranged. Get this set up before the family meeting on improving mornings.

If they're old enough to be home alone—let them stay home. I know you think they will never go to school, but that is not the case. They may enjoy testing this, seeing what it's like to be at home alone, watching daytime TV, but it gets dull pretty fast, especially if no one is angry at them or insisting they go to school. Honestly. If they don't want to go to school, the issue is not dawdling—something at school is amiss.

So there is the road map to getting your children to school sans pink slips. Of course, the entire success of this plan hinges on your attitude. If you think "ah ha!—finally a parenting tool sooo strong even the morning dawdler will be defeated MWAAAAaaa!" then, it won't work. Your children will see you are just trying new ways to control them. You actually have to share power with your children and have faith in them to manage their life if they're given a chance to practice and learn it. Sweet.

BUT WHAT IF . . .

What if you get them out the door, but they walk at a glacial pace?

Maybe your kids want to walk slower and enjoy the scenery and your company. Start the journey earlier so you can take a thermos of coffee and be more leisurely in your walk.

Make time to play. You can make it part of your routine to play in the schoolyard a half hour before the bell. Maybe plan to meet another parent there for picnic breakfasts. Your child may find a playdate motivating. Certainly the extra half hour will take the time pressure off.

Don't fight. If your child plants herself on the ground and refuses to budge, sit down beside her and start reading a book or checking your emails on your BlackBerry. Let her know you'll be ready to walk again whenever she is. The first time she may sit for a *long* time, but if you never fight and never get upset, this will probably only happen a few times. Remember, it's your job to escort her to school, it's her job to get there on time.

Inform the school. For a lot of parents, it's embarrassing to drop our children off late; we think the school will believe we are not taking our parenting responsibilities seriously. To alleviate your tension, and to make it clear to your child that you're committed to having her manage her own morning responsibilities, speak to your child's teacher about it, in your child's presence.

Sample Script

"Mr. Bennett, Harriet is learning to manage her mornings. She has her own alarm clock and even posted her morning schedule on her door. She's doing a great job of it so far [show of faith]. If she is late a few times while she gets the glitches worked out, I hope you'll understand and support her."

The teacher will hear this and know you are doing a great job of helping your child become responsible. He will not judge you for the times your child arrives late.

SWITCHING SCHOOLS

I get a lot of questions about switching schools. Here is a typical email:

"Alyson, I started my daughter in a special French program, but I don't know if it's a good fit for her. Her brother did the same program and really excelled, but she is struggling. I am thinking of moving her to a regular public school. I'm worried, though, that she'll feel she is not getting the same special programming as her brother. What should I do?"

Parents have major concerns about making what feels like a momentous decision. It's a big change and they worry about making a wrong choice, with potentially negative consequences.

Allow me to offer some reassurance:

- You don't need to make the decision alone.
- You don't need to feel it's a permanent, irreversible decision.
- You can trust your child to cope with change.
- You should trust yourself to know you are making the best informed choice that you can at the moment, and as new information presents itself, you can respond to it and alter your course.

I think we parents tend to conceptualize decisions around our children as being either right or wrong. It may be better to think of schooling choices as a best-fit process. Keep a "let's experiment and see" attitude.

From a psychological perspective, children decide for themselves what to make of a situation. You are projecting when you worry that your daughter may think her brother is getting preferential treatment. Your daughter might think she is! Talk to the kids, take their input into consideration, but be sure that you are the ultimate decision maker. It's unfair to ask your children to decide for themselves which school they want to go to. Too much pressure. That is a parent's responsibility.

Here is what I said to my kids (and yes, it was at a family meeting).

- -

Sample Script

"We want to make your schooling the best experience possible. Obviously, we are interested in your input—it's your school, after all. But there are many factors to be considered. You must trust us, as your parents, to make this decision. You must know we are here to look out for you and we would never force you to be in a situation that you didn't like. However, it's pretty common to love where you are, and anything new or different may seem odd. It takes time to meet and make new friends, learn how the new school works. We promise that whatever decision we make (with your input) will be open to reassessment. In a few months, we can discuss how it's going. If it's not working out, we can change our minds."

- -

🌱

• •

It's freeing to know you can change your mind. It's easier to be courageous and take chances if you know you can recover them. Parent and child alike.

• •

THEY'RE AUTOCRATIC—WE'RE DEMOCRATIC

I am often confronted with this question: "You're teaching us how to raise our children in a democratic way at home, but their school is still autocratic. Won't that be a problem?"

Imagine if we had the same worry when it came to emancipating women or slaves. Regardless of the challenge, it's the right thing to do. We can't bring about social change without pioneers leading the way.

Rest assured it will *not* be a problem. Your children will not be at a disadvantage because they think of themselves as social equals and want to be treated with respect. In fact, they are less likely to be bullied or bully, less likely to take drugs, break the law or be sexually active at a young age, and they will most likely avoid or survive a host of other issues that plague youth.

Children raised with democratic methods will quickly find their place in the classroom and get busy doing what the needs of the situation demand: studying, queuing up in line, putting up their hands to ask a question and so forth. They are not preoccupied with overcoming inferiority feelings. They are less likely to misbehave. They know how to cooperate, solve problems and see another's perspective. It's unlikely the teacher will have an issue with your children.

However, your children may have an issue with their teachers. They may be more vocal about perceived injustices or breaches of respect. Isn't it wonderful that they don't accept disrespectful treatment? By anyone? Have faith. When *your* children encounter injustice or poor treatment, they'll know what to do. They've been trained!

Because they've grown up with family meetings, they know the process that needs to be observed when a person is unhappy with the current state of affairs and wants to mobilize change. They are apt to ask for a meeting with their teachers to discuss their issues, and will probably present a few solutions they have already thought up. Your child may teach the teacher a thing or two.

CHAPTER 13

EXTRACURRICULAR ACTIVITIES—THE DEMOCRATIC WAY TO MANAGE THE ANGST

The Overscheduled Child · The Dropout Kid
· Goes to Lessons but Won't Participate

Parents are told that children who participate in enrichment experiences will enjoy many benefits, like learning good sportsmanship and building self-esteem. But what we don't spend much time talking about is how this cultural tradition also has some serious downsides for kids and their families. Here are just a few:

- *Huge expense*—when most families carry an oppressive debt load
- *Time consuming*—in an already time-strapped culture
- *Loss of family time*—our children now spend little time with their own parents and siblings; the majority of their day is in the care of teachers, coaches and mentors, even if they have a stay-at-home parent
- *Destruction of "Team Family"*—we've had to sacrifice family activities like doing dishes, shoveling the driveway, cutting

the grass and such, that serve to connect children to the most important team they'll ever "play" on: Team Family

- *Loss of vital family dinner-table time*—"bread-breaking" is largely replaced with drive-through burgers and tacos en route to an activity, which is unhealthy on two fronts
- *Loss of unstructured free play*—this is so developmentally important, especially for stimulating creativity and connections with others
- *Overtired children*
- *Anxious children*
- *Increased fighting*—for example: "Where is your bag?" and "We're late—get a move on."

Who needs a kid who can paddle a kayak and speak Mandarin if his family life is eroding around him?

"It is no measure of health to be well adjusted to a profoundly sick society."

—Jiddu Krishnamurti

Although parents feel they're failing their child somehow if they don't provide enough enrichment, many of the benefits of extracurricular activities are simply not worth the cost to family functioning. Let's look at some of the common areas of concern parents have so that you can find the balance between engaging your child's interests with good programming and allowing your child the benefits of a happy, healthy family life.

THE OVERSCHEDULED CHILD

So you want to know if, indeed, your child is overscheduled? I've Googled the other experts' answers and I find them less than helpful. For example:

Limit number of activities by child: Some experts suggest two activities per child at any one time. Well, if you have three kids, and between them they are in competitive dance, rep hockey and synchronized swimming, you're toast.

Some experts recommend you simply look for signs of stress in your child, such as trouble sleeping or irritability.

Although these are all symptoms the child may have, they give no indication of how the parents or the family relationships are being affected. How about watching out for these signs:

- Dad's a basket case, wondering how he'll ever afford all this since he needs to pay for lessons, two cars, a cleaning lady and a lawn-care service now that no one is home to do all that.
- Mom is in therapy, wondering why she has lost a sense of her self since becoming a mother. She gives her whole life to managing her kids' schooling and activities.
- The dog has become incontinent for no apparent medical reason and the siblings can't remember each other's names!

SOLUTIONS

Ask yourself, how is the entire family functioning? Can you be objective and take a barometric reading of sorts? Can you feel the atmospheric pressure of your own family? If you were a stranger coming to your house for the first time and standing in the foyer watching you all, what would you "feel" from this family?

Posing these questions is a good exercise. After all, we're talking about the environment our children are growing up in. Just as sure as you protect them from lead paint and urea-formaldehyde, you have to protect kids from toxic social environments too. Some households are just too frantic, stressed, fractured and fast-paced to be conducive to good mental health and strong relationships. We're wired to move a whole lot slower than modern society's expected pace. Get off the crazy treadmill.

Parents seem to like to get permission from the "experts" on their parenting practices. I am giving you permission now. Trust yourself and your own assessment of when it's too much for *any* of you. You are not putting your children at a disadvantage. In fact, you are being wise. I am endorsing the benefits of focusing your time commitments within the family instead of outside it. There is no better gift you can give your children than a slow, simple, happy and supportive home life. If you can sprinkle some extracurricular on top of that, go for it.

THE DROPOUT KID

You just spent $300 on dance classes—and that doesn't include the required specialty shoes and tights—and now she wants to drop out. What to do? You don't want kids to think they can just give up. We have to teach children to honor their commitments, and that when you start something you finish it—don't we?

UNDERSTANDING THE PROBLEM

If your child has signed up for an activity and, after attending the first few sessions, decides she doesn't like it, I suggest you probe for why, what's up? There seems to be three types of glitches that get in the way, and rarely is it the dreaded inability to make a commitment. Instead I encounter these three challenges:

1. Something is bothering them that is easily solvable.
2. They discover they don't like the activity as much as imagined.
3. They discover they aren't immediately the best in the class.

Let's see if we can help on all fronts.

SOLUTIONS

Here are the three areas of concern and the suggested solutions for each.

1. *Something is up.* For the child with something bothersome going on, probe for the underlying issue and work together to find solutions to the problem that is holding the child back from participating. If the public change room is an issue, they could

change at home or wear their swimsuit under their clothes. If they can't see the instructor from the back of the class, you could see about moving them to the front row.

2. *Not enjoyable.* If the activity was just not as enjoyable as the child had imagined it would be, that's understandable. Allow the child to drop the class. People make mistakes. No harm, no foul, glad they tried! After all, we sign them up for things so they'll learn what they like and don't like. There are sure to be a few misses over the years. I would sure hate for a child to say no to trying new things because she fears if she doesn't like the activity she'll be sentenced to months of enduring it, since her parents won't allow her to drop out.

To minimize the likelihood of an activity mismatch, try to be proactive using some of these tactics:

- Check it out first. If your child has a friend currently enrolled in a similar class, ask if your child can come as a guest. She may discover, for example, that gymnastics requires a *lot* of waiting while other people have a turn on the equipment. It's not all just bouncing on a trampoline, after all. Better to know that *before* enrolling.

- Check the policy. Does the class have a dropout period so the child can try it before committing for a full season or year? Be sure to ask. Some places are very reasonable, others are brutal. Shop around. Read the contract.

- Aim for lower upfront costs. If your child is interested in an instrument, can you borrow or rent one before buying one? Is there a used or borrowed gymnastics leotard you can obtain while your tot is deciding if he likes the class? The minute you are out of pocket, you're more likely to be upset if the child decides he doesn't want to continue.

3. *Not doing well enough.* Many children (and adults) have no tolerance for the inevitable mistakes required of being a beginner.

Some kids have the mistaken belief that they must be first and best or perfect—ergo, they also believe that if they are not, they must be worthless. This is obviously faulty thinking, but until we change that underlying belief, the child will probably only choose activities that she can master and excel at almost immediately.

The solution is to correct the faulty thinking and mistaken value through encouragement. Encouragement means to literally give our children the courage to be imperfect. They need to believe they are worthy right now as they are! Not when they are perfect or best or hit some other standard.

Often, parents mistake praise for encouragement. After all, most of us grew up being praised so it's the language we know. However, praise is actually the culprit in enforcing ideas about the importance of perfection, and erodes a stable sense of confidence in our worth. Instead, we want to de-emphasize perfection and instead pass along non-judgmental messages that emphasize the value of effort and improvement over "best" and "perfect."

- -

Encouragement versus Praise

When we praise we send the message "You're good when . . ." It's a conditional regard for the child that supposes some are better than others.

When we encourage we send the message "Right now, as you are, you are already all you need to be." Unconditional regard for the child says all people are valued, and it doesn't need to be earned, and it can't be lost. This frees our children from spending energy on "looking good" and allows them to tackle the task at hand.

For more on the language of encouragement, see chapter 15.

- -

How to Be Encouraging

During the child's lessons, the instructor is in a position to be encouraging. At home, you can be encouraging by implementing some of these ideas:

1. Stop being so perfect yourself! Model making lots of mistakes and laughing them off.

2. Stop being critical of yourself (and others).

3. Notice (and dampen) your own ambitious drive and need for success.

4. When your child flogs himself for making a mistake, correct his attitude: "You seem disappointed that you didn't get the goal, but did you notice how much you've improved? All your hard work is paying off." This puts the focus on his effort and improvements rather than the end results.

5. Downgrade the emphasis placed on the final achievement. Sure, it's great to reach a goal, but often accolades are paid only once a child "achieves"—rather than focusing on the process. Hey, you won! I noticed you really get the hang of passing and skating backwards. Those practice drills are really working.

6. Correct the notion that mistakes are failures. Remind your child that the most successful people are the ones who can stick it out. Find one of his heroes in business, sports, science or the arts and share stories of how many "failures" happened before that person "made it."

Tactical Tip

When picking activities try to customize the experience to best suit the individual style of your child. Pay attention to the style of class and instruction that your child enjoys:

- Does your child seem to enjoy one-on-one or group lessons better?

- Does she prefer a more relaxed, recreational class, or does she get engaged only when it's a serious undertaking?

- Some children care a lot about who the instructor is and others couldn't care less. If the teacher matters to your child, work with her to find a good partnership.

- Some children (especially those more perfectionist firstborns) prefer individual sports to team sports, so instead of soccer, hockey or T-ball, consider golf, swimming or tennis. That way, if the child loses, he disappoints only himself and not others, and it's only his performance that impacts the outcome of the game.

- Is there a way to learn or develop the same interest that doesn't involve signing up? Wayne Gretzky's dad flooded a rink in the backyard and he and his son played shinny together.
- Have you tried learning something together? I took piano lessons with my dad, and I was better than him! It was "our thing," and I loved that. Cooking classes? Art classes? Get creative!

GOES TO LESSONS BUT WON'T PARTICIPATE

You can get Jill to her swimming lesson, but you can't get her in the pool! She just sits on the side. Why do you even bother bringing her? Should you just take her out of lessons and try again when she is older?

UNDERSTANDING THE PROBLEM

Many parents stay and watch their children's lessons. While we want to support them and show them we care, it usually leads to misbehaviors. Just like being a parent volunteer in the classroom, our presence changes their behavior. Attention seeking and power struggles abound. The child may say behaviorally, "You can drive me here, but you can't make me participate." In which case, the goal is power. Or, it may be that if the child fusses about getting in the water, mom will fuss and stay closer by on the pool deck instead of retreating to the observation balcony, in which case it achieves undue parental attention.

SOLUTIONS

Acknowledge the child's power. Let the child know it's okay if she wants to sit out that day. You've completed your obligation of getting her to the class. She can decide if she wants to sit or participate. Without the added benefit of your reaction, the child may decide that participating is a better use of her time. Plus, the instructor is more likely than you are to engage the child in the class. However, the instructor will only be effective in doing that *after* you leave. When you are not there as an audience, the parent-child dynamic that is keeping the child from participating is no longer in force.

Find connection time. Find more connection time at other times of the day, preferably in advance of the swim lesson.

❧

If, after implementing these strategies, the child still doesn't participate after a few classes, ask her if she would like to drop out. Point out that she doesn't seem to want to be in the class. Be prepared for the answer—yes, please, I want out! Respect that decision without being angered.

Tactical Tip

Make your own dropout policy with your child. She needs to feel she has an exit strategy if the activity is just unbearable to her. For example: "How about we try piano until December, and if you still don't like it, then let's not continue." This will often win the cooperation of your child to hang in at least that long—if you have chosen the strategy together.

But be reasonable. Don't say: "You must take piano until you get your Grade 3, and then you can decide if you want to continue." Whose agenda is this, anyway? Remember, it's *extra-curricular*, not mandatory.

CHAPTER 14

KIDS AND COINS—THE DEMOCRATIC APPROACH TO MONEY MATTERS

Mommy, Buy This for Me! ("Dammit" Implied) · Complaining about the Amount of Allowance · Savings or "Slavings"? · Loses Money

We live in a consumer culture. Unless you want to move to a place that still relies on bartering, your children are going to have to learn financial literacy as part of their life preparation. Given the typical financial state of parents these days, this may be a "do as I say, not as I do" rule. (Don't you wish you'd had some better financial preparation yourself?) Let's try to help the next generation do better than us.

To that end, I am working with the Bank of Montreal and their BMO SmartSteps for Parents program, a great online resource you might want to check out too, at www.bmo.com/parents launching in spring 2011.

In this chapter, I'll tackle parents' most common problems, and the issues that seem to plague us all.

MOMMY, BUY THIS FOR ME! ("DAMMIT" IMPLIED)

Do you have one pant leg longer than the other from the constant tugging?—"Mom, mom, buy me this book. Mom, mom, buy me some Timbits. Mom, mom, buy me this Barbie." You don't want to spoil them, and you probably don't want a big scene in public either. What to do?

UNDERSTANDING THE PROBLEM

How else *would* they be able to make these purchases without demanding, pleading, begging and, yes, the ultimate form of demanding, tantruming? Most children don't have procurement alternatives. Left with no other means, they do what they can—they get creative and use a mistaken approach, a misbehavior, and usually that's effective. Cry and you might just get that Barbie. Whine and you might get daddy to buy you some Timbits. But is that how we want our children to go about this? I don't think so.

SOLUTIONS

Start an allowance. We have to find constructive avenues for purchasing so our children don't have to wear us down as their only methodology. That means it's time to start them on a small allowance. Now when they pull your pant leg, you can reply, "That's something you can buy for yourself with your allowance." Fight averted. You'll also be surprised at how many things your kids don't actually want when they have to pay for it themselves.

BUT WHAT IF . . .

My child is only 4. I really can't see an allowance for a 4 year old making any sense. I didn't have an allowance till I was 10. Four year olds don't understand money.

It's true that children are not born with an innate understanding of the Dow Jones Index or international money markets. Hell, they can't even tell the difference between a quarter and a nickel. But we can teach them. This is how their understanding begins. There are many things for children to learn as they develop financial literacy. You can't just wait until they are about to go off to college and expect them to get up to speed in one year. They have to start early, with simple practices that build one on top of another over time. A small allowance is simply a first step.

And remember, money is associated with power. Take away a person's money and you take away his or her power. Inversely, as soon as you begin a small starter allowance, it's a baby step forward along a continuum of growth, knowledge and skills development that helps in the reach for autonomy, self-direction and self-determination.

Have 'em create a wish list. If your child asks you to buy things all the time, rather than labeling ("You are so spoiled") or judging ("You have enough of those silly Webkinz") or insulting ("Do you think I'm a money tree?"), simply say, "Let's put that on your wish list." Now you're affirming your child instead. That's encouraging. Plus, it will diffuse what could have turned into a fight. We kept a list in the back of our family-meeting book. My kids still like going back to see what they wanted when they were little.

Remember, it's called a wish list for a reason. You are *not* promising to buy these things at a later date. But now those recorded items are a reference list of ideas for friends or family members trying to think of things your children would like for a birthday or holiday gift.

Modeling. What are your buying habits? Some parents shop every single day. Consumer habits are modeled, and if the next generation picks up our habits, we've got a global crisis on our hands. Check out the great project called "The story of stuff" at www.storyofstuff.com with your children. Maybe you'll learn something too.

Be clear and consistent. To help reduce meltdowns over your saying no to requests, be sure your child has clear expectations about what you're willing to buy and when. Too often we say things like, "If you are a good girl at the mall today, I'll buy you something." Or its companion punishment, "No, you can't have that because you were a bad boy today." Ouch. Perhaps we're in a good mood and feel generous one day and we feel pinched and stingy the next. With no clear understanding, our kids are likely to feel we are acting arbitrarily, being gatekeepers, lording our power, and this will surely lead to misbehavior. You can give them the heads up, "We're going to the mall, but we won't be buying anything for you today. It's a "no-gifts trip." Now stick with your statement. Firm and friendly all the way.

COMPLAINING ABOUT THE AMOUNT OF ALLOWANCE

Do your children moan that you're cheap? Do they argue that all their friends get a bigger allowance than them? You calibrate the amount with age. Isn't that standard? A dollar per year? Yes? No? HELP! How much is the right amount for allowance?

UNDERSTANDING THE PROBLEM

The phrase "But my friends do" is not going to win any arguments with me. It's a good time to learn to say: "Every family is different; in our family we do it this way. We can discuss changes at the family meeting if you'd like." So many families struggle to do what's best. But renting limousines to take students to Grade 6 graduations and paying $10k for sweet-sixteen parties tell me that keeping up with the Joneses is not the best way to determine your parenting practices, or your family's budgetary constraints.

Allowance is about teaching money-management skills and increasing the child's autonomy and independence. Allowance should be based on a reasonable spending budget. I don't see any connection between the age of the recipient and the money he receives. That is illogical. This does nothing to help your child learn to develop a realistic budget.

Instead, a budget should reflect the family's socio-economic status. A good budget is an itemized list of things that you, the parent, are currently purchasing on behalf of your child that you feel the child is now ready to purchase for himself. It should never cost you additional money to put your child on an allowance. Instead of *you* buying his scholastic books, he is buying his own. The same amount of money would have been spent. Some families can afford more than others. Don't be ashamed or hide that fact. If you hold your chin up in a self-respecting manner and say, "We can't afford that amount, sorry," you're teaching your child to have a positive attitude about the reality of the family's income. If you feel guilty, you're teaching him to be ashamed of the family's income level—PSHAW!

The child's budget will change over time, aligning with his growing abilities to manage money and make purchasing decisions independently. You may even have a younger child whose allowance is bigger than that of an older sibling because in drafting his budget he included a bus pass, while the older sibling doesn't take the bus.

As a parent, you can show your child how to draft a budget and submit it to you for approval. If he submits a proposed budget that includes $10 a week for candy, you can say the budget has not been approved. Let the child know you'd be okay, though, with $2 a week for candy.

But What If . . .

Alyson, I know my candy-holic smart child would submit a budget of $10 for books and $2 for candy and then promptly spend $12 on candy. How can I control this?

Just like any other budget, if you get $10 for books and don't use the $10 on books, you lose the money in that category or line item. Keeping your spending in line with your budget is all part of the lesson. Remember, we are doing all this so our children learn. Learning requires making mistakes. Let them learn by experiencing the consequences. And let them learn while the stakes are low. No getting angry required. Just let them know that the next allowance is $2 to reflect the fact that the book budget wasn't being used.

Sample Starter Allowance

Preschooler

- *Candy.* The amount depends on how much you let the child consume. If you've been buying her a pack of sugar-free gum at the grocery store, she could begin making this purchase on her own. Cost: $1.25.
- *Juice.* If you always buy her a juice after swim lessons, she could buy this on her own. Cost: $2.
- *Toys.* Toys are expensive, but if you go to garage sales, the dollar store or Walmart, your child could probably find some item for $2. Better yet, she can begin to understand that some things cost "three allowances" and now she has impetus to wait and save. Teaching saving and patience develops emotional intelligence, too. The child will also learn that the dolls you buy at the dollar store fall apart after a month, while the expensive Mattel babies keep their limbs a lot longer. Do you see all the great benefits of even a small allowance?

- -

True Story

When my children were preschoolers and getting a small allowance, they saved up their money for months to buy me a gift for mother's day. They were so excited and proud. If their dad had taken them shopping and spent his own money, it would not have been the same experience of truly giving.

- -

School-aged Child

It's easy to forget just how expensive common items like a DVD can be. Track your current spending for these items on your child's behalf before you decide to allot money for some or all of the following items:

- Books
- Milk, lunch or pizza money at school
- Bus money
- Toys/games/hobbies

- Music/iTunes/DVDs
- Movies/entertainment/online bling like buying items at FarmVille.
- Money to buy presents for others
- Money for charitable activities of their choice
- Savings

Tween

Probably many of the same items as listed above will appear on a preteen's budget; however, the amounts may increase as the tween's money competency improves. In addition, it's time to consider adding:

- Clothing allowance
- Cell phone budget

Teen

Eventually, as part of their money-management training, your child needs to start understanding about the workforce and earning money through a part-time job. Working a few hours while going to school has all kinds of benefits for a young adult. Parents should cap their teens' allowance budget, pay only for essentials and allow teens to take responsibility for paying for their own nonessentials. They'll be wanting higher ticket items, like March Break school trips, a used car, expensive hair highlights and what not, so they'll be motivated to supplement their allowance with a paycheck if we limit or cap what we're willing to pay for.

Chores and Allowance? A Marriage Made in Heaven, or Oil and Water?

What's a parent to do when their kid happily made his bed for a dollar a week and then grandma goes and gives him $100 in a birthday card? Thanks, grandma. Now he refuses to do his chores. Worse, you ask him to help you unload groceries from the car and he says, "How much will you pay me?" Good Lord, really?

Yes, we want to teach our children about money and the way the world works. But home and work are not parallel systems. Our homes are social units that work solely based on volunteerism. Try paying your spouse for sex if you don't agree and see how that goes over.

Families are not a free market economy. In the workforce it's a "paid for services rendered" system, but home is a community bound by relationships, where you pitch in and help. And gosh darn it, they help you too! It's reciprocal, kind and caring, and not at all about bean counting. Yech!

I suggest that you separate these concepts so your children learn that they get money in the form of an allowance because they need money to function in the consumer world. They do their part around the house because it's needed. They're part of the team. In a community we all pitch in, and no one unfairly burdens another. If you want to have some of the wildebeest cooking on the fire, you had better help with the hunt. We *need* each other's help to survive. That's why we help mom unload the groceries.

But What If . . .

Oh sure, now you tell us we shouldn't be paying for chores. How are we supposed to get off the fee-for-service system once we've started it?

I suggest that at your family meeting (yes, you'll need to read up on those in my book *Honey, I Wrecked the Kids,* or check out the boxed feature in chapter 5 of this book) you simply share your thoughts. Tell your kids that the way labor and money are being handled has not been sitting well with you and you'd like to revisit it. Explain your rationale. Share this chapter in the book with them if it helps.

If you are revisiting this issue, it may be time to start the allowance-with-budget strategy. Your kids may be pleasantly surprised to find they get *more* money on an allowance system. Usually kids appreciate this system because when you do work to help, it feels better than doing work to get paid, so be sure to share lots of appreciations for their contributions on a regular basis. Don't you wish you were appreciated more for the meals you make and cleaning and car pooling you do? We could all do better at showing our gratitude.

SAVINGS OR "SLAVINGS"?

Does your child complain you're "taking" her money when relatives give her cash on her birthday and you force her to put it in her savings account instead of buying the skateboard she wanted? After all, isn't a hundred bucks too much for a 10 year old to "blow"? You don't even think skateboarding is safe. Saving it would be much more responsible, wouldn't it?

Going back to first principles of democracy: If the child gets a gift of money, it's *her* money. Possession is nine-tenths of the law, isn't it? What right do you have over it? You may ask the gift giver to clarify what he intended the money to be used for. If he stipulated "education savings," great! It goes into a Registered Education Savings Plan (but by the way, that sucks as a birthday gift—ya gotta throw in a Toblerone bar at least). However, if it's for a new bike, you need to honor the gift giver's intentions. If he said, "I didn't know what Harriet would like for her birthday, but here's $100 for her to pick something for herself," then it's fair game. She decides.

BUT WHAT IF . . .

Harriet wants to buy a paintball gun?

You'll have to set limits and boundaries around paint-ball guns. Example:

> "You can buy a paint gun, that is your right, but the age in our house for using a paintball gun is 10, so it's gonna sit collecting dust till then; maybe you want to choose something else you can use right away."

> Or, if she buys $100 worth of candy, that's fine too, but the family rule is still one treat a day.

> "You can use your money to buy whatever you want, but our family rule is one candy a day, so those last few pieces could be mighty stale."

All I am saying is, so long as it's legal to sell to minors, you're not in a position to stop them from buying it, but you still are able to use family meetings to set house rules about behaviors.

I want my kids to learn about savings, but I know if I use my parental powers to snatch what is rightfully theirs, then they are not really onboard and they're gonna feel I'm abusing my power. It's unlikely they'll be learning what I hoped to teach. Problems will surely ensue. If it were me, I'd be burning through that savings account as soon as I got my hands on it, feeling it was my due. Gotta find another method.

Teaching a child to save can be broached when she wants something that costs more than her allowance. If she wants the $100 skateboard but only gets $10 as an allowance, she could:

- Ask for an increase in allowance. (You decide yea or nay, but budgets should be assessed regularly.)
- Save up (in a jar or with a savings account).
- Earn additional money through babysitting, delivering papers, selling old toys at a garage sale, etc.
- Put it on a wish list (and pray).
- Ask parents to match the savings (again, you can say yea or nay).

- -

It Worked for Us

My daughter is saving for a trip to Kenya next summer to build schools with Free the Children. You can imagine that a 15 year old saving all that money herself would take forever. She is working actively on all fronts. "Money for Africa" is on her wish list; she is also fundraising and earning money through sales of a music CD of original songs she wrote and recorded. I have offered to match the funds she can raise or save herself. All of this is possible because she *really* wants to go to Kenya. And years of financial-literacy training have prepared her for this. She understands how expensive it is, that the funds must be earned and that it's her responsibility, although my helpfulness is an appreciated bonus. She has experienced earlier success saving for smaller-ticket items, and each of those experiences gave her proof she could do this. There is no sense of entitlement, and the pride she'll feel in getting herself to Kenya on this mission will be so much more than if I just cut a check and send her.

The moral of the story? When your kids have a desire to buy something they can't afford, seize the day. This is a teachable moment.

- -

Remember, inspire instead of force. You'll always come out ahead.

LOSES MONEY

I had a mom ask for my advice. She had given her daughter $20 to spend on books at the book fair. She warned her daughter to put it someplace safe, knowing how forgetful her daughter was, and still the daughter lost it. Her question to me: Should mom replace the money?

My kids were standing beside me listening to the story. It was patently clear to them: no!

One of the important lessons we have to learn about money is that it's finite and when it's gone, it's gone. We have to respect money and take care of it. We have to keep an eye on our purses and wallets. The best way to learn to be mindful of your money is to experience the natural consequence of losing it. Argg!

We can share that we feel really badly for our child. Maybe share a story of when you lost your wallet at some point. Or coach her around the things to do to help keep attentive to where her money is. Coaching helps our children build skills and strategies.

However, if you replace the missing funds, your child is learning that you'll bail her out. Money loses its value again, and our kids are likely to remain careless. Heck, there is no reason to change your behavior if the money fairy just replaces the money.

BUT WHAT IF . . .

My child doesn't lose his money, he just conveniently "forgets" it.

Some children are notorious for forgetting to bring along their cash—"Dad, can you lend me $20 and I'll pay you back at home?" If you lend the money and upon arriving home your child immediately grabs his wallet and repays you, then great, he was a good loan risk. If, however, he doesn't immediately pay you back, or you have to go all bounty hunter on him, I would simply let him know that you only lend money to people with a good credit history. Until then, the answer is no. If she wants that belly button ring and she don't have her money, bummer, she'll have to go back and get it another time. Of course, the only way to improve your child's credit history with you is for you to offer another chance, so let the child try again after experiencing a few disappointments.

CHAPTER 15

SIBLING FIGHTING—AND THE DEMOCRATIC APPROACH TO ENDING IT

Fighting in the Car · Mommy, He Stole My Toy! ·
Can't or Won't? · The Physical Factor: When Siblings
Physically Fight · My Toddler Is Too Rough with the
Baby · Name-Calling and Being Mean · Is Jealous

I can't stress enough how important it is for parents to understand the family dynamics that are at play when raising more than one child. I wrote a chapter on the subject in *Breaking the Good Mom Myth* under the myth "Good mothers manage sibling conflict." Our "myth-conception" is that if siblings are fighting, we should step in and make them stop. We believe if we let them fight, we're not "doing our job."

To the untrained eye, it seems there is an "aggressor" and a "victim." We feel that one child is innocent, defenseless and in need of saving while the other is acting in ways that are wrong or unfair and require us to step in and punish them. Unfortunately, this is not the case. In fact in *all* cases of conflict, both parties are equally responsible for the creation of the discourse. Why? Because either child can choose to act in ways that either lead the interaction toward peace or toward escalating conflict. If it goes the way of conflict it's because both parties are complicit in taking it that way (or choosing to *not* act in ways to prevent it).

Punishing only one child for a crime actually committed by both will lead to resentment, fracture the sibling relationship and cause one child to want to hurt the other all the more.

I know that this dynamic is not always clear to see for parents. It requires some understanding of family dynamics, birth order, subtle ways we reinforce and lock our children into roles, and how we inadvertently take sides or show favoritism. Yes, it's complicated.

For our purposes here, I'd like to recap the key concepts to keep in mind as we implement strategies for the common problems this chapter covers, from fighting in the car to pilfering each other's possessions.

SIBLING FIGHTING CHEAT SHEET

Here are the main ideas you'll need to know, even if you just take me on my word.

- Conflict between any two people is inevitable, but how we respond to our children's fights determines if they will learn to resolve conflicts or become life-long rivals.
- Children are the caretakers of their own relationships. They must learn how best to deal with each other independently.
- Children can choose to either fight or get along. Either child can guide the course of the interaction toward peace. If neither chooses to, the fight ensues with both parties' agreement.
- It takes two to agree to fight: it's a form of cooperation, just on the negative side of life.
- Children need to be taught basic problem-solving strategies for learning to get along. However, most fighting is not due to a skills deficit but is purposeful, goal-directed behavior.

- Fighting has benefits. Here are the purposes it serves:
  - Gains parental attention and involvement (well-behaved children get ignored too often, while conflict is sure to keep you in the room).
  - Reinforces each child's role in the family; that is, to make one look good and the other look bad.

With these basic concepts in hand, let's look at the common kafuffles and how to respond in ways that will help our children get along.

FIGHTING IN THE CAR

It's just a short trip across town to the karate studio, but it seems the minute you put those kids in a car, it's like putting two vipers in a pit. Fight! Fight! Fight! Before you invest in a new vehicle with a third row of seats—to separate the siblings—let's get to the real reason your kids are duking it out in the backseat.

UNDERSTANDING THE PROBLEM

In a car, there are three factors that lead to car quibbles:

1. Kids are restrained and bored.
2. Kids are in forced close proximity.
3. Parents are a captive audience.

Just like kids know we are more likely to cave if they have a tantrum in public and humiliate us, they also have figured out that parents are less tolerant of shenanigans in the car. They've discovered that car fighting is a sure way to reach their (mistaken) goal of parental involvement and attention. So they fire up right away with some irksome behavior toward their sib. Of course, being only inches away, we overhear them, and as our "fair" brain kicks in, we put on the white powdered wig, grab our gavel and prepare to dispense justice.

"Josh, stop complaining; it's Taylor's turn to pick the song, you picked yesterday."

"Stop kicking, Jade! That's not nice."

But let me ask you this: In each altercation whose problem is it? Who isn't getting his song played? Who is being kicked?

The second you start interfering and working your parenting powers to make things fair between your children is the very same moment you are inadvertently taking sides. You're speaking up for one of them. It becomes two against one.

This is how we groom our victim-role children to be passively uncooperative. Why take a stance against your sibling when doing nothing gets mom or dad to fight your battles? Of course, that only fuels our belief that children can't defend themselves (rather than they won't). It becomes a self-fulfilling prophecy.

SOLUTIONS

Fire yourself. Ask yourself, "Whose problem is this?" If it's not yours, the rule is: mind your own business (MYOB). It's not your job to make your children get along. So fire yourself.

Zippy One-Liner: "It's not my job to solve this—you'll need to work it out together."

Ignore. Ignore their bickering until it becomes a safety issue for you. Screaming, chucked library books, the distraction of your seat being kicked; now *you've* got a problem! Apply a logical consequence.

Apply logical consequences. Calmly state the NOTS (needs of the situation), offer choice and follow through firm and friendly. For example: "It's unsafe to drive when there is fighting. Can you calm yourselves? Or do I need to pull over?" If they continue, pull the car to off the road and start reading a book or check emails on your BlackBerry until they are calm again and you can resume driving. If things don't de-escalate quickly, the children are still convinced you are an audience to their antics, so move even farther away from the war zone. Get out of the car and state, "I'll be waiting out here; let me know when it's safe to drive again."

Once your children realize that you are not interested at all in their fight and that you're not invested in making them get along, they are left with the simple formula: get along = car goes; fight = car stops. Mom and dad are not in the equation at all—it's the kids' behavior alone that controls the gas pedal.

Eventually, the kids will grow tired of waiting or fighting and come to the realization that they need each other to get along in order to get off the shoulder of the road and get on with the day. It may take a while the first time, so know that you may have to be late for that karate lesson.

However, if you commit to this tactic without fail, each and every time they fight, I promise you that while you may be inconvenienced a few times, you'll have done the hard work of teaching your children to get along in the car. Isn't that worth being late? This is an investment in your future that will gain you hours of happy car rides.

Word of warning: your children will test you from time to time. A fight will break out in the car a few months from now, just when you thought all this was behind you. Instead of falling back into the verbal reminders and getting involved because you think "they know better," simply pull the car over. They'll know what it means. You won't have to say a thing.

Bust boredom. Fighting children want your attention and involvement. Instead of giving it to them through negative means, find positive ways to interact. Play "20 Questions" or "The Alphabet Game," where everyone hunts for the letters of the alphabet in order ("There is an A on that license plate" or "I see a B on that street sign for "Baseline Drive"). Tell knock knock jokes. Have ideas like these up your sleeve, or assign the job to the kids so it doesn't always have to be your burden and creativity at work. There are lots of ideas online they can research for fun during car travel.

Problem solve at the family meeting. Remember that in times of conflict, people are not in the problem-solving frame of mind. If your children have recurring issues in the car, like who rides shotgun or what station to listen to on the radio, put these issues on the agenda for the family meeting, where problem solving happens best.

MOMMY, HE STOLE MY TOY!

You hear a frantic voice and see that your daughter is crying because her brother has taken her Barbie. Surely that is wrong. You should step in now, right?

UNDERSTANDING THE PROBLEM

A stolen Barbie, an old stuffed animal, a set of markers, a bike, a binder, an iPod, a favorite jean jacket or ball cap. It really doesn't matter what it is. Kids take their siblings' stuff without getting permission. What's up with that?

Well, as parents we believe things must be "fair" and if we see someone taking another person's belongings without permission we consider that "breaking the law," and feel bound to right that wrong. We reprimand the thief. In short order, children learn to taunt each other with their possessions, refuse to share and then tattle on their siblings when they take things. It's a formula for getting your sibling put in the doghouse and making yourself look good. It's also a surefire way to engage parents.

SOLUTIONS

Just imagine for a moment, if you didn't get entangled in their issues with one another. Imagine if the two are left to deal with each other on these matters. Here is the better outcome you're now making possible as they experience the reality of social contracts, of sharing or respecting each other's property:

1. If I don't share with my sibling, she won't share with me, either. I guess I should start sharing more if I want some of her stuff.

2. If I take something of hers without asking, I am just inviting her to take from me without asking at another time, and I don't like that, either. I'd better get her permission first.

3. I had better treat my sibling nicely so she doesn't take my possessions in anger. I really need her to get along with me!

Ultimately, all such social agreements are just hand shakes and people having the good will to honor them. They're more likely to want to cooperate with each other because of the inherent benefits. If we withdraw our services of being deputy dog law enforcer, they'll no longer get the benefit of getting each other in trouble and looking good. Conflict loses its benefits.

Now, let's walk through a typical situation so you can see how that would look:

If you saw the incident from the kitchen, say, and no one has come to ask you for help, leave it. Ignore it. Mind your own business. You are not needed. Let them work it out between them.

If, however, your child comes running into the kitchen upset and looking for you, she is tattling on her sibling and hoping to get them in trouble with you. Don't let the child reach her goal. Instead, offer emotional support and redirect. Be empathetic without rescuing or solving the child's problem. After all, someone you love has a problem; it's okay to be caring. Not getting involved doesn't have to feel like cold abandonment. Try active listening (see chapter 10).

Zingy-One Liners. "He didn't listen when you said, 'No,' and that feels disrespectful."

Name the child's feelings and put words to the problem. You're showing her you understand her plight. That alone is very supportive. She feels your strength and presence.

But each of these lines should be followed with: "I am sure you can work it out with him." You're loving but not rescuing. The problem ownership stays with the proper people—the sibs.

CAN'T OR WON'T?

If your children are young, and you feel they still need training on basic skills of speaking up or taking turns, you can step into the situation, but be sure to wear your educator hat, not your Judge Judy wig.

Instead of reprimanding the Barbie snatcher per usual, direct your energy to the person who feels wronged. Teach this child how to step up and deal with life. Show her it's not helpful to just be a puddle of tears and hope that other people will solve her problems. We want assertive children who tackle problems, not kids who whimper and assume all is lost and out of their control. Encourage her to find her own voice, speak up for herself and learn to take herself and her own power seriously.

Kids need to learn that they can influence situations all on their own, by deciding what they can do differently, rather than wishing and praying the other person changes. Coach them to speak up and respond to their sibling.

The two-arm technique. I recommend the two-arm technique for teaching children to speak up. I learned this method during my nursery school teacher training with Althea Poulos. It goes like this:

Get both children together (I know, like herding cats, right?), you holding one in each arm so they are facing each other and with you down on your knees at their eye level. Now try the following:

- -

Sample Script

Mom: Didi, you look upset, do you need to speak up and say something to your brother? You can say, "I don't like that."

Didi will either take the prompt and say, "I don't like that" or stare dumbfounded at your new tactic.

If Didi doesn't speak up, carry her message:

"I see from your sister's face that she is telling you she is upset and doesn't like that." (When said this way, the message is still coming from Didi, not from mom).

Now, to coach the thief:

Mom to Theo: "Theo, it looks like you want Didi's Barbie too. Can you use your words and ask for a turn? Can you say, "Can I have a turn please?"

Theo will either repeat the phrasing or, again, be in total shock and wondering what the heck is taking place, since you've not done this before. He is still expecting you to put him in a time-out for misbehaving.

Mom: "Theo seems interested in your Barbie. He's hoping you'll share with him. How would that be?"

Didi: "No!"

Mom to Theo: "It sounds like your sister is still upset and not feeling much like sharing with you right now. Is there something you could do to make her feel better? People don't usually feel much like sharing when they're mad at the person. It's easier to share when people are getting along."

Theo shrugs.

Mom to Didi: "Theo is not sure what he could do to make things better with you. Do you have any ideas?"

Didi: "I just got it! It's new. I don't want to share it."

Mom: "Sounds like it's pretty special and you'd like it just for your own. What could you do so your brother is more likely to respect your wishes?"

Didi shrugs.

Mom: "Would you like a suggestion? Maybe if he knew that sometime he might get a turn later, he'd be less apt to take it without permission. Would you be willing to let him play with it for a bit later today or tomorrow? Maybe there is something of his you'd wish you could use and you could swap? Or maybe some other idea you have?"

See if either child is interested in working something out. If they don't, the process is over, but you might let them know, "If the Barbie is becoming a problem between you, we'll have to put it away until you two figure something out."

I can hear readers thinking "What? That sounds unfair." Actually, it's the best response for keeping both children on a level, power-wise. It's known as putting them in the same boat.

- -

Putting them in the same boat. If an item becomes a source of conflict, and it is put away until a solution is reached, then both children realize they are equally able to get the other's item removed simply by creating a fight. Even a small child who can't speak is now able to have equal power over her older, bigger, wiser, stronger brother.

That levels the playing field—it's actually an equalizing tactic and not unfair at all.

This teaches them that they need the other's cooperation to get an item back and to keep it. They're now invested in getting along with the other instead of being pitted against one another trying to get the other in trouble. By implementing this tactic you are providing a reason, and a benefit, for the need to get along.

Examples:

> "If you can't decide on which TV show to watch, the TV will go off until you agree."

> "If you can't share the tub toys peacefully, the tub toys get removed."

I promise you, the technique of putting both children in the same boat not only works like a charm, you're also teaching a very important lesson: your sibling is your keeper, not your enemy, and you had better work *with* him, not against him. That will foster cooperation and a close relationship.

But What If . . .

I noticed that my one daughter, Chloe, has a hard time getting her turn, and rather than fight with her sister, she simply acquiesces. It doesn't seem fair.

If you notice one child is incapable of getting her way, or always acquiesces to an overbearing sibling, don't feel sorry for the child and fall back into fighting her battles. Instead, put the problem on the family agenda and work though a more equitable solution—together, outside the time of conflict.

For example, instead of fighting over what DVD to watch, and Chloe always giving in to her sister's choice, you might decide instead to try alternating whose night it is for picking the movie. I know another family whose solution was to have one child pick three DVDs and then the sibling child selected from one of those three, so the final selection was for sure something they both liked. It's not the solution that counts so much as implementing ideas the children come up with themselves.

THE PHYSICAL FACTOR: WHEN SIBLINGS PHYSICALLY FIGHT

What about the kids who get physical with each other? Yelling is one thing, but are you suggesting we let them bludgeon each other to death?

UNDERSTANDING THE PROBLEM

When parents learn that allowing children to work out their own problems is a better approach, they feel more comfortable ignoring their children's fights. But, from the child's perspective they are no longer reaching their goal of getting their parents' attention! They liked the way things were before. It was working for them! So, they redouble their efforts. They intensify the fighting to make it more aggressive and physical, trying harder to engage you.

Since physical fights are harder to watch, let alone ignore, we often break our rule of non-involvement and step in to break it up. They learn that you will ignore them *until* the fight gets physical, so now instead of resolving their fights, they actually learn to fight harder to reach their goal.

SOLUTIONS

To avoid the situation getting more aggressive and physical, try one of these strategies.

Give them permission to fight. Honor that fighting is their choice to make and you can't change that. They decide to fight or they decide to get along. It's up to them. State clearly: "I see you two are really wanting to have a fight. This is not a fighting house—take it outside to the yard, please. I am going to take the dog for a walk."

The reason this works is twofold: they hear your commitment to not stopping them, and you won't be around to (potentially) cave in and get involved. If they continue to fight when they're alone, they have already become rivals and family counseling might help heal their relationship. However, the more common result is the children deciding that as mad as they are at their sibling it's not worth getting hit and kicked if they don't get the larger payoff of mom's reactions. De-escalation and resolution usually follow quite quickly.

Put them in the same boat. If you have to break up a fight because that is the only thing that feels right for you, then do so, but put them in the same boat to honor that the fight is co-created by both children: "I see you can't be together without someone getting hurt. Take some time apart in your own rooms to cool down. You can regroup when you are able to be together and not fight."

But What If . . .

I am okay with a certain amount of roughness, but what if someone really does get hurt? Shouldn't the other face some consequence for that?

It's not the children's intention to *really* hurt each other. Well, yes, they want to hurt each other—but not injure each other. They could be far more violent if they wanted to be.

In fact, a child doesn't twist an arm until it breaks, just until the sib screams for mercy. If the sibling does get injured, it's an accident, and the instigator feels awful about it. Under all the bravado, he does love his sibling and will react to that sibling's pain, tears and blood with terrific remorse and empathy if, and only if, we don't distract him from it.

How do we distract these kids? Parents fly off the handle and start admonishing them:

"Look what you did now!"

"I told you someone would get hurt, but you didn't listen!"

"I've had it with you and your bad behavior—you're a bad boy— look what you've done!"

These sentiments shut down the child's natural empathy and kick in ego defenses to protect himself from verbal attack. Now the child is likely to be mad at you *and* mad at his sibling. Any gains in empathy are lost, and more harm is done to all the relationships.

Instead, say: "I see your brother is hurt; what could you do to help? Can you get a bandage? Come with us to the hospital and keep him company while he waits for his stitches; hold the ice bag for him." Bones and skin will heal, and their relationship will mend if they are allowed to make these reparations. Don't let your anger get in the way of that. You'll be surprised how loving and supportive they can be. It could even be a bonding moment if we keep our upset in check.

But What If . . .

What if one child doesn't defend himself? Or one is really big and the other is out-powered?

The same rules apply. Remember that both children have allowed things to escalate to this point. Along the way, either child could get creative and do something to de-escalate the situation. The smaller child will learn not to provoke so hard, or to back off earlier if he sees that it can lead to physical fighting. The instigator will learn not to act in ways that will lead to him being hit or bitten. By being left to resolve the situation on their own, kids realize that how they participate in fights can change the outcomes.

MY TODDLER IS TOO ROUGH WITH THE BABY

The baby is in the bouncy chair eating Cheerios and babbling when your toddler runs over and pinches his arm. Surely you don't think that was provoked or that the baby can defend himself.

Understanding the Problem

With our littlest kiddos, the behavior is usually one of two things.

Undue attention seeking. Your toddler doesn't really want to hurt the baby; she just knows this is an action that is sure to get your attention. The toddler has learned that all she has to do is come close to the baby and your vigilance goes up, you're quick to verbally remind her, "Gentle hands," "Don't touch the baby," or "Let him be." These reminders and nagging, and stopping what you are doing to come over to protect the baby, are easy attention grabs. Some kids learn to touch electrical sockets or pull the cat's tail—your kid discovered that the new baby was the thing you can't manage to ignore.

Finding connection through mistaken means. Toddlers don't have all the social skills of a preschooler and may want to connect with the baby, but how does she do that with a pink blob that only babbles and drools? Maybe by squeezing and pinching them . . .

Solutions

Ignore the behavior, not the child. What would happen if you didn't respond? The baby would cry and the toddler would look to see your reaction to the crying. If you didn't look or respond or come over, the toddler would be left with a crying baby. Even to a little toddler, that quickly becomes distressing, and she may learn not to get herself in that situation again.

However, we have to be aware the toddler is seeking our attention, and so we have to engage her in other useful ways. This is where *distraction* and *redirection* work so beautifully.

Examples:

"Connor, can you help mommy stir the batter?"

"Shelby, can you get your crayons and coloring book and join me at the table?"

No words about how to treat the baby are necessary—we're on to coloring and baking! Mistaken approach gone, proper approach taken.

Use actions—not words. If you feel safety is an issue and you must keep the baby safe, move the baby to a playard, or take the toddler by the hand and move him away from the baby and engage him in something else. These are actions that resolve the situation without using words at all.

Take Time for Training (TTFT). If the toddler's pinching and squeezing is an attempt to connect with the baby, rather than constantly saying what *not* to do (which is a verbal correction and gets discouraging when it comes time and time again), Take Time for Training about other ways to play and connect with the baby. For example: "Can you spin the mobile for your sister? She loves it when you do that! You are so good at making your sister smile; can you make those noises she likes to hear?"

Catch 'em being good. Children move in line with our expectations, so be sure to notice and comment when your toddler is being gentle with the baby.

Examples:

"You have such gentle hands."

"You really know how to be kind and gentle with your sister, don't you?"

"You are showing your sister how caring you are."

When a child hears these messages, she internalizes them and comes to believe she is, in fact, caring, gentle and kind. This will increase the likelihood of seeing more of these behaviors and attributes.

- -

It Worked for Me

Nursing the baby seems to invite misbehavior in the baby's toddler siblings. It's a time when you are busy with the baby, and the act of nursing itself is intimate and loving, so it can raise feelings of insecurity in your toddler. Those feelings of insecurity can lead to what looks like misbehaviors.

I was able to use nursing time as a special time for my toddler by making it our reading time. We had a basket of books that my daughter Zoe would bring to the couch, and we would snuggle side by side while I nursed her baby sister, Lucy. I could read to Zoe while nursing Lucy, and so this time felt more like Zoe time. It worked like a charm for me.

NAME-CALLING AND BEING MEAN

It's an all-day and all-night affair. The kids tease and call each other names, pull the chair out when the other person is about to sit down and just never leave each other alone. It's all so mean-spirited.

Understanding the Problem

There is a lot of socializing happening between these kids; it's just all negative. If they really didn't like one another, why waste energy on your siblings at all?

There is a competitiveness that underlies all these shenanigans—the constant pulling of each other's chain, the pushing of each other's buttons. They are vying for position, upsetting one another so one looks like top dog and the other is low man on the totem pole.

Solutions

Make more time for family fun. Find cooperative, all-ages games to play together, such as charades, Pictionary, bowling with a total family score, doing a puzzle together or strategy games that you have to work together to solve. Break the Safe by Milton Bradley and Family Pastimes make games that are meant to be cooperative instead of competitive. Help build up the relationships in the family and replace antics with more directed fun.

Practice active listening and coaching. You have to be willing to accept that your children will have hard feelings about their siblings from time to time. You need to hear those feelings, too. If Cassandra called Matthew a jerk, you can say, "Sounds like you're really upset with your brother. Maybe you could let him know how you're feeling. He might be more receptive to hearing what you say if you let him know he's made you mad rather than calling him a name." Or, "Do you think the reason your brother does that is to get your goat? To make you upset? If he enjoys getting a rise out of you, maybe he'd be less inclined to do it if you showed him a different reaction, like not getting so upset. Then what fun would it be?"

Reduce competition in the family. Find ways to reduce competition in the family. Mom and dad set the tone. Are you competitive with your partner? You might think not, but ask yourself this: Do you have to "win" or "be right"?

How do you resolve your own interpersonal conflicts as a couple? By reaching mutual agreements or fighting till someone wins? How do you get your way? What do you do when you don't get your way?

Let's face it—we're not always the best models of cooperation. We don't always embody egalitarian, mutually respectful relationships, either. We may not pull out a chair from beneath our spouse, but did you go behind your partner's back and buy that new vacuum without getting the okay to spend that money from the family budget, knowing if you asked, your spouse would say no? You might not have called him "dumb dumb" or "penis breath," but did you say he was a lazy slob for not cutting the grass? Isn't that name-calling?

Let's try to model better treatment of our loved ones and reduce competition in the family. Here is how:

1. Don't compare siblings to each other. ("Ashley has such a clean room. Why can't you keep yours picked up?" "Ashley got all As on her report card; what is your problem?")
2. Don't label them. ("He's my scholar." "She's my athlete.")
3. Don't set your children up to directly compete with one another. No "First one to the car is a winner!" or "Fastest one to eat their supper is the winner!"
4. Don't praise. Use encouragement instead. Praise is all about passing judgment and children meeting your mark. It invites competition. Encouragement is nonjudgmental and will stimulate cooperation instead.

Praise versus Encouragement

	PRAISE	ENCOURAGEMENT
Dictionary definition*	1. to express favorable judgment of 2. to glorify, especially by attribution of perfection 3. expression of approval	1. to inspire with courage 2. to spur on; stimulate
Hidden parental message	You're okay when . . .	You're okay no matter what.
Addresses	The doer: "You're a 'good girl.'"	The deed: "You did a good job."
Recognizes	Final completed perfect task: "You did it right."	Effort and improvement: "Your hard work is paying off. You've really come far."
Who owns the accomplishment	Parent: "An A! I am so proud of you."	Child: "An A! You must be feeling so proud of yourself."
Child's likely response	To seek change in order to get approval from others.	To seek change in order to better self.
Locus of control	External: "What do others think of me?"	Internal: "What do I think of me?"
Teaches	What to think; evaluation by others.	How to think; self-evaluation.
Goal	Conformity: "You did it right."	Self-understanding: "What do you think? Feel? Learn?"
Effect on self-esteem	Feel worthwhile only when others approve of him or her.	Feel worthwhile without others' approval.
Mistakes	Mistakes are bad and to be avoided. Mistakes are evidence you are not perfect. Praised children will avoid tasks they can't excel at immediately. When effort or struggle is required, they stop or evade instead of trying harder.	Mistakes are not bad at all, but rather just inevitable and embraced as being opportunities to learn. We are all imperfect humans. The encouraged child has the courage to be imperfect and sally forth.

Competition	Stimulates the need to beat others at any cost to ensure he or she is being judged as "better" or superior to others.	Stimulates the desire to do one's best, since child is not concerned with being judged or held back by mistakes. In fact, as a good mistake maker, the child learns more and achieves more in the long run.
Long-range effect	Dependence on others	Self-confidence, self-reliance

Adapted from *Positive Discipline in the Classroom Teacher's Guide*, by Jane Nelsen and Lynn Lott, www.empoweringpeople.com

Switch Up Praise for Encouragement

PRAISE	ENCOURAGEMENT
"All As. You're so smart!"	"All As. You worked hard."
"Your bedroom looks great."	"You worked hard getting your bedroom in order. Way to go! That must feel good."
"What a beautiful picture!"	"Tell me about your picture . . ."

Table adapted from Jane Nelsen Positive Parenting Program

For more on the art and language of encouragement check out my earlier books.

IS JEALOUS

"Mommy loves you more!" "I can't do anything right!" "*She's* daddy's favorite." "He's such a momma's boy," "I hate my sister!" "You'd never do that for me!" Do you hear any of these complaints?

UNDERSTANDING THE PROBLEM

Sometimes a child feels a deep-seated jealousy toward her sibling. This stems from the child feeling that the other is preferred in her parent's eyes and fearing being loved less.

We have to identify how we are accidentally showing favor to some and marginalizing others. I've already discussed not comparing children, not taking sides and reducing competition in the family. But there are more subtle ways that we show a greater interest in one child than another.

SOLUTIONS

Here is a checklist to see how you're doing in keeping up your relationships with all your children:

1. Do I know the teachers' names, classes, homework and upcoming school events of each of my kids?
2. Do I know their friends' names?
3. Do I share a hobby or activity or interest with them all individually?
4. Do I listen openly to each child's viewpoint and value everyone's different opinions? Or just those who agree with my viewpoint?
5. Do I feel the same excitement when I see each of my children?
6. Do I give chores and responsibilities to each child? Or do some get excused, while others are expected to set an example, or help their siblings such that they may feel burdened?
7. Do I have the same expectations of each child, or are some held to a higher or lower standard?
8. Do I respond to each child the same? Or are some given a harsher treatment?

If you answered no to any of the questions above, you know where to focus your efforts. If you feel things are not improving, it's worth the investment of time and money to get some family counseling.

CHAPTER 16

THE BEST PRACTICES DEMOCRATIC FAMILY CHECKLIST

We started this journey with the understanding that misbehavior is really just our children's mistaken approach to finding a sense of belonging, mastery, autonomy and purpose. The mistaken beliefs about themselves and how to accomplish these goals need to be corrected. Besides the "in the moment" responses this book offers, we can work on long-term objectives between misbehaviors. Here is a list of best practices you should be working toward incorporating into your family life to achieve a democratic family rich in mutual respect, caring and cooperation.

BEST PRACTICES FAMILY CHECKLIST

- ☐ De-stress your family. Reduce your commitments, live within your means, simplify, downsize, slow down and relax.

- ☐ Create opportunities for family fun together—all of you. Engage in noncompetitive family fun times as much as you can squeeze in.

- ☐ Create rituals and traditions for your family.

- [ ] Spend special time with each child, but especially your discouraged and misbehaving child.

- [ ] Find each child's unique qualities and strengths. Help them develop these attributes in ways that can benefit the family and others.

- [ ] Give children jobs and responsibilities.

- [ ] Find ways for children to participate in and contribute to daily family life.

- [ ] Establish a budgeted allowance.

- [ ] Hold weekly family meetings as a place to make family decisions together.

- [ ] View difficulties as problems that need solutions instead of problems that require consequences.

- [ ] Adopt an attitude that views mistakes as opportunities to learn, rather than failure.

- [ ] Encourage instead of praise.

- [ ] Act in self-respecting ways and treat others with respect.

- [ ] Model a healthy, cooperative, loving relationship to your children by having one with your partner.

- [ ] Give gratitude and focus on what is working, and downgrade what isn't—yet.

- [ ] Maintain an "others/community" focus instead of a "me" or "us" focus.